the brain and

the meaning of life

the brain and
the meaning of life

Paul Thagard

PRINCETON UNIVERSITY PRESS

PRINCETON AND OXFORD

Library of Congress Cataloging-in-Publication Data

Thagard, Paul.
The brain and the meaning of life / Paul Thagard.
p. cm.
Includes bibliographical references and index.
ISBN 978-0-691-14272-2 (hardcover : alk. paper) 1. Life. 2. Cognitive science. I. Title.
BD431.T28 2010
128—dc22
2009025312

British Library Cataloging-in-Publication Data is available

2253

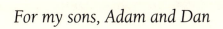
For my sons, Adam and Dan

Contents

Preface   xi

Acknowledgments   xv

1. We All Need Wisdom   1

   Why Live?   1
   Sources of Wisdom   3
   Philosophical Approaches   5
   The Relevance of Minds and Brains   6
   Looking Ahead   8
   Conclusion   12

2. Evidence Beats Faith   13

   Faith versus Evidence   13
   How Faith Works   14
   How Evidence Works   20
   Evidence and Inference in Science   23
   Medicine: Evidence or Faith?   27
   Evidence, Truth, and God   32
   A Priori Reasoning and Thought Experiments   35
   Conclusion   40

3. Minds Are Brains   42

   The Brain Revolution   42
   Evidence That Minds Are Brains   43
   Evidence for Dualism?   54
   Objections to Mind-Brain Identity   59
   Who Are You?   63
   Conclusion   64

4. How Brains Know Reality   67

   Reality and Its Discontents   67
   Knowing Objects   69
   Appearance and Reality   72
   Concepts   76
   Knowledge beyond Perception   81
   Coherence in the Brain   85
   Coherence and Truth   90
   Conclusion   92

5. How Brains Feel Emotions   94

  Emotions Matter   94
  Valuations in the Brain   95
  Cognitive Appraisal versus Bodily Perception   98
  Synthesis: The EMOCON Model   100
  Emotional Consciousness   105
  Multilevel Explanations   108
  Rationality and Affective Afflictions   111
  Conclusion   116

6. How Brains Decide   119

  Big Decisions   119
  Inference to the Best Plan   121
  Decisions in the Brain   123
  Changing Goals   126
  How to Make Bad Decisions   133
  Living without Free Will   137
  Conclusion   140

7. Why Life Is Worth Living   142

  The Meaning of Life   142
  Nihilism   143
  Happiness   146
  Goals and Meaning   149
  Love   152
  Work   158
  Play   161
  Conclusion   165

8. Needs and Hopes   168

  Wants versus Needs   168
  Vital Needs   169
  How Love, Work, and Play Satisfy Needs   171
  Balance, Coherence, and Change   176
  Hope versus Despair   177
  Conclusion   182

9. Ethical Brains   183

  Ethical Decisions   183
  Conscience and Moral Intuitions   184
  Mirror Neurons   188
  Empathy   190
  Moral Motivation   192

Ethical Theory 195
Moral Objectivity 201
Responsibility 204
Conclusion 206

10. Making Sense of It All 209

Connections Made 209
Wisdom Gained 213
What Kind of Government Should Countries Have? 215
How Can Creative Change Be Produced? 217
What Is Mathematical Knowledge? 221
Why Is There Something and Not Nothing? 224
The Future of Wisdom 226

Notes 231

Glossary 251

References 255

Index 271

Preface

When I was fifteen, I read a book that dramatically transformed my life, launching an intellectual journey that has taken me through philosophy and cognitive science, the interdisciplinary field that investigates how the mind works. I was shelving books in my job at the public library in Saskatoon, Saskatchewan, when I noticed a volume by Bertrand Russell, *Why I Am Not a Christian.* For a Catholic high school student and former altar boy, this was an incendiary title, especially given my growing doubts about what I was being told by my school's nuns and priests. I devoured Russell's demolition of the standard arguments for the existence of God and started reading similarly skeptical philosophers such as John Stuart Mill and Jean-Paul Sartre. Around the same time, I shelved another book in the library's careers section about the pleasant life of a university teacher and formed the ambition to become a philosophy professor.

Amazingly, this dream came true, and more than forty years later I can look back on a wonderful academic expedition that has taken me not only from religion to philosophy, but also on to psychology, artificial intelligence, and neuroscience. Today, I feel the same excitement about current developments in the understanding of how brains make minds as I did about my first discovery of philosophy. In the last decade, the explosion of experimental and theoretical results in neuroscience has generated much insight into how people think, feel, and act. These results have major implications for traditional philosophical problems, and also for everyday issues of how people can best lead their lives.

This book is an extended argument that brain science matters for the most fundamental philosophical issues about knowledge, reality, morality, and the meaning of life. I will show how metaphysical and ethical questions, once the favored territory of religious thinking, can be better illuminated by a grasp of how brain processes enable us to perceive the world and reason about how it is and should be. The result of many emerging ideas about minds as brains is a conceptual revolution as significant as the leap of Copernicus to place the sun rather than the earth at the center of the cosmos, and the leap of Darwin to mark humans as animals originating from evolution rather than divine creation.

Unlike the Copernican and Darwinian revolutions, the current change is not associated with any one thinker, so I will call it the *Brain Revolution*. Mounting evidence in neuroscience and psychology requires the abandonment of many traditional ideas about the soul, free will, and immortality. For many people, such a transition is fraught with pain, but I will try to show how life can have meaning and value within the framework that I call *neural naturalism*. Naturalism is the view that we can best address philosophical questions by taking into account scientific evidence and theories rather than by seeking supernatural sources. Many branches of science are relevant, from physics to anthropology, but we shall see that neuroscience is especially relevant for issues about the nature of mind and meaning.

Naturalism has substantial advantages over both religious faith and conceptual reasoning based on thought experiments. Science alone cannot answer inescapable philosophical questions, but it can collaborate with philosophy to establish general theories about reality and morality. This book shows how brains can arrive at knowledge of the real world and make good decisions about how to act, in ways made meaningful by the activities of love, work, and play.

I have tried to write this book without jargon or obscurity, so that it can be understood by intelligent readers with no special background. The book is written at two levels. I have tried to make the main text as broadly accessible as possible, explaining key ideas without distracting references to the relevant literatures in philosophy and science. For scholars I have provided

extensive notes and references that relate my discussions to these literatures and provide suggestions for further reading. At the end of the book, a
glossary gives partial indicators of the meanings of key terms. Supplemen-
tary material such as Web links can be found at http://press.princeton.edu/
titles/9152.html.

Acknowledgments

For comments on earlier drafts, I am grateful to Jonathan Aycan, William Bechtel, Chris Eliasmith, Lloyd Elliott, Scott Findlay, Carole Lee, Abninder Litt, Josef Nerb, Cameron Shelley, Peter Slezak, Terry Stewart, and Joanne Wood. Thanks to my editor, Eric Schwartz, for helpful suggestions and enthusiastic support, and to Lauren Lepow for skillful copyediting. Thanks to John Michela and Jennifer La Guardia for useful suggestions about goals and needs. Vicki Brett helped with the references. Figures 3.1, 3.2, and 5.1 were produced by Peter Sylwester, adapted with permission from figures in Sylwester (2007). Thanks to Don Addis for the use of his cartoon in the preface. I have benefited substantially from funding by the Natural Sciences and Engineering Research Council of Canada.

the brain and
the meaning of life

we all need wisdom

Why Live?

Why don't you kill yourself? Albert Camus began his book *The Myth of Sisyphus* with the startling assertion "There is but one truly serious philosophical problem and that is suicide." A French novelist and philosopher who won the Nobel Prize for literature in 1957, Camus said that judging whether life is or is not worth living amounts to answering the fundamental question of philosophy. If life is meaningless, there is no point to pursuing traditional philosophical questions about the nature of reality, knowledge, and morality.

Why life is worth living is indeed an urgent question, but it is rarely the question of suicide. The question of why you don't kill yourself arises only if you think that there are reasons why you *would* kill yourself, and people's lives are rarely so miserable that such reasons become prominent. If depression, disease, and despair were the overwhelming character of everyday life, then people would have a daily struggle about whether to go on at all. Unfortunately, such a struggle is not rare among young adults: an American survey of university students found that 10 percent said they had seriously considered suicide during the preceding year.

Most of us face the much less drastic question of *how* to go on, of how to live our lives. Then the question of the meaning of life is not the skeptical one of whether there is any meaning at all, but rather the constructive one that can have informative answers concerning what aspects of life make it worth living.

For most people today, religion provides a major source of answers to such questions about the meaning of life. When I was a child in Catholic school in the 1950s, I learned from the Baltimore Catechism that "God made me to know Him, to love Him, and to serve Him in this world, and to be happy with Him forever in the next." From a religious perspective, meaning arises not from any meager aspect of our daily lives, but from our profound connections with God, who brought us into existence and who provides the possibility of eternal happiness. However, for Camus and others like myself who have abandoned the beliefs produced by our religious upbringings, the theological answer to the meaning of life is implausible. Does this imply that life is absurd, ridiculous, and pointless, so utterly devoid of meaning that suicide should be a daily preoccupation of everyone?

Not at all. The eminent clinical psychologist Martin Seligman remarked that the three great realms of life are love, work, and play. For most people, these realms provide ample reasons to live. If your life is rich with love of family and friends, with work that is productive and pleasant, and with varieties of pastimes and entertainments that bring you joy, then the general issue of the meaning of life need rarely trouble you, eliminating Camus' extreme question of suicide. In chapters 7 and 8, I will use evidence from psychology and neuroscience to show how love, work, and play make life meaningful for most people, whether or not they are religious.

In the absence of the threat of absurdity, narrower issues about the meaning of life arise when the three realms conflict. For example, couples with young children often experience severe conflicts between love and work, when the intense needs of children compete for time and energy with the demands of career development. Young adults need to figure out how to render compatible the delights of playful pastimes such as sports and music with the imperative to get a job and support themselves. One of the few advantages of growing older is that the reduction of family responsibilities and the satisfaction or diminishing of career goals can make conflicts between the realms of love, work, and play much more manageable. I will describe how the meaning of life is no single thing such as a devotion to God, but rather depends on multiple dimensions that shift in importance over the course of a person's life. Hence life need never sink into the kind of absurdity embraced by Camus when he was writing in his twenties.

My aim in this book is to use experimental and theoretical research in psychology and neuroscience to provide a much richer and deeper understanding of how love, work, and play provide good reasons for living. Thus an answer to Camus' philosophical question about the meaning of life becomes tied to scientific findings, which many philosophers and religious thinkers would consider cheating. They think that philosophy should be concerned with truths that are eternal and absolute, not with the messy and sometimes transient findings of empirical science. Unfortunately, philosophy has been no more successful at finding such eternal truths than religion has been. In contrast, I will try to show that neuropsychology is richly relevant not only to the question of the meaning of life, but also to questions that I think are just as fundamental, concerning the nature of reality, knowledge, and morality.

Without any ranking, here are what seem to me to be the most fundamental philosophical questions:

- What is reality?
- How do we know reality?
- Why is life worth living?
- What makes actions right or wrong?

In contrast to Camus, I think that it is useful to address the question of the meaning of life *after* considering the nature of our knowledge of reality, although we will see that all these questions are intimately interconnected. For example, the question of why life is worth living raises issues about the moral legitimacy of ends such as love, work, and play. Moreover, issues about the nature of knowledge and reality are crucial for the pursuit of questions about morality and the meaning of life. We need to know what persons are and how they can gain knowledge in order to be able to figure out how to assess the objective value of human lives and the rightness or wrongness of actions.

Sources of Wisdom

The word "philosophy" arose from Greek words for love of wisdom, but what is the wisdom that philosophy is supposed to be seeking, and how can it be found? Wisdom is not just knowledge, as there are many pieces of knowledge of little general importance. I know that Toronto is a city in Ontario, but would hardly claim that this knowledge makes me wiser. Rather, we should think of wisdom as knowledge about what matters, why it matters, and how to achieve it. Knowing what matters should guide us to acquire other kinds of important knowledge rather than acquiring a wealth of beliefs that may be true but rather trivial. At the deepest level, wisdom involves knowing not only what kinds of things are important to human beings, but also *why* they are important. For example, to be wise you need to have some understanding that love matters to people, that there are psychological and biological reasons why love matters, and that there are better and worse ways of finding love.

All people need wisdom of this sort in order to conduct their lives effectively, but wisdom may take on different forms as people go through the stages of life. Small children have scant need for wisdom, fortunately, as their needs and plans are normally taken care of by parents and other caregivers. But adolescents and young adults face important transitions, from play as their major focus to concerns with careers and families that elevate the importance of work and love. Finding coherence among work, love, and play is key to finding satisfaction and happiness in middle age. As people grow older, they need to figure out how to shift this balance in keeping with changes in family responsibilities and diminished capabilities due to reduced health.

The ancient Greek philosopher Epicurus eloquently expressed the need for wisdom across the life span:

> Let no one be slow to seek wisdom when he is young nor weary in the search of it when he has grown old. For no age is too early or too late for the health of the soul. And to say that the season for studying philosophy has not yet come, or that it is past and gone, is like saying that the season for happiness is not yet or that it is now no more. Therefore, both old and young alike ought to seek wisdom, the former in order that, as age comes over him, he may be young in good things because of the grace of what has been, and the latter in order that, while he is young, he may at the same time be old, because he has no fear of the things which are to come. So we must exercise ourselves in the things which bring happiness, since, if that be present, we have everything, and, if that be absent, all our actions are directed towards attaining it.

In chapter 7, I will challenge the assumption of Epicurus that happiness is the meaning of life, and I prefer to write of the health of the mind or brain rather than the soul. But I agree wholeheartedly that old and young alike ought to seek wisdom.

Wisdom operates at different levels. Most generally, it concerns recognizing major goals such as love, work, and play. In addition, much wisdom consists in knowledge about how to accomplish these goals. For example, learning from experience how to have a good romantic relationship contributes to satisfaction of the goal of having love in one's life. Moreover, wisdom includes many kinds of knowledge that complement more specific information about primary goals and how to accomplish them. In particular, knowing how to keep yourself healthy by eating well is valuable for ensuring that illness won't prevent the pursuit of major goals. Wisdom of a particularly deep sort concerns knowing why some goals such as love, work, and play are so important to people. Chapter 8 will argue that love, work, and play are the meaning of life because they help to satisfy vital human needs.

Where can we look for all these kinds of wisdom? Philosophers have sought wisdom for thousands of years, but there is little consensus about what they have learned. The philosopher Jerry Fodor joked that anybody who thinks that philosophers have access to large resources of practical wisdom hasn't been going to faculty meetings. My own approach to wisdom is unusual in that I use experimental psychology and recent research in neuroscience to develop a systematic account of what matters to people and why it matters.

Philosophical Approaches

The approach to philosophy that I favor, attempting to answer fundamental questions by relating them to scientific findings, is called *naturalism*. Many philosophers since Plato have scorned naturalism, arguing that science cannot provide answers to the deepest philosophical questions, especially ones that concern not just how the world is but how it ought to be. They think that philosophy should reach conclusions that are true *a priori*, which means that they are prior to sensory experiences and can be gained by reason alone. Unfortunately, despite thousands of years of trying, no one has managed to find any undisputed a priori truths. The absence of generally accepted a priori principles shows that the distinguished Platonic philosophical tradition of looking for them has failed. Wisdom must be sought more modestly.

Sometimes, however, philosophy gets too modest. The highly influential Austrian/British philosopher Wittgenstein asserted that philosophy is unlike science in that all it should aim for is conceptual clarification. In his early writings, he looked to formal logic to provide the appropriate tools, and in his later work he emphasized attention to ordinary language. He claimed that philosophy "leaves everything as it is." Much of twentieth-century philosophy in English devoted itself to the modest goal of merely clarifying existing concepts. But no one has learned much from analyzing the logic or the ordinary use of the words "wise" and "wisdom." We need a theory of wisdom that can tell us what is important and why it is important. Such theorizing requires introducing new concepts and rejecting or modifying old ones.

My approach in this book is to seek wisdom that is natural, not in the health food sense of being free of chemical additives, but in the scientific sense of being guided by experiments and theories. Philosophical naturalism is more intellectually ambitious than conceptual clarification, but rejects Platonic and religious ambitions to seek truth in supernatural realms. In chapter 2, I will give a sustained argument why we should base our beliefs on scientific evidence rather than on faith. Psychology and neuroscience are particularly rich sources of evidence relevant to the four central philosophical questions about reality, knowledge, meaning, and morality, so I call my approach neural naturalism.

The Relevance of Minds and Brains

Experimental psychology and neuroscience are still young fields of investigation, dating back only to the late nineteenth century. My goal in this book is to show how they can contribute to answers to central philosophical questions about the nature of reality, knowledge, morality, and especially the meaning of life. My arguments will be largely empirical, tying philosophical issues to experiments and theories in neuropsychology.

Like other sciences such as physics, psychology and neuroscience are both experimental and theoretical. Attempts to understand the mind are ancient, going back more than two thousand years to Greek thinkers such as Plato. Attempts to understand the physical world are similarly ancient. But experimental science began to flourish only in the seventeenth century, when thinkers such as Galileo showed the advantages of basing conclusions about the physical world on evidence derived from systematic instrument-based observations and carefully designed experiments. Galileo used the newly invented telescope to make novel observations of the planets, achieving unexpected discoveries such as the moons of Jupiter. He also conducted experiments to determine how falling bodies behave on inclined planes. The superiority of experimental approaches to the world over traditional ones based on authorities such as Aristotle and Thomas Aquinas became increasingly apparent. Common sense, tradition, and the Catholic Church said that the earth is the stationary center of the universe; but the evidence collected by Galileo, Kepler, and others combined with the theories developed by Copernicus and Newton to make inescapable the conclusion that the earth moves.

Psychology, however, became experimental only centuries later, when Wilhelm Wundt and others established laboratories for systematically investigating mental operations. Early psychological theories were crude, because ordinary language provided a very limited vocabulary for explaining how the mind works. A major theoretical breakthrough took place in the 1950s, when emerging ideas about computing began to provide analogies about how minds can operate using representations and mechanical processes. These ideas developed hand in hand with new experimental techniques such as the precise measurement of how fast people react to different stimuli. Today the interdisciplinary field of cognitive science develops computational theories intended to explain the results of many different kinds of psychological experiments.

Neuroscience also blossomed at the end of the nineteenth century, when new techniques for staining cells made it possible to identify how neurons constitute the brain. The Spanish biologist Santiago Ramón y Cajal developed what came to be called the neuron doctrine, the idea that the brain's functions are largely carried out by its nerve cells. Through the first part of the twentieth century, psychology and neuroscience developed largely independently of each other, but began to converge in the 1980s through a combination of experimental and theoretical advances. A major experimental advance was the invention of brain-scanning machines that make it possible to observe the operation of different brain areas while people are performing mental tasks. A major theoretical advance was the development of computational ideas about how neurons can interact to generate complex representations and processes. Together, these advances made possible the field of cognitive neuroscience, which is the theoretical and experimental study of the neural processes that underlie human thinking. Combining psychological and neurological experiments with computational theories that explain their results takes the scientific study of mind far beyond what casual introspection can tell us about mental phenomena. The main thrust of chapters 3–10 is to show the relevance of results in cognitive neuroscience for philosophical problems about reality, knowledge, meaning, and morality.

Looking Ahead

In summarizing the rest of the book, I run the risk of seeming to assert dogmatically a host of views that have not yet been defended. But I want to give the reader a good idea of where the book is going and how it all fits together. Such fitting together is a holistic, parallel process that is not easily grasped through the unavoidably serial process of reading successive chapters, but I will try to portray the whole picture in a preliminary form here and more thoroughly in the concluding chapter that will tie together preceding arguments. This look ahead will be rough and incomplete, but should serve to introduce some key ideas for providing naturalistic answers to philosophical questions.

What is reality? My answer will be that we should judge reality to consist of those things and processes identified by well-established fields of science using theories backed by evidence drawn from systematic observations and experiments. This view is highly contentious, as it rules out both religious faith and a priori arguments as sources of knowledge about reality. Chapter 2 will provide an argument why philosophy, like medicine and science, should be evidence based rather than faith based. Tying reality to the results of scientific investigations does not in itself rule out spiritual entities such as gods, souls, and angels, for there could be observations and experimental results that are best explained by theories postulating the existence of such entities. Historically, however, the development of naturalistic explanations in terms of physics, biology, and other sciences has rendered supernatural explanations dispensable. I will describe how theories in physics and biology have demolished theological arguments for hypotheses about divine creation to explain the origin and nature of the universe. Chapter 3 will similarly argue that neuropsychological theories are now sufficiently powerful to make it plausible that minds are brains, so that hypotheses about the existence of the soul are as superfluous as ones about gods and angels. Reality is what science can discover.

In arguing for a scientific approach to reality, chapter 2 also provides the beginnings of an answer to my second major philosophical question, concerning how we know reality. I will go into detail about how scientific thinking works, including how observations and experiments constitute evidence that can be explained by competing scientific theories. Evidence-based medicine provides an accessible example of the advantages of using science rather than faith or a priori reasoning to reach conclusions. Philosophy and science are not restricted merely to what can be observed, but instead can go beyond observation to develop theories about things and processes that surpass the reach of human senses and available instruments. We can use a reasoning process called inference to the best explanation to justify the adoption of theories that go well beyond what we directly observe.

Chapter 2 will not depend on any neuropsychological findings, but the argument in chapter 3 that we should identify minds with brains will set the stage in the following chapter for a discussion of how brains know reality. Here I will draw heavily on recent experimental and theoretical results in neuroscience to explain how brains represent the world, using both sensory processes such as vision and reasoning processes such as inference to the best explanation, enabling scientists to develop knowledge that goes beyond our rather limited senses. Chapters 2, 3, and 4 propose integrated answers to some of the most central questions in metaphysics (the theory of reality) and in epistemology (the theory of knowledge). Scientific reasoning is the best way to gain knowledge, and minds are brains equipped with all the observational and inferential capacities we need to comprehend how the world works. Thinking is multimodal, requiring both verbal and sensory representations, and multidimensional, employing representations that acquire meaning by relations to each other and to the world.

To address ethical questions about the nature of morality and the meaning of life, we need to go beyond the cognitive processes described in chapters 2–4 to consider how the brain accomplishes emotional feelings and makes decisions. Chapter 5 defends a theory of emotional consciousness that serves two purposes. First, it fulfills a promise in chapter 3 to show how it is possible to give a naturalistic explanation of consciousness. Second, it provides the basis for the attempts in chapters 6–8 to describe the neural basis for meaningful decisions and moral judgments. I will argue that our emotional feelings are the result of parallel brain processes that involve simultaneous cognitive appraisal of the situations we face and internal perceptions of the states of our bodies. Our everyday decisions about what to do are tied in with the same kinds of processes, which generate the gut reactions that tell us what actions to pursue. According to chapter 6, decision making is inference to the best plan, selecting actions that accomplish our goals, which are emotionally marked neural representations of desirable states of affairs. Such inferences require a dynamic interaction of cognition and emotion. Good decision making requires the ability to adopt, abandon, and revalue goals on the basis of experience.

With theories about reality, knowledge, and decision making in place, we can return to the question that began this book: why is life worth living? For chapter 7, I draw on recent findings about the neural processes involved in love, work, and play to offer an account of how these realms can provide all the meaning to life that people need. Just as chapter 4 discussed the meaning of mental representations such as concepts in terms of multiple dimensions, chapter 7 defends a multidimensional, neural-based view of the meaning of life. Chapter 7 also completes the account in chapter 6 of how brains make decisions by describing how love, work, and play constitute major goals that affect what actions people choose.

Philosophy addresses normative concerns about how things ought to be, not just descriptive matters of how things are. Chapters 6 and 7 touch on normative issues about how people should think and act, but these are addressed more thoroughly in chapters 8 and 9. Chapter 8 shows how love, work, and play deserve to be meaningful because they contribute to vital human needs for relatedness, competence, and autonomy. Love, work, and play satisfy requirements that people need to live as human beings, and so provide the meaning of life normatively as well as descriptively. Finding a balance among competing goals and needs is not easy, but the prospect of satisfying even some of them is enough to generate hope, which is the opposite of the despair that leads to thoughts of suicide. From the perspective of neural naturalism, hope is a brain process that combines cognitive appraisal and physiological perception to produce a positive feeling about future goal satisfaction.

In chapter 9, I argue that moral judgments are produced by neural processes of emotional consciousness. Understanding the neural basis for moral judgments does not in itself answer the philosophical question concerning what makes actions right or wrong. But it does rule out two sorts of answers that have been historically influential. My naturalistic approach is incompatible with what is still the dominant cultural view, that morality derives from religious teaching. The theory of ethical intuition that I derive from my neural account of emotional consciousness is also incompatible with philosophical views that seek the basis for morality in indubitable ethical intuitions or a priori reasoning.

I will argue for an ethical position that allows us to judge the morality of acts by considering their consequences for all involved, subject to constraints that emanate from our neural constitutions, biological nature, and social needs. Inferences about how things ought to be cannot be simply derived from empirical matters, but we can nevertheless draw objective normative conclusions by coherently producing inferences to the best moral plan. Normative conclusions about the meaning of life and about human rights can be based on biological and psychological evidence concerning vital needs. Although my approach is deeply biological, it rejects many claims made by evolutionary psychologists concerning an innate basis for specific kinds of behaviors.

Finally, in chapter 10, I review the big picture of how a naturalistic approach to mind based on psychology and neuroscience provides answers to fundamental philosophical questions. As chapter 3 and 4 argue for knowledge, and chapter 9 argues for morality, inference is a matter of fitting all relevant conclusions into a coherent whole, and I will try to display what I think is the overall coherence of neural naturalism. Whole systems of philosophy are out of fashion, but I try to show the general fit, with each other and with scientific findings, of my conclusions about realism, coherence, moral consequences, and the multiple dimensions of the meaning of life. I will sketch the beginnings of naturalistic answers to some additional important questions. What kind of government is desirable? How can brains be creative? What is mathematical knowledge? Why is there something rather than nothing? My treatment of these questions will be highly preliminary, but it will point to avenues for future collaborations between philosophy and science.

Conclusion

Plato said that philosophy begins in wonder, but he was only partly right. For many thinkers such as Camus, philosophy begins in anxiety, the intense and hard-to-overcome feeling that life may be meaningless, absurd, irrational, futile, and lacking in morality. Modern science helps enormously to satisfy the feeling of wonder, by providing answers to questions about what is strange and surprising in the natural world. But science may seem to be helpless to deal with anxiety about lack of meaning in people's lives, and indeed may even increase such anxiety. Suppose physics is right that our universe began around fourteen billion years ago in a big bang that produced billions of stars; and suppose biology is right that human beings are just a kind of highly evolved ape. Then our lives cannot have the special, central place in the universe promised by religion based on faith, and by philosophy based on a priori reasoning. Hence it is unsurprising that the Brain Revolution encounters opposition from those who fear its practical as well as its intellectual consequences.

This book aims to show that neural naturalism can serve to satisfy wonder about the nature of mind and reality, and also to alleviate anxiety about the difficulty of life in a vast and apparently purposeless universe. Philosophy and neuropsychology can do little to remove the many hardships that people face as their lives develop, with inevitable bouts of failure, rejection, disease, and eventually death. But together philosophy and science can paint a plausible picture of how minds, even ones that are merely brains, can apprehend reality, decide effectively, act morally, and lead meaningful lives enriched by worthwhile goals in the realms of love, work, and play. To begin this picture, we need to understand how scientific evidence provides a better source of knowledge than does religious faith or pure reason.

Chapter Two

evidence beats faith

Faith versus Evidence

When you have a medical problem, where do you look for information that might help you deal with it? Perhaps you consult a medical expert such as your family doctor, or maybe you go looking on the Web to see what practitioners of alternative medicine have to say about it. Or else you might ask a religious leader to whom you look for medical as well as spiritual guidance. My preference in medicine as well as philosophy is to look for scientific evidence rather than religious faith or a priori reasoning, but what justifies this preference? Isn't it just a matter of having faith in science rather than in religion?

No: this chapter will provide good reasons for basing beliefs and decisions on evidence rather than on faith. After a brief history of the conflict between scientific evidence and religious faith, I will describe how faith and evidence differ in the way they affect beliefs and decisions. I will use medicine as an informative area in which the superiority of evidence over faith is clear, and generalize this superiority to other domains, including philosophy. Although the tradition of a priori reasoning in philosophy is not usually allied with religious faith, I will argue that its reliance on intuitions and neglect of evidence is similar to faith-based thinking. The currently common use of thought experiments in philosophy is akin to reasoning based on faith rather than on evidence.

Plato and Aristotle, long the most influential philosophers, saw no deep conflict between reason and religion. Both included theology as a crucial part of their thinking about the nature of reality and morality. They differed in that Plato argued for the superiority of a priori knowledge based on abstract ideas, whereas Aristotle's approach was more empirical, drawing much more on what was known at the time about the physical and biological worlds. Medieval philosophers in various religious traditions—Averroes for Islam, Maimonides for Judaism, and Thomas Aquinas for Christianity—attempted to integrate their religious views with Aristotle's philosophical approach. Whereas much of Aristotle's work was based on empirical observations of the physical, biological, and social worlds, medieval discussions of Aristotle tended to treat his writings as a kind of sacred text almost as venerable as the Bible or Koran.

Veneration of texts was challenged by the scientific revolution of the sixteenth and seventeenth centuries. After the Royal Society of London was formed in 1660, its motto became "Nullius in verba," Latin for "nothing in words." This phrase expressed the determination to base conclusions on experimental methods such as those used by founding members Robert Boyle and Robert Hooke. Such methods contrasted starkly with reliance on sacred religious and philosophical texts, although many scientists, like Isaac Newton, remained religious. In the eighteenth century, however, the conflict between science and religion became explicit in the writings of philosophers such as Voltaire and David Hume. Today, most leading scientists are atheists or agnostics, either denying the existence of God or expressing doubts about it. At the other extreme, religious fundamentalists in both the Christian and Islamic traditions reject science as propounding views that are not just false but also evil.

Some thinkers today attempt to reconcile science and religion, either by loosening religious doctrines in ways that make them compatible with scientific findings, or by delegating different areas of responsibility to science and religion. For example, the biologist Stephen Jay Gould argued that science and religion occupy separate areas of concern, with science having responsibility for empirical matters such as whether evolution occurred, but with religion remaining autonomous and paramount for questions of morality and meaning. My view is that even morality and meaning are better approached via scientific evidence than by religious faith. Let us now look at the difference between faith-based and evidence-based thinking.

How Faith Works

According to the Website adherents.com, 84 percent of the more than 6 billion people in the world today support some religious group. The largest religions are Christianity, with 2.1 billion members in various denominations, and Islam, with around 1.5 billion. Both of these religions believe in just one god, unlike the third largest religion, Hinduism. And both have central texts, the New and Old Testament Bible for Christians, and the Koran for Muslims. They also have historically important religious leaders, such as St. Paul for Christians and Muhammad for Muslims, as well as contemporary leaders such as the pope and cardinals for Catholics and ayatollahs for Shiite Muslims. Christianity and Islam both have subgroups, with many different kinds of Protestants opposed to Catholics, and Sunni Muslims often in conflict with Shiites over doctrines and practices.

Religious faith is a belief in, trust in, and devotion to gods, leaders, or texts, independent of evidence. For example, Catholics believe in God and saints such as Mary the mother of Jesus, and they also trust the pope and the Bible as sources that reveal the word of God. A belief is faith based if the source of its acceptance is supposed communication from a deity, leader, or text. If you are religious and have a moral dilemma about whether to lie to a friend, you can pray to God, consult a religious leader such as a priest, or read a religious text such as the Bible. Your aim is to get a faith-based answer that will tell you what you are morally obliged to do. Faith can also propose answers to factual questions, such as the age of the universe: fundamentalist Christians consult the Old Testament and their ministers and conclude that the universe began around six thousand years ago, in contrast to the fourteen billion or so years that scientific evidence suggests.

Religious faith is enormously important to the lives of billions of people, but it faces three serious problems as a means of deciding what to believe or what to do: variations among religions, falsity of religious beliefs, and evil actions based on religion. The first problem is that religions vary greatly in what gods, leaders, and texts they propose to believe in, and faith provides no basis for choosing among them. Should you have faith in the single Christian God, or in the dozens of Hindu gods such as Shiva? Who is a better guide to life, St. Paul or Muhammad? Should you listen to the Catholic pope or to a Protestant minister? Should you seek wisdom in the Bible, the Koran, or the Book of Mormon? There are major disagreements within and across various religions, and faith provides no way of settling such disagreements other than simply shouting that your faith is better than the others. Religious faiths cannot all be right, but they can all be wrong.

For most people, the religious faith that they acquire is an accident of birth. Consider two prominent examples, former American president

George W. Bush and Arab leader Osama bin Laden. Many of Bush's beliefs and decisions are based on his religious faith, which derives from his Christian Protestant background. He became more deeply religious in his early forties, giving up drinking and undertaking serious study of the Bible. Osama bin Laden has a very different set of beliefs and values, but they are also heavily faith based, deriving from his Muslim upbringing and subsequent study. Obviously, there are many Christians who do not share Bush's attitudes, and many Muslims who do not share bin Laden's, so religion is not the only determinant of their beliefs. But it is equally obvious that the particular faith that most people acquire is the result of their family circumstances. From a child's point of view, acquiring the parents' religious views makes sense, as the parents are the source of many kinds of reliable information. Once children are exposed to particular religions, their doctrines can become highly coherent with their other beliefs and personal goals. Such intense coherence can make it very difficult for a religious adherent to understand or take seriously opposing religious views, including atheistic ones that reject religion altogether. If faith is to be a source of knowledge, it cannot be accidental or arbitrary.

The second obvious problem in using religious faith as a basis of belief is that there have been many cases where beliefs based on it have turned out to be false. For example, the Catholic Church rejected the Copernican ideas of Galileo as heresy, but today even fundamentalists grant that the earth moves around the sun. Biological evolution was initially rejected as incompatible with the Bible, but today most Christians acknowledge that evolution occurred. Before modern medicine, many people believed that diseases are God's punishment for bad acts, but now we know that they have natural causes. Not all proponents of religion would accept these revisions, but many have recognized that theological descriptions of the motions of planets, the origin of species, and the causes of diseases are erroneous. Scientific beliefs have also turned out to be false, in accord with the expectation, discussed below, that new evidence and new hypotheses will lead to changing beliefs.

Religious faith meshes with tendencies in human thinking that are very natural even though they often lead to errors. One is confirmation bias, which is the tendency to notice only examples that support our beliefs while ignoring evidence that conflicts with it. For example, when religious leaders or texts make predictions, people tend to notice events that confirm those predictions, rather than events that refute them. Confirmation bias is a pervasive part of human thinking, as when people retain social stereotypes by noticing only cases that support the views they already hold.

An even more powerful kind of support for religious beliefs is motivated inference, which is the tendency to use memory and evidence selectively in order to arrive at beliefs that facilitate our goals. Belief in God can enable people to feel better about many things they desire, such as immortality, divine love, freedom, personal success, and the group identity and social support of their religious community. Unfortunately, the fact that a potential belief would help to accomplish your goals provides no reason for embracing the belief as true. Motivated inference and confirmation bias work together to make it very hard to change your mind even in the face of evidence that goes against what you want to believe.

The philosopher Charles Taylor proposes to discuss belief and unbelief, not as rival theories to account for existence and morality, but as different kinds of lived experience involved in understanding the fullness and richness of our moral and spiritual life. But without theories that can be supported by evidence, there is no reason to prefer one kind of lived experience over another, or to think that the experienced richness is anything but illusion based on our motivations to believe that there is more to the universe than there actually is. These motivations are powerful, offering reassurances of life after death and a divine plan ensuring that everything happens for a reason. But lived religious experiences can be explained as the result of psychological factors that are not signs of a reality that transcends scientific theorizing. Your lived experience may tell you that your life is full because of a caring God, but in the past people have felt just as strongly that the earth is flat, that the sun revolves around it, and that earthquakes are divine punishments.

The third serious problem of religious faith is that there have been many cases where actions based on it have turned out to be evil. To take just a few examples of faith-based intolerance, prejudice, and persecution, consider Christian crusader massacres, anti-Semitic pogroms, and the murder of thousands of people by Al-Qaeda in September 2001. All of these actions were supported by faith in preferred gods, leaders, and texts. Faith often produces an inordinate degree of certainty that fosters intolerance, as in the following joke:

I was walking across a bridge one day, and I saw a man standing on the edge, about to jump. I ran over and said: "Stop. Don't do it."

"Why shouldn't I?" he asked.

"Well, there's so much to live for!"

"Like what?"

"Are you religious?"

He said, "Yes."

I said, "Me too. Are you Christian or Buddhist?"

"Christian."

"Me too. Are you Catholic or Protestant?"

"Protestant."

"Me too. Are you Episcopalian or Baptist?"

"Baptist."

"Wow. Me too. Are you Baptist Church of God or Baptist Church of the Lord?"

"Baptist Church of God."

"Me too. Are you original Baptist Church of God, or are you Reformed Baptist Church of God?"

"Reformed Baptist Church of God."

"Me too. Are you Reformed Baptist Church of God, Reformation of 1879, or Reformed Baptist Church of God, Reformation of 1915?"

He said: "Reformed Baptist Church of God, Reformation of 1915."

I said: "Die, heretic scum," and pushed him off.

Faith often tells people that the beliefs of those who disagree with them are not only false but immoral, so that heretics deserve not just argument but punishment as well.

Religious faith has also been used to justify social inequality, as in the Christian doctrine of the Divine Right of Kings. If the authority and legitimacy of the monarch derives from God, then it cannot be challenged by people subject to tyrants. Similarly, the Hindu ideas of karma and reincarnation may seem benign, but have helped to legitimize the oppressive Indian caste system. If you are born into a miserable life, it must be because you did something horrible in a previous one. Religions focus people on eternal rewards, diverting them from the need to change conditions in their current lives.

Faith is usually used to support major religions, such as the variants of Christianity and Islam, but also contributes to a host of practices observed by people who consider themselves spiritual rather than religious. New Age beliefs in phenomena such as astrology, channeling, reincarnation, psychic experience, numerology, angels, crystals, and holistic health are supported by selective personal experience and attention to dubious authorities. Books by popular authors such as Deepak Chopra and Andrew Weil play the same role of fostering faith as do the Bible and Koran for adherents to Christianity and Islam, providing answers to difficult life questions whose appeal owes much more to confirmation bias and motivated inference than to careful marshaling of evidence.

An egregious example of New Age motivated inference is the 2006 best-selling book *The Secret,* which trumpeted the "Law of Attraction," according to which a person's thoughts attract corresponding positive or negative experiences. People find very appealing the idea that they can dramatically change their lives merely by positive thinking that improves their financial status and romantic relationships. Unfortunately, support for the law of attraction relies only on motivated inference, confirmation bias, and confused allusions to allegedly related scientific facts about energy, vibrations, and quantum physics. New Age spirituality does not defer to deities to the same extent as do traditional religions, but it has the same arbitrary reliance on leaders and texts as sources of ideas that are emotionally appealing but unsupported by evidence.

Evidence-based thinking can also lead to false beliefs and evil actions, but there are crucial differences. When disagreements occur, scientists do not have to resort to empty pronouncements about whose faith is stronger; instead they can attempt to assess competing beliefs with respect to the available evidence. It can take years or decades for scientific disputes to be resolved, but the method of resolution is not in dispute: collect more evidence and determine which of the conflicting views fits with it best. Strikingly, this process can lead to the abandonment of beliefs previously held, as has occurred in scientific revolutions and in much more mundane cases where scientists have been led by evidence to change their minds. Faith-based thinking provides no basis for resolving disagreements by changing minds, but evidence-based thinking does. Let us now look in more detail at how it works.

How Evidence Works

To begin with a familiar use of evidence, consider the reasoning in criminal investigations frequently portrayed in books, movies, and television. Such reasoning has been performed by Sherlock Holmes, the detectives in Agatha Christie novels, the investigators in TV shows such as *CSI* and *Law & Order*, and many other fictional characters. Reasoning to identify the criminals responsible for illegal actions is also performed by real-life investigators and prosecutors, as in the famous case of O. J. Simpson, a football player and movie star whose ex-wife was killed in 1994. Los Angeles detectives collected many kinds of evidence, such as Simpson's bloodstained glove, that led many people to conclude that he was guilty. Nevertheless, a jury in 1995 acquitted Simpson on the grounds that the prosecution had not shown beyond a reasonable doubt that he had killed his ex-wife. The jurors were legitimately influenced by evidence that racist members of the Los Angeles Police Department had fabricated some of the evidence. But it also appears that some of the jurors were motivated to find Simpson not guilty because of his achievements in football and movies.

Such motivations aside, here is how legal reasoning is supposed to work. Detectives and forensic investigators of a crime collect all the available relevant evidence, such as fingerprints. The best evidence is gleaned by carefully conducted observations, as when investigators thoroughly go over the undisturbed crime scene using techniques such as dusting for prints, collecting hairs, and taking photographs. Evidence can then be supplemented by scientific tools for analyzing blood and DNA. Contrast these kinds of evidence with information unlikely to have any connection with the actual crime, such as a psychic who reports seeing a killing in a dream.

On the basis of evidence and information about the victim, investigators form hypotheses about who committed the crime, and evaluate these hypotheses according to how well they explain the full range of evidence. A hypothesis is a guess about what might have caused something to happen. For example, the hypothesis that Simpson killed his ex-wife provides an explanation of why her blood was found on his glove. The explanation here is causal: the event of Simpson's stabbing her could have produced blood that got onto his glove. The job of the defense is to propose alternative explanations, in this case that the blood on Simpson's glove was planted there by police officers, and that Nicole Simpson was killed by drug dealers rather than by O. J. The jury is supposed to impartially determine whether the hypothesis that the accused committed the crime is the best explanation of the full range of evidence, beyond a reasonable doubt. Philosophers call this kind of reasoning *inference to the best explanation*.

Such reasoning is commonplace in everyday life. You use it whenever you are puzzled by the behavior of someone you know, as when a normally good-natured friend treats you in a hostile matter. In such cases you naturally seek explanations—for example, your friend is depressed because of troubles at work or school. An alternative hypothesis might be that you inadvertently said something that your friend found insulting. You need, then, to collect additional evidence that might tell you whether work stress or a perceived insult is the best explanation of your friend's hostile behavior. We use similar reasoning in dealing with mechanical problems. When your car won't start and you have to take it for repairs, the mechanic's job is to find the underlying breakdown that is the best explanation of what's wrong. Mechanics carry out a number of tests to try to figure out whether it is the battery, the ignition, or some other component that is preventing your car from starting.

Similarly, when you go to the doctor with a medical complaint—say, a pain in your stomach—your doctor collects additional evidence by probing your abdomen and possibly ordering tests such as blood work and X-rays. Your doctor's diagnosis is an inference to the best explanation about what underlying disease is responsible for the full range of evidence, including both your reported symptoms and the test results. The television show *House* portrays an obnoxious but brilliant doctor who every week has to find an unusual diagnosis for a patient suffering from an unusual range of symptoms. Dr. House is carrying out the same kind of reasoning as would Sherlock Holmes and your automobile mechanic: collecting evidence and trying to find out the best explanation for it.

Legal and medical hypotheses often involve multiple layers of explanations. Detectives looking for evidence that a suspect is guilty of a crime collect observations, such as fingerprints on the murder weapon, that are explained by the hypothesis that the suspect did it. But they also investigate possible motives that would explain *why* the suspect did it: perhaps the suspect was angry at the victim because of a previous fight. Similarly, a

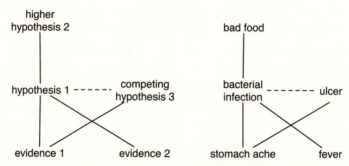

2.1 Structure of inference to the best explanation, with a higher hy
pothesis explaining a hypothesis that competes to explain the evidence. The solid lines indicate explanatory relations, whereas the
dotted lines show competition between alternative explanations.

doctor looking for the best explanation of your stomach symptoms will try
to ascertain not only the condition that caused them, but also what might
have caused your condition. For example, your having eaten some exotic
food might explain how you got a gastrointestinal infection that is the cause
of your stomach pain.

Figure 2.1 depicts the structure of how hypotheses such as those about
diseases serve to explain observed evidence and are themselves explained
by higher-level hypotheses. The general case is on the left, and a very simple medical example is on the right, with solid lines indicating explanatory
relations and dotted lines indicating competition between hypotheses. In
the general case, hypothesis 1 is highly coherent because it explains two
pieces of evidence and is explained by a higher hypothesis 2, which makes
hypothesis 1 superior to a competing hypothesis 3 that explains only one
piece of evidence. Similarly, in the stomach example on the right of figure
2.1, the hypothesis that the ache is caused by a bacterial infection wins
out as the best explanation both because it explains more evidence than
does the competing ulcer explanation, and because it can be explained by
the hypothesis of having eaten bad food. Choosing the best explanation
requires not just counting the pieces of evidence explained, but also evaluating which of the competing hypotheses have most overall coherence with
all the available information.

Evidence and Inference in Science

Of course, television shows and simple medical examples hardly constitute proof that inference to the best explanation is the right model for how people assess evidence, but I have used them as familiar illustrations. Much more seriously, we can consult the history of science for many examples of inference to the best explanation. Darwin's *On the Origin of Species* is a brilliant long argument for his theory of evolution by natural selection, showing that it provides a better explanation of evidence such as the fossil record than does divine creation. In physics, the acceptance of Newton's theory of gravitation, Einstein's theory of relativity, and quantum theory can all be understood as instances of inference to the best explanation. To take a more recent example, debates about why the dinosaurs became extinct sixty-five million years ago involve acquiring and assessing evidence that can be explained by competing hypotheses. The view that the dinosaur's demise was primarily the result of the collision of a massive asteroid with the earth is currently accepted because it explains such facts as why the fossil occurrence of dinosaurs stops at a level of sediment that contains the element iridium, which is commonly found in asteroids.

Inference to the best explanation in science has the same basic structure as does reasoning in law, medicine, and everyday life. In all these domains, you should collect as much relevant evidence as you can, consider higher-level hypotheses and alternative ones, and accept the ones that provide the best overall explanation of the evidence. A particular explanation describes how a hypothesized event or process might have caused what was observed. However, scientific instances of this kind of reasoning differ from everyday ones in several important respects involving mechanisms, mathematics, social structures, systematic observations, instruments, and experimentation.

First, explanations in science employ detailed mechanisms, which are descriptions of systems of interconnected parts that produce regular changes. To understand how a bicycle works, you need to identify its parts—the frame, pedals, wheels, chain, handlebars, and so forth—and how they connect to each other. The interrelations among the parts produce regular changes, as when pushing on the pedals moves the chain, which moves the wheels. Similarly, explanations in physics identify parts of things like atoms and subatomic particles, with relations between them such as forces that lead to motion and other changes. Explanations in biology identify parts of organisms—for instance, cells and proteins—whose biochemical interactions produce living processes such as reproduction. In psychology, explanations are increasingly becoming mechanistic as knowledge accumulates about how neural processes produce thought and behavior, as we will see in chapter 3. Biological and psychological explanations employ mechanisms that are far more active, complex, and adaptive than are the simple machines familiar in everyday life.

Second, science often uses mathematics in its formulation of hypotheses and explanations that connect them with observations. In fields as diverse as atomic physics, population genetics, and cognitive psychology, mathematics provides an indispensable tool for overcoming human cognitive limitations by efficiently representing the relationships among various quantities. Writing F = ma in Newton's laws of motion says no more than that force equals mass times acceleration, but it enormously facilitates applying it and other mathematical principles in derivations that connect theories with the evidence for them.

Third, the social structures of science enforce the logical prescriptions of inference to the best explanation more stringently than is found in everyday life. Scientists are just as prone as anyone else to confirmation bias and motivated inference, inclining them to pay more attention to evidence that supports their own theories. But they know that it will be hard to publish their favorite views in peer-reviewed journals unless they take into account a wide range of relevant evidence and alternative hypotheses. Detectives, doctors, and people explaining their friends' behavior should also consider all the evidence and alternative hypotheses, but they can often get away with much more selective kinds of thinking because they don't have to deal with reviewers and editors. Moreover, the social reward system of science encourages novelty, with incentives for those who generate exciting new theories and evidence. In contrast to conservative social organizations such as most religions, change in beliefs is not only tolerated but expected through introduction of new evidence and explanations. Science is recognized as approximate and fallible, allowing for the development of new and better theories rather than the dogmatic maintenance of orthodoxies.

Fourth, scientists are trained not to focus on just those observations that fit with their biases, but rather to conduct systematic observations that collect broad and representative samples of relevant data. Astronomers scan the skies systematically, making a broad range of observations that furnish evidence for evaluating competing theories about the nature and origins of the universe.

Fifth, whereas ordinary people gain evidence only from their senses such as sight, scientists use instruments to observe things and events that are out of reach of direct sense experience. Since the seventeenth century, scientists have been able to use telescopes, microscopes, X-ray machines, and many other kinds of instruments to make systematic observations of things that are too far away, too small, or too hidden to be directly perceivable.

The sixth and probably most important way in which evidence-based inference in science differs from everyday life is the use of experiments. All people learn from perceiving the world and make inferences about what best explains what they observe. But the use of carefully designed and controlled experiments is relatively recent in human history. Rough experiments were performed by ancient Greek and medieval Arab thinkers, but laboratory experiments with quantitative measurements began only around the seventeenth century. Galileo was one of the pioneers. Although he may never have conducted the famous experiment of dropping heavy and light balls from the Tower of Pisa, he did employ inclined planes to test the Aristotelian doctrine that weight does not affect the speed of descent. He used musical beats to measure the time it takes heavy and light balls to roll down a plane, and concluded that heavy and light balls fall at the same rate.

Such laboratory experiments have several advantages over more casual observations. First, experimenters perform planned manipulations, changing only a small number of the features of a situation in order to be able to identify causes and effects. Second, experiments are repeatable by different scientists; they can duplicate the same situation and events to see whether the results are the same even if the experiments are done at different times by different people. Third, the experimental situation can be designed to make possible precise quantitative measurements rather than vague qualitative ones. Precise and repeatable observations furnish evidence that can be challenging to different hypotheses, so that the results of laboratory experiments greatly aid the contribution of evidence to inference to the best explanation.

All inferences from observations presuppose a kind of inference to the best explanation. You cannot, for example, directly infer from "I see a bear" to "There is a bear that I see." That there actually is a bear in front of you is just one possible explanation of why you seem to see one; other possible explanations are that you are misled by a picture of a bear or by a large dog, or that you are hallucinating. Similarly, even from many observations of bears with teeth you cannot directly infer that all bears have teeth, for the best explanation of your many observations might be that you have been presented with an unusual sample of bears. However, if you have carried out many observations under good conditions and have evidence against alternative explanations, then you can be justified in concluding in the particular case that there is a bear, and in the general case that bears have teeth.

Laboratory experiments create special situations that help to rule out ways in which observations may be unreliable. For example, it is fortunate that Galileo conducted his falling balls experiment on inclined planes rather than only at the Tower of Pisa, where interfering factors such as gusts of wind might have produced less reliable results. For our theories to be well justified as the best explanation of what is observed, we need assurance that the observations are correct, which requires that the best explanation of their occurrence comes from the reality of what is observed rather than bias, chance, or incompetence. I will return to the importance of experiments in discussing evidence-based medicine later in this chapter. A much fuller discussion of how brain mechanisms make possible the perception of reality is found in chapter 4.

In science as in everyday life, inference to the best explanation often licenses inferences that go far beyond what can actually be observed. For example, when you think that a friend might be depressed, you are hypothesizing a mental state that you cannot directly observe. In law, a jury may conclude that someone had a malicious intention and therefore deserves to be convicted of murder rather than manslaughter. The jury members cannot see the past or current intentions of a suspect, but they can reasonably infer them from the suspect's behavior. In medicine, the occurrence of a disease may sometimes be perceived, but often it must be inferred. For example, a diagnosis of Alzheimer's disease cannot be directly confirmed without an autopsy that identifies plaques in a patient's brain, but it can nevertheless be established in a living patient by inference to the best explanation of behavioral symptoms such as severe memory loss. In all these cases, we accept a hypothesis as the best explanation of the evidence even though we cannot directly observe what is hypothesized.

Science also very frequently goes beyond the observable. Positivism is the philosophical view that such leaps are illegitimate, that science should stick to what can be observed with the senses. But why should observation be restricted to what the human senses, with their particular evolutionary limitations, can perform? There are other species that have a broader range of visual, auditory, or olfactory sensing than humans have. Humans have excelled, however, in developing instruments that vastly expand our sensory abilities, from telescopes to electron microscopes to brain-scanning machines. Chapter 4 will have much more to say about how brains have the capacity both to observe the world and to make inferences that go beyond observation.

The scientific leap beyond what is directly observable has had enormous theoretical and practical benefits. Physics and chemistry tell us that objects consist of atoms whose constituents include protons and electrons. We can observe atoms only by using electron microscopes, presupposing that there are electrons, which are not at all observable. But we have ample reason to believe that electrons exist, because the theories that postulate their existence have so much explanatory power. Countless phenomena of electricity and magnetism are best explained by the hypothesis that matter includes extremely small negatively charged particles. Without electrons, we have no credible explanation of how electric lights turn on and how computers enable us to process information.

In sum, the scientific use of evidence is radically different from and more effective than religious faith. Science uses explanations that are mechanistic and mathematical, observations that are systematic and made by instruments more powerful than human senses, and experiments that generate evidence acutely relevant to the choice of the best explanatory hypotheses.

Medicine: Evidence or Faith?

To further illustrate the nature and value of basing beliefs on careful collection and evaluation of evidence, consider the practice of medicine. When

I first heard of the movement for evidence-based medicine, my initial re-action was: what, there's another kind? I was shocked to learn that many medical treatments are based more on lore and common practice than on rigorous tests of efficacy. The movement for evidence-based medicine was started by visionaries such as Archie Cochrane, David Sackett, and Gordon Guyatt to make medical practice more scientific. They argued that the high-est standard of medical evidence should be the randomized, double-blind, placebo-controlled clinical trial. Suppose you have the medical hypothesis that vitamin C helps prevent colds. You might start taking the vitamin your-self and noticing when you get colds, or you might convince a bunch of friends to take vitamin C and track their health. However, such evidence would not be worth much, as you would unavoidably be prone to confir-mation bias and motivated inference, which incline you to notice the suc-cesses of vitamin C and ignore the failures. Most people who try something new from their health food store such as an herbal or homeopathic remedy are similarly prone to confirmation bias and motivated inference. The best explanation of conviction that a treatment works may well be such biases, rather than the actual efficacy of the treatment.

If you really want to know whether vitamin C prevents colds, you need to conduct a clinical trial that is controlled, which means that in addition to having a group that gets vitamin C, you have another group that does *not* get vitamin C. Having these two conditions allows you to assess whether the group that got vitamin C had fewer colds than the group that did not. If the vitamin C group gets fewer colds than the control group, then you have some grounds for thinking that the best explanation of the observed cold reduction is vitamin C, rather than bias or chance in the observation.

Another way to reduce bias is to randomize your controlled study by picking a homogeneous population of people and dividing them randomly (say, by flipping a coin) into two groups, one of which takes vitamin C and one of which does not. Otherwise, if people could simply choose whether to take vitamin C, it might be that this choice is made by people who are gen-erally health conscious and therefore would get fewer colds for other rea-sons. Similarly, you do not want people's doctors to decide who gets vitamin C, because the doctors may have a selection bias that would assign more or less healthy or compliant people to the vitamin C condition. If your study finds that people who take vitamin C get fewer colds, the best explanation of this finding should be that people really do get fewer colds, not that there was a biased selection concerning who took the vitamin.

The demand of inference to the *best* explanation also justifies the ideal requirements that randomized, controlled trials be double-blind and placebo controlled. Double-blind means that neither the participants in the study nor the experimenters know who is in the treatment condition or in the control condition. Otherwise, it might happen that people who know they are in the treatment condition might get better because of their expectations. The placebo effect is well known in medicine: giving patients a biologically inert treatment such as a sugar pill can help them have less pain or improve in other ways, even though the pill has no direct effect on the underlying disease. Thus in your vitamin C study you would want to make sure that participants in both conditions receive identical pills, so that they cannot tell whether or not they are getting the vitamin. Moreover, in addition to keeping the participants blind to whether they are getting vitamin C, you should ensure that the people giving the vitamin or placebo to people do not know who is getting what. Otherwise, experimenters who know who has taken vitamin C might expect that group to do better and treat them differently, perhaps leading them to actually have fewer colds. Double-blind experiments using placebos help to rule out the hypothesis that an observed effect of vitamin C is due to biased expectations of the participants or experimenters rather than to the causal efficacy of the treatment.

I hope this makes it clear why well-designed controlled clinical trials are a particularly good form of evidence: they give us strong grounds for thinking that the best explanation of medical observations is a hypothesis concerning the real cause or effective treatment of a disease, rather than an alternative hypotheses such as bias or chance. Strictly controlled experiments also set the highest standard of evidence in other scientific fields such as physics, molecular biology, and cognitive psychology. Unfortunately, there are many real-world domains—among them, astronomy, economics, and ecology—where controlled studies are difficult to carry out. In economics, for example, no one has the power or ethical justification to divide a set of countries randomly into two groups in order to see what kind of monetary policy is most effective. Similarly, in medicine there are often biological or ethical reasons why it is difficult to conduct randomized, controlled clinical trials. For example, surgery can rarely be conducted in a double-blind fashion, as the surgeon will know whether the patient is in a control condition, and cutting into a patient as a control condition is ethically dubious.

Although randomized, controlled trials are rightly touted as the highest standard, there is room for other kinds of data in evidence-based medicine, which allows a hierarchy that includes additional forms of investigation such as retrospective studies of natural cohorts. A large population whose use of vitamins and medical history was tracked over a long time may provide some evidence for accepting or rejecting the hypothesis that vitamin C prevents cold. In medicine and other areas of experimental science, it would be rash to rely on a single study to justify acceptance or rejection of a hypothesis. Rather conclusions about the value of a medical treatment should be based on systematic evaluation of whether its efficacy is the best explanation of many studies, including wherever possible the best designed, randomized, controlled clinical trials. Incidentally, carefully controlled clinical trials seem to show that taking large doses of vitamin C does *not* actually help to reduce the occurrence or severity of colds.

Many people, including even some doctors, have only a weak understanding of the rationale of evidence-based medicine. Some doctors continue to espouse the advantages of "clinical experience," which may indeed sometimes be a source of reliable observations about effective treatments for diseases. But it is very difficult to separate the reliable from the anecdotal or spurious, given that doctors are prone to cognitive and emotional biases just like other people. The situation is even worse for those who base their personal medical treatments on advice from naturopaths, health food personnel, and self-appointed medical gurus, most of whom have little acquaintance with good evidence. Even if a recommended treatment seems to work for you, you have no reason to believe that you are witnessing anything but a placebo effect or biased observation. It is possible that your favorite herbal remedy, homeopathic treatment, or chiropractic manipulation actually has some general medical efficacy, but there is no way of knowing without evidence derived from well-designed clinical trials.

Few people today rely solely on religion for medical treatment. Members of the Church of Christ, Scientist insist on spiritual healing instead of medical treatment, but their numbers are small and shrinking. Priests, ministers, rabbis, and Muslim imams consult doctors rather than merely relying on the power of divine intervention to cure their maladies. Of course, religious leaders also advocate prayer, but experiments have found that heart patients do not benefit from prayers for their recovery. Hence we have good reason to prefer evidence-based medicine over faith-based medicine.

Evidence-based medicine is not always easy. As I mentioned, it is often difficult to conduct the kinds of carefully controlled clinical trials that are most useful for determining the efficacy of medical treatments. Another worry is that many trials are conducted by pharmaceutical companies with a strong financial interest in showing that their own drugs are effective, raising difficult issues about bias arising from motivated inference. It is dismaying but not surprising that published tests are more likely to support the effectiveness of a drug if they are conducted by the company that sells it. American drug companies spend more money on marketing than they do on research and development. Hence it is no simple matter, institutionally or individually, to practice evidence-based medicine, but its advantages over faith-based medicine for patient health remain indisputable. Similarly, the advantages of evidence over faith in the pursuit of physics, chemistry, and biology are easily documented. Chapter 3 will argue for an evidence-based approach to psychology as well.

Medicine provides a telling example of the superiority of evidence over faith as a road to knowledge, but it would be good to have a more general argument that using evidence to make inferences to the best explanation is a method that reliably leads to true conclusions. There are often cases in everyday life and in science where evidence and inference lead us astray. Sometimes we fail to understand other people because we reach false conclusions about their mental states. In medicine many theories have turned out to be false even though they seemed to be the best explanation available at the time. The Hippocratic theory that diseases are caused by imbalances in the four humors of blood, phlegm, and yellow and black bile dominated medicine for two thousand years, and more recently accepted theories such as the association of stomach ulcers with stress have been overturned. Physics and chemistry have also had dominant explanatory theories that are now rejected, such as the views that light moves through an invisible medium called the ether, and that combustion occurs because burning objects emit a firelike substance called phlogiston. If evidence-based thinking using inference to the best explanation is so unreliable, maybe it really isn't much better than faith-based thinking.

The fact that inference to the best explanation of evidence can go astray is no reason to reject it, as long as it often gets things right and there is no alternative method that has a better record of achieving important truths and avoiding errors. I have already argued on the basis of technological successes that we have good reason to believe that the kind of evidence-based inference used in science does often achieve at least approximate truth; chapter 4 contains a fuller argument that science attains at least approximate knowledge about reality. In medicine we can point to the fact that the life expectancy of human beings is now double what it was two centuries ago, a testament to the truth of the germ theory of disease as providing ways of preventing and treating infectious diseases. The cases where accepted theories have been overturned point to a strength rather than a weakness of evidence-based thinking, which can progress by acquiring new evidence and developing new theories that explain it. Faith-based thinking has no such motivation to improve on what has already been laid down by sacred texts. In contrast, science thrives on belief revision and theory improvement spurred by experimental advances. Hence medical theory and practice should be based on evidence rather than faith.

Evidence, Truth, and God

It might be possible, however, to use evidence to support faith-based thinking. This support could come in either of two ways, through the use of evidence to justify claims for the existence of God or through the provision of evidence that faith-based thinking at least makes people happier than does evidence-based thinking. Some philosophers and scientists have thought that the existence of God does not have to be a matter of faith but rather can be justified on the basis of evidence. The two most compelling arguments for divine existence offer explanations of the origin and design of the universe. According to the cosmological argument, the world must have had a cause, which we can identify with God. Although this argument can be put in deductive form, it is most defensible when stated as an inference to the best explanation, with the hypothesis that God created the universe providing an explanation of how the universe began. Similarly, the argument from design is most convincing as a claim that the complexity of the biological world is the result of an intelligent designer who created all forms of life.

Although these two arguments are usually treated separately, they have greatest force when combined into one big coherent inference to the best explanation. We should conclude that God exists because that supposition provides the best explanation of both the existence and the complexity of the universe. This argument does not justify any particular religion, since it does not establish whether the god that is supposed to have created the world is Islam's Allah or the Catholic Trinity or the ancient Greeks' Zeus. But it would provide a basis for saying that there is some creator.

Unfortunately for the theist, this mega-argument for God's existence fails because science provides alternative, competing explanations. Darwin's theory of evolution by natural selection was momentous because it furnished a strong alternative explanation of biological complexity, one that has become all the more successful because of the development of allied theories of genetics and molecular biology. Understanding of proteins, genes, and ecological populations meshes with Darwin's basic insight to provide explanations of biological changes that are far more detailed and more fully supported by evidence than is the alternative theory of intelligent design. Scientific cosmology has found experimental support for the big bang theory that the universe began about fourteen billion years ago with an explosive expansion that continues today. This theory explains evidence that galaxies are becoming more distant, that there is microwave background radiation, and that the relative proportion of light elements in the universe is what early expansion would have produced. Where the big bang came from remains speculative, but recent work in string theory suggests a possible explanation in terms of the operations of space-time objects called "branes" (see chapter 10 for further discussion).

Even without that additional theory, the combination of biological evolution and big bang cosmology possesses far more explanatory power than does the hypothesis of divine creation. Modern evolutionary theory, including molecular biology and genetics in addition to natural selection, can explain a vast array of facts about the nature and development of organisms. Cosmology and allied areas of physics explain in detail a great many facts about the nature and history of the universe. Hence defenders of religious belief are forced to fall back on evidence-free and embarrassingly arbitrary rationalization by faith. They have yet to give plausible explanations as to how one might reconcile the hypothesis of creation by a benevolent God with the existence of natural disasters such as earthquakes and human-produced tragedies such as wars that together cause so much suffering in the world. The reconciliations that are offered—for instance, that God has a plan that we cannot hope to understand—are merely reaffirmations of faith.

For many people, the strongest evidence for the existence of God is their own personal lived experience of religious awe and devotion. There are, however, plausible psychological alternatives to the hypothesis that religious experience results from divine communication. Similar incidents can be induced by drugs such as LSD and by magnetic brain stimulation, taking on forms heavily influenced by personal cultural background. Hence religious experience can be explained as a kind of emotional consciousness arising from neural mechanisms described in chapter 5.

Even if empirical evidence beats blind faith as a road to truth, perhaps religious faith is a better route to satisfaction of personal goals than is scientific investigation. For many people, religion is a great source of comfort and reassurance that things will work out. There are even some studies suggesting that religious people are happier, although it is difficult to separate religiosity from other associated factors that also promote happiness, such as membership in a supportive community. Historically, religion has been more sociologically successful at providing a great many people with answers to questions about the meaning of life than alternative available sources, such as literature or philosophy, have been. In chapter 7, I will argue that evidence drawn from neuroscience and psychology can provide highly useful guidance about the achievement of happiness and a meaningful life.

If faith-based approaches to knowledge are inferior to evidence-based approaches, why does religion still dominate the thinking of the vast majority of people? I think the answer is a combination of testimony and motivated inference. As I remarked above, children acquire their first acquaintance with religious doctrines from their parents, who are generally reliable sources. Most of our beliefs do not derive from our own observations but rather depend on the testimony of others. Hence it is natural to acquire belief in God and the practice of faith from parents and other teachers to whom we are exposed long before we make any acquaintance with the systematic, evidence-based methods that science brings. In addition to testimony, religious beliefs, including looser ones about spirituality, are supported by motivated inference. We want to believe in religion and faith because they provide solace in a threatening world and reassurances about immortality, a caring God, religious community, and ultimate meaning. Chapter 5 will provide a neural account of emotional intuition that illuminates why faith can be such a compelling generator of belief.

A Priori Reasoning and Thought Experiments

Much philosophical discourse is based on neither empirical evidence nor faith. Many philosophers since Plato have sought a priori knowledge of necessary truths. One major method for trying to establish such truths is thought experiments, which are stories that are supposed to show what has to be true because of the nature of the concepts involved. I now argue that philosophical attempts to establish a priori conceptual truths are no better than faith-based thinking and need to be supplanted by arguments tied to evidence.

Besides the cosmological and design arguments for the existence of God, there is an a priori argument defended in different versions by such philosophers as Anselm, Descartes, and Leibniz. The ontological argument of Anselm says that God is by definition the greatest being conceivable, but if that being did not exist we could conceive of a being that is still greater because it does exist. But a being greater than the greatest being conceivable is a contradiction, so God conceived as the greatest must exist. Conceivability is also a major part of arguments that there is more to mind than just the body. Descartes claimed that he could easily imagine himself not having a body, but could not imagine not having a mind, since doubting that he thinks would still be thinking. He concluded that thinking, rather than having a body, is the essence of being a person. Variants of this argument survive today in philosophical claims that consciousness cannot be a physical process, as we shall see in chapter 3.

Such arguments assume that what we can conceive or imagine can tell us something about reality, that our minds have some way of grasping not only how the world is but how it has to be. But what we can imagine is determined by the concepts and beliefs that we already have, not by any kind of absolute faculty of conceiving. Most people cannot conceive of space as having more than three dimensions, but if you have learned the concepts and mathematics of string theory in physics, you can start to think of space-time as having ten or more dimensions. Some people find it hard to imagine ceasing to exist, but if they abandon the concept of a soul and begin to think of themselves in terms of perishable brains and bodies, then it becomes much easier (although not pleasant) to conceive of one's total demise. The history of thought is full of cases where what was conceivable changed as a function of the availability of new concepts and theories. The atom was once defined in terms of its indivisibility, but now we divide atoms into myriad subatomic particles. Some dictionaries still define marriage as the union of a man and woman, but same-sex marriage has become common in a few countries like Canada and the Netherlands.

Plato assumed that beliefs arrived at by thought alone would be true because he thought that they would arise because of the ability of souls to grasp ideal heavenly forms (ideas). But if minds are brains rather than souls (as chapter 3 argues) and if concepts are neural processes rather than ideal entities (as chapter 4 argues), then a priori beliefs can be false. A priori beliefs, if there are any, would need to be based on innate ideas, concepts that we have at birth. It is indeed possible that humans do have some such concepts that have arisen through evolution because they make organisms more successful at surviving and reproducing. But such evolutionary advantages do not imply that the concepts are anything more than useful approximations to reality, or that beliefs derived from them are true.

For example, babies may be born with concepts of space consistent with assumptions of Euclidean geometry, but Einstein's general theory of relativity implies that space is non-Euclidean. It may be useful to arrive in the world with the innate belief that all snakes are dangerous, even though some species of snakes are harmless. The theories that best explain the observations that we can now collect using telescopes and other powerful instruments may supersede theories aligned with concepts that evolved merely to support survival and reproduction. Hence even if we can generate a priori arguments that everyone would assent to, we shouldn't trust them in the absence of consideration of the much broader range of evidence available to scientists today and not to our evolutionary ancestors.

A priori reasoning based on what is conceivable is not the same as faith, in that it does rely on arguments rather than on blind trust in a deity, leader, or text. But it has the same arbitrary nature as faith. Just as what people adopt as their particular brands of religious faith depends largely on their upbringings and associates, so what people take to be true a priori—what they can imagine—depends on what they have already learned. Thus theists look for a priori justifications of God and dualists look for a priori grounds for rejecting materialism, the view that nothing exists except for matter and energy. Few materialists, however, look for a priori grounds for the existence of matter and energy while rejecting God and the soul; materialists are usually naturalists, defending their conclusions on the basis of evidence and inference to the best explanation.

I used to think that there is at least one a priori truth, identified by the American philosopher Hilary Putnam: Not every statement is both true and false. But then I heard it said of a postmodernist philosopher that he defined truth as whatever your contemporaries will let you get away with. I don't think this is a good definition of truth, and will argue in chapter 4 for a more traditional view that truth is correspondence with reality. But this highly relativist view is at least conceivable, and it allows the possibility that your contemporaries might be so gullible that they could be convinced of every statement and its negation. Then it would be conceivable that every statement is both true and false! Hence while I agree with Putnam that not every statement is both true and false, and would even argue for the much stronger view that *no* statement is both true and false, I cannot view either of these claims as ones we know entirely by reason.

If you stretch your mind a bit, even violations of the law of noncontradiction become conceivable. Some Hegelians and Marxists claimed that, to understand motion in the light of Zeno's paradox, we need to consider that an object is both in a place and not in that place at the same time. A contemporary philosopher has asserted that paradoxical statements like "This sentence is false," which is false if it's true and true if it's false, are best understood as *both* true and false. I think there are better ways to understand motion and logical paradoxes than by allowing a statement to be both true and false; indeed, I would say that the principle of noncontradiction is true, in our world. But the fact that some people have had the audacity to conceive exceptions to it provides grounds for doubting that it is true a priori. You may insist that no one can *really* conceive it as false because you cannot, but there is nothing more beyond this than there is in the religious faith that no one can really doubt that a god created the universe.

One of the motivations for using a priori reasoning is to arrive at necessary truths, ones that hold not only in our world but in all possible worlds. But what determines whether a world is possible? If possibility is conceivability, it is arbitrary, because conceivability is merely relative to what you already believe. Logical possibility is usually defined as consistency with the laws of logic, but we have just seen that even violation of the principle of noncontradiction is conceivable, so we do not know a priori what the laws of logic are. Hence the notion of necessary truths is just as empty as the notion of the a priori. Both serve merely, like faith-based assertions, to provide ill-founded support for what people happen already to believe. The concept of necessity is a vestige of theology and should be dispatched to the dustbin of history, along with deity and monarchy. In the next chapter, I will discuss how the most common philosophical argument against identification of mind and brain appeals to this illegitimate notion of necessity.

Surely, as some philosophers will reply, at least the truths of mathematics must be necessarily true and knowable a priori: we can't really imagine that 1 + 1 isn't 2. But Douglas Hofstadter considers the exercise of imagining what the world would be like if 13 were not a prime number. The philosopher Immanuel Kant claimed that the truths of Euclidean geometry were necessary and a priori, but in the nineteenth century non-Euclidean geometry was developed and even became part of physics in Einstein's theory of relativity. I do find it hard to imagine that 1 and 1 might not make 2, but I also find it hard to imagine that carrots might not be orange. Once again, what we can conceive or imagine depends on what else we believe, not on some absolute direct access to what has to be true.

Much philosophical writing assumes that thought experiments like Descartes' imagining himself without a body can reveal conceptual truths. Some have even argued that scientists such as Galileo used thought experiments legitimately to establish necessary truths. Galileo cleverly refuted the Aristotelian assumption that heavy objects fall faster than light ones by imagining what would happen if a heavy object were tied to a light one, creating a still heavier object. But he also did extensive experiments measuring the motion of objects of different weights on inclined planes.

I grant that thought experiments can be useful in science and philosophy for revealing inconsistencies in opposing views, and they can also be helpful for developing new hypotheses, as they were for Einstein when he imagined himself chasing after a beam of light. But I know of no case in science where a theory was adopted merely on the basis of thought experiments. Galileo's physics legitimately won out over the Aristotelian view because of the amassing of large amounts of observational evidence for it. Without such evidential evaluation, use of thought experiments becomes merely the trumpeting of one philosopher's intuitions over another's, a process no more conducive to truth than the professions of faith by advocates of rival religious sects. For every thought experiment there is an equal and opposite thought experiment.

Thought experiments are often viewed as tools for conceptual analysis, but the idea that the job of philosophy is to clarify concepts rests on several mistakes. First, it assumes that philosophy should be happy with examining our current set of concepts, a conservative view that conflicts with the history of science, which shows the value of drastically revising empirically inadequate concepts such as planet, force, air, and life. As in science, the point of philosophy should be to improve concepts, not to analyze them. Second, the idea of philosophy as conceptual clarification assumes that concepts can be examined independently of the theories in which they are embedded. But we see from the history of science that concepts like the ones just mentioned change when theories change: adoption of new theories leads to adoption of new concepts. Chapter 4 will develop a neural theory of concepts that will show how their meanings mesh with both theory and observation.

Hence this book does not attempt to analyze concepts such as wisdom or the meaning of life, any more than it uses thought experiments or a priori reasoning. These mainstays of philosophical deliberation have little to tell us about the nature of knowledge, reality, morality, or meaning. Rather, in the naturalistic tradition of philosophers such as Aristotle, John Locke, David Hume, John Stuart Mill, Charles Peirce, John Dewey, and W.V.O. Quine, I will try to tie philosophical conclusions to the best available evidence, especially to new findings in psychology and neuroscience. Philosophy can be experimental and theoretical much as science can, but with greater generality and emphasis on normative issues to be discussed.

Conclusion

This chapter has attempted to provide good reasons for a naturalistic, evidence-based pursuit of knowledge that matters. Faith-based approaches to the meaning of life are limited because they provide no grounds for choosing among the large array of religious faiths available. George W. Bush and Osama bin Laden have their different faiths, but no basis of arguing that one is any better than the other. Faith has been used to support many beliefs that we have good grounds to deem false, such as placing the earth at the center of the universe. Faith has also been used to support many practices, such as religious wars and torture, that from a broader perspective are more in tune with evil than with good. Faith provides no way of resisting natural error tendencies in human thinking, including confirmation bias and motivated inference.

In contrast, although evidence-based thinking is fallible, it has an effective method of correcting errors, by systematically collecting new evidence, developing new explanatory hypotheses, and selecting the best. Experimental methods such as those used in evidence-based medicine have the advantage of making inference to the best explanation more effective by helping to identify cases where observations are the result of bias, error, or chance. Inference to the best explanation enables us to go beyond the limits of human sensory observations to accept theories about nonobservable entities such as viruses and electrons. Done carefully, such inference does not suffice to justify belief in God.

The philosopher Karl Popper is often cited as having shown that the crucial difference between science and nonscience is falsifiability. Scientists are supposed to make bold conjectures and then devise experiments that can refute them. Then the point of scientific evidence is not to show that theories are true, as in inference to the best explanation, but rather to show that they are false. According to Popper, what makes metaphysical theories bogus is that they are not falsifiable in this way.

As a philosophy of science, however, Popper's view has many problems. No theory is strictly falsifiable, because a theory can be used to make predictions only in conjunction with other assumptions, such as experimental conditions and the reliability of instruments. Hence when a prediction fails, a scientist cannot know whether to infer the falsity of the theory or that of one of the assumptions. Historically, scientific theories are refuted only when a better theory comes along to provide a better explanation of the experimental evidence. Popper's view of method expects scientists to aim to show that their own theories are false, but such intentional self-refutation rarely happens. The reason is not just that scientists grandiosely seek their own personal success; rather, the aims of science include arriving at theories that accurately describe reality and provide informative explanations of observed phenomena.

Therefore, the hallmark of science is not falsifiability but use of evidence in inferences to the best explanation. Inference to the best explanation can lead us to conclude that many metaphysical theories are not only falsifiable but false. For example, I argued earlier in this chapter that, based on available evidence, we should conclude that there are no gods. Similarly, chapter 3 argues that the hypothesis of the existence of the soul can be judged to be false because of much greater evidence for the alternative view that minds are brains.

Philosophical attempts to establish truths by a priori reasoning, thought experiments, or conceptual analysis have been no more successful than faith-based thinking has been. All these methods serve merely to reinforce existing prejudices. In contrast, evidence-based thinking often forces us to realize that our old theories and the concepts embedded in them are inadequate, leading to the development of new ones that fit much better with the full range of observations. That is why our search for wisdom should not be based on faith or pure reason, but instead requires attention to all the relevant evidence, especially what can be learned from research in psychology and neuroscience. A crucial step in this search is the recognition that minds are brains.

minds are brains

The Brain Revolution

Your brain is a mass of cells inside your skull and weighs around 1.4 kilograms, or 3 pounds. Common sense insists that your mind, with all its amazing powers of thinking and feeling, cannot just be your brain. The contrary belief that minds are souls is firmly held by the large majority of people who belong to theistic religions, and by many philosophers since Plato and Descartes. They allow that the mind may be closely associated with the body and especially with the brain, but insist that mind and brain are not the same because they have different properties. Your brain has mass, consists of matter and energy, and ceases to function when you die; whereas your soul weighs nothing, is not subject to physical laws, and survives your death. Most people today are dualists, believing that a person consists of both a spiritual mind and a physical body.

In contrast, most psychologists and neuroscientists are materialists and believe that minds are brains: the mind is what the brain does. General acceptance of this view would amount to the most radical conceptual revolution in the history of human thinking. Previously, the two most sweeping scientific revolutions were Copernicus's rejection of Ptolemy's view that the earth is the center of the universe, and Darwin's rejection of the religious view that humans were specially created by God. According to modern astronomy, the earth is just another planet circling the sun, which is just one of billions of stars in billions of galaxies. According to Darwin, humans are just another biological species evolved through natural selection. The Brain Revolution now in progress is even more threatening to humans' natural desire to think of ourselves as special, for it implies that our treasured thoughts and feelings are just another biological process. Unsurprisingly, even some nonreligious thinkers find disturbing the view that minds are brains, despite mounting evidence for such identification. Not only immortality but also highly compelling doctrines of free will and moral responsibility have been tied to the idea of minds as souls. The lure of dualism is powerful.

This chapter will argue that the hypothesis that minds are brains has far more explanatory power than does its main competing hypothesis that minds are souls. Later I will also consider two prominent materialist views that resist identifying minds with brains: the functionalist view that minds can be processes in many different physical systems, and the embodiment view that minds are states of the whole body. I think that neither of these views contradicts my main claim that human minds are brains, which is, however, radically incompatible with the commonsense view that minds are not physical objects.

Philosophers call the claim that states and processes of the mind are identical to states and processes of the brain the *identity theory*. Mind-brain identification follows a long line of theoretical identifications that have marked scientific progress: sounds are waves; combustion is chemical combination with oxygen; water is H_2O; heat is motion of molecules; lightning is electrical discharge; light is electromagnetic energy; influenza is a viral infection; and so on. Each of these identities is part of a larger theory that was accepted because it provided a better explanation of the relevant evidence than did competing theories. Similarly, I will argue that the claim that minds are brains is part of a rich theory that provides explanations for many mental phenomena, including perception, memory, learning, inference, and emotion. Once this identification is established, we can consider the radical implications for traditional philosophical questions about reality, knowledge, morality, and personal meaning. Eventually, we will be able to learn from the neural processes that underlie love, work, and play why they are such important realms of human life.

Evidence That Minds Are Brains

We believe that water is H_2O and that lightning is an atmospheric electrical discharge because these identifications are parts of accepted theories with substantial explanatory power. The connection between lightning and electricity was first noticed in 1746 when the Dutch physicist Peter van Musschenbroek developed the Leyden jar as a way of storing static electricity. Benjamin Franklin's famous kite experiment in 1752 provided the first direct evidence that lightning is a discharge of electricity. This hypothesis explained not only why sparks flew from the key that Franklin had attached to the kite he flew in a thunderstorm, but also a broad array of observations about lightning, such as its bright flashes, its production of loud sounds, and its ability to injure people. Demonstrating that minds are brains is more complicated but is based on the same kind of reasoning, providing a large array of evidence for which this hypothesis is part of the best explanation.

How Brains Explain

It was not always obvious that brains have much to do with thinking. Aristotle believed that the primary organ supporting thought was the heart rather than the brain, whose main function was to cool the blood. By the sixteenth century, however, rough connections between the brain and thinking were generally recognized—for example, that vision and hearing depend on brain anatomy. Understanding of how brains work began only at the end of the nineteenth century when the development of new chemical techniques for staining cells made possible identification of the cells that constitute brains. It was decades before the electrical nature of brain cells— neurons—was appreciated. Only with the development of computers did it become possible to formulate and test detailed hypotheses about how the interactions among large numbers of neurons might be able to support different kinds of thinking.

When the psychologist Stephen Pinker was on the TV show *The Colbert Report* in 2007, Stephen Colbert insisted that he explain, in five words or fewer, how the brain works. Pinker's brilliantly concise response was "Brain cells fire in patterns." Neurons are different from the cells that make up other bodily organs in that they build up electrical charges; they can pass these on to other neurons that are connected to them. Firing is a kind of electrical discharge. The flow of electrical charge in neurons is only a few millivolts, compared to as much as a billion in lightning flashes, and also differs in being directed along pathways formed by the thousand or so connections that a neuron has with other neurons. These connections are called synapses. Figure 3.1 depicts how one neuron can send messages in the form of electric signals to another neuron by means of synaptic connections.

A firing neuron does not simply send a spark across to another neuron but rather sends a chemical signal in the form of neurotransmitters that flow

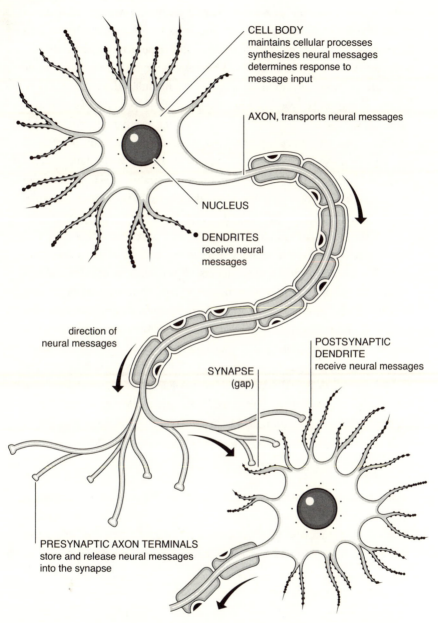

CELL BODY
maintains cellular processes
synthesizes neural messages
determines response to
message input

AXON, transports neural messages

NUCLEUS

DENDRITES
receive neural
messages

direction of
neural messages

POSTSYNAPTIC
DENDRITE
receive neural messages

SYNAPSE
(gap)

PRESYNAPTIC AXON TERMINALS
store and release neural messages
into the synapse

3.1 A functional model of two connected neurons.

from the firing neuron across the synaptic gap to the neurons to which it is connected. Using these signals, one neuron can either excite the neurons to which it is connected, increasing their electrical activity, or inhibit the activity of the connected neurons. Whereas a lightning flash is like a single trumpeter producing a loud sound with no intended direction, the synaptic connections between neurons enable them to perform like a trained orchestra with many coordinated musicians. Just as a band performance is a complex pattern of activity in a group of musicians, a brain function is accomplished by patterns of coordinated firing activity in interconnected neurons. The brain is not like a symphony orchestra that has a conductor to keep everyone synchronized, but more like a bunch of jamming jazz musicians whose coordinated playing emerges from their dynamic interactions.

At first it seems incredible that patterns of electrochemical activity in a bunch of cells could generate thought. Then again, it is also not obvious that a hundred musicians playing together could produce a beautiful symphony, or that billions of tiny water molecules in a cloud could accumulate a huge electrical charge that generates bright flashes of lightning and loud rolls of thunder. But much is coming to be known about how patterns of neural firing can produce complex kinds of perception, memory, learning, inference, language, and other mental functions. In what follows I will be extremely introductory. I don't need to convince neuroscientists or cognitive psychologists that minds are brains, so the explanations that follow are aimed at people new to the idea that thinking might be explained neurologically.

Perception

First consider our senses of sight, hearing, smell, taste, and touch, which are major sources of information about the world. Much is known about the physical basis of how these senses work, because they can be studied in nonhuman animals whose senses seem to operate much as our own do. Here is what happens when you see a tree. Light reflects off the tree and into your eyes, where photons stimulate some of the millions of nerve cells in the retina at the back of your eyeball. These cells then send signals along your optic nerve to the back of your brain to the occipital lobe, which begins a complex process of interpreting the retinal input using a series of regions that include parts of the temporal lobe (see figure 3.2). Eventually,

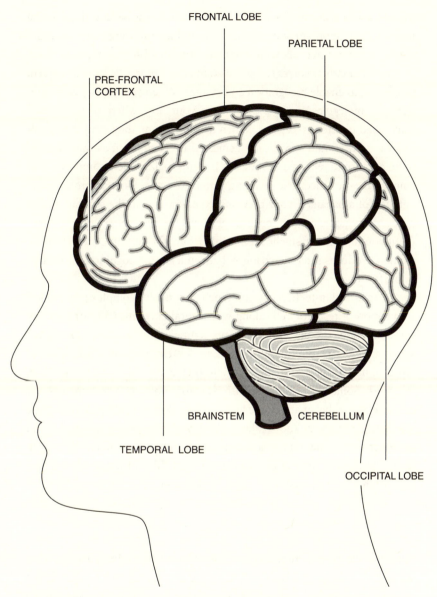

FRONTAL LOBE

PARIETAL LOBE

PRE-FRONTAL
CORTEX

BRAINSTEM   CEREBELLUM

TEMPORAL LOBE

OCCIPITAL LOBE

3.2 Rough sketch of some major regions of the brain. For a more detailed diagram, see
figure 5.1.

the result is a pattern of activation of neurons in the several regions that reactivates an approximation to the pattern of neural firing that constitutes your concept of a tree, allowing you to identify the observed object as a tree.

Smell similarly involves the stimulation of receptor cells and subsequent processing to enable recognition and storage. When you sniff a banana, for example, molecules of it are drawn into your nose where they stimulate cells called olfactory receptors. When these cells fire, they send the signals to areas of the brain specifically dedicated to smell, such as the olfactory bulb, but also to related areas such as the amygdala, which is important for emotional experience. The resulting pattern of activation may produce recognition of a banana if your previous experiences with the substance have produced synaptic connections that generate a similar pattern of activation. Or, if you have never smelled a banana before, the resulting pattern of activation produces synaptic changes that can lead to recognition of bananas in the future.

The senses of taste, hearing, and touch also involve complex processes of stimulation of receptor cells along with neural encodings and transformations. Similarly, the perception of pain, temperature, balance, and internal states such as gastrointestinal fullness are increasingly well understood in terms of how dedicated brain areas interpret signals from various kinds of receptors. Some animals have sense receptors not found in humans—for example, those that enable some fish to detect electric fields. Although there is still much that is unknown about how brains perceive sights, smells, and other sensations, neural explanations of perception are sufficiently rich to justify thinking of perception as a collection of different kinds of brain processes. Chapter 4 discusses further how brains perceive the world.

Memory

Similarly, the basic neural mechanisms of memory are increasingly being worked out. When you have an interesting experience such as attending a concert, your neurons fire in patterns that together capture your experience of the concert. Forming a memory of the concert requires changes in your neural connections that will enable you to retrieve a memory of the concert in the future. To understand memory, we need neural theories of both storage and retrieval.

Storing memories in the brain is not like saving a computer file, which can immediately produce a record that can be fully re-created in its original form. The perceptions that form your experience of the concert are first captured by neural populations in your hippocampus, a brain area so crucial that people with damage to it sometimes become incapable of forming any new memories at all. But permanent storage of your concert memory requires interactions between the hippocampus and regions of the cortex, the outer layer of the brain. Storage in both areas is another case of learning, as described in the next section, produced by changes in the synaptic connections between neurons.

Retrieval of a memory works by reactivating a pattern of firing in a population of neurons. Suppose someone starts telling you about another concert that is similar to the one you went to, perhaps because the bands played the same kind of music. Hearing about the new concert may produce a pattern of firing in roughly the same populations of neurons that encoded the various aspects of the old concert. The newly generated pattern of firing will then generate additional neural activity by virtue of synaptic connections, possibly producing a pattern of firing that is roughly similar to your original experience. That activation of a firing pattern of neurons constitutes your recalling the memory.

Many different kinds of experiments support the hypothesis that memory is a brain process. I have already mentioned the sad case of people with damage to the hippocampus who are unable to form memories. When people with Alzheimer's disease lose their memories, autopsies show buildup of plaques that have destroyed neural connections. Brain scans measuring the flow of blood to regions as small as a few millimeters show what anatomical areas become active when people are presented with stimuli of different kinds similar to ones they remember. Together, such experiments provide strong evidence that when you remember something, it is because your brain has revived patterns of neural activation.

Learning

Even snails and slugs can learn. The American neuroscientist Eric Kandel won a Nobel Prize for his research on how learning works in the sea slug, *Aplysia*. These slugs have only a few thousand large neurons, so Kandel was able to map out the connections among them and investigate the chemical mechanisms responsible for the formations of these connections. Sea slugs don't learn much, but they are able to modify such behaviors as eating and withdrawing from noxious stimuli. Kandel showed in the 1960s how these behavioral changes result from changes in synapses, the connections between neurons. For example, when a sea slug is exposed to a new substance and given an electric shock, its neurons undergo chemical changes that alter its behavior, enabling it to avoid the substance.

Much later, Kandel was able to show that sea slugs experience Hebbian learning, a process hypothesized by the Canadian neuroscientist Donald Hebb. This kind of learning is captured in a slogan that summarizes how two neural connections are formed: what fires together wires together. Consider two neurons with a weak synaptic connection that are both made to fire by the same stimulus. According to Hebb, there should be a mechanism by which their firing at the same time wires the neurons together by increasing strength of the synaptic connection between them. From the work of Kandel and many other researchers, we now know that this kind of learning occurs in sea slugs and also in animals with much more complex brains.

Cognitive neuroscience is still far from having a full explanation of all the different kinds of human learning right up to the most creative leaps made by human scientists, inventors, and artists. But thanks to research by Kandel and others, there is no doubt that many kinds of learning are the result of identifiable brain processes. Conditioning and Hebbian learning occur in humans as well as lower animals. The psychiatrist Norman Doidge has written an accessible book about neuroplasticity, the enormous adaptability of the human brain that is the result of its learning mechanisms. We do not need to have a fully worked-out account of every kind of human learning to note the substantial ongoing explanatory successes of the hypothesis that learning is a brain process.

Inference and Language

Most cognitive science research on inference, problem solving, and language has developed psychological rather than neurological explanations. But progress is rapidly being made on neural explanations of high-level thinking, and I will give only a few examples. John Anderson is a psychologist well known for his computational models of problem solving, and he has increasingly tied these models to the operations of particular brain areas. Vinod Goel has used brain scanning to identify neuroanatomical correlates of high-level reasoning. Jerome Feldman has proposed a neural theory of the learning and application of language.

Reading is a practically important example of inference and language, and a leading researcher on dyslexia has recently reviewed the current state of knowledge of how brains manage to read. Maryanne Wolf points out that literacy is a recent development in human history, going back only about five thousand years, to the Sumerians. There is no evidence that the brain evolved special functions to support reading; rather, reading is like many other cultural developments in using neural mechanisms that evolved for other reasons. Wolf describes how successful reading requires interactions among several brain areas, including occipital, temporal, and frontal regions. Difficulties in reading can arise because of problems with particular areas, such as the angular gyrus, but also because of interactions between or among different areas. Neural explanations of reading ability and dyslexia are still sketchy and provisional, but the prospects for further advances in the understanding of these and other features of language use appear strong.

In order to have a full neural theory of human thinking, we would need to have explanations of how the brain carries out the most high-level, creative kinds of thought. Theories are just beginning to be developed of how the brain manages its most impressive feats, like solving challenging problems, writing novels, composing music, and creating scientific theories. There are rough ideas about how the brain manages to be creative, but nothing yet that could count as a mechanistic explanation. How does the brain form new scientific concepts, such as sound wave, electron, and gene? How can groups of neurons generate new hypotheses, like the idea that species evolve by natural selection? More mundanely, how do neurons carry out basic forms of inference such as deduction, generalization from examples, and analogy? The present shortage of available answers to these questions is not evidence against the hypothesis that minds are brains. That much remains to be understood about thunderstorms does not undermine the fact that identification of lightning with atmospheric electrical discharge has had great explanatory success. Every scientific theory is incomplete in that there are some relevant phenomena that it cannot explain, but such gaps become evidence against a theory only when an alternative theory arises that can fill them by explaining the phenomena. The view that minds are souls cannot explain creativity and high-level inference either, and lacks any prospects for explanatory progress.

Drugs and Diseases

The impressive connections between mental processes such as perception, learning, memory, and reading and specific brain processes are evidence for the identification of mind and brain only if brain changes cause mental changes. But perhaps there is only correlation here rather than causation. The fact that ice cream consumption and drowning frequency are correlated does not show that one causes the other, as they have a common cause in high temperatures. A dualist could argue that all the empirical studies described above merely show that brain processes correlate with mental ones without brain's being the exclusive cause of mind. In scientific reasoning, the best way to show causation rather than mere correlation is to introduce an intervention, showing that manipulating one factor leads to a change in another factor. In psychology and neuroscience, there are both technical and ethical reasons why it is often hard to show that manipulating the brain can produce mental changes.

However, people frequently engage in such manipulations when they take drugs that have psychological effects. If you use recreational drugs such as alcohol or therapeutic drugs such as antidepressants, you are producing a physical change in your brain that changes your mental state in predictable ways. A quick review of how drugs affect the brain and thereby change mental states provides evidence that the connection between brain and mind is causal and not just correlational.

Much is now known about the neural and molecular mechanisms that draw people to recreational drugs. When you have a glass of beer, wine, or whiskey, the alcohol quickly affects your brain chemistry. Because of increased concentrations of the neurotransmitter dopamine, there is increased activity in the nucleus accumbens, a brain area associated with feelings of pleasure. Alcohol also increases activity of the neurotransmitter GABA, which enables some neurons to inhibit the firing of other neurons. You then get greater inhibition of neural firing, which in small doses of alcohol can produce relaxation but in large doses can lead to lack of coordination, slurring of words, and even passing out. Other neurotransmitters that are altered by alcohol include serotonin and norepinephrine. Extensive studies with animals and humans support the following causal chain: drinking alcohol changes your brain processes and thereby changes your thinking. Similarly, we know that people become addicted to smoking cigarettes because nicotine stimulates acetylcholine receptors and increases dopamine levels, producing a physical dependency.

The neuropsychological mechanisms triggered by illegal drugs are also well understood. Stimulants such as cocaine and amphetamines, including the popular drug Ecstasy, increase brain concentrations of the pleasure-inducing neurotransmitter dopamine, as well as other energizing neurotransmitters such as norepinephrine. Dependency on such drugs can arise because depletion of these neurotransmitters produces cravings for more of the drug. Opiates such as heroin stimulate special receptors in the brain leading to release of dopamine and subsequent feelings of pleasure and relaxation, producing strong inclinations toward addiction. Enough is known about how such powerfully addictive drugs work that we can confidently say that people use them to manipulate mental states by changing their brain states.

In psychiatry, drugs used to treat mental illnesses also perform such manipulations. For depression, millions of people take drugs like Prozac and Zoloft that inhibit the reuptake of the neurotransmitter serotonin. How these drugs alleviate depression may involve the production of new neurons in the hippocampus as well as increased availability of serotonin in the synaptic gaps between existing neurons. Other antidepressants, such as MAO inhibitors, affect neurotransmitters in different ways. Bipolar disorder, formerly known as manic depression, can be effectively treated with lithium, which affects various neurotransmitters. The often devastating disease schizophrenia can sometimes be treated with drugs like Thorazine and Risperdal that inhibit dopamine and also can affect levels of other neurotransmitters. Increasing concentrations of dopamine can alleviate the symptoms of Parkinson's disease.

Thus the use of recreational and therapeutic drugs provides overwhelming evidence that changing brain processes causes changes in mental processes. Of course, the precise effects of drugs often depend on expectations, as when people get more drunk than normal on a small amount of alcohol just because of their social surroundings. So it is legitimate to say that mental processes cause brain processes too. After all, the mind-brain identity theory just says that mental processes are brain processes, and there is no problem in saying that brain processes cause other brain processes. More importantly, these expectation effects provide no evidence for reintroducing the soul or other nonmaterial substance into explanations of brain changes, because beliefs can be understood as neural processes.

In this section I have only scratched the surface of the kinds of explanations that neuroscience is increasingly able to give of diverse kinds of thinking. Those wanting more detail should consult textbooks and journals in cognitive neuroscience and psychopharmacology, which will provide pointers to thousands of experiments that investigate the neural bases of perception, memory, learning, emotion, and other mental processes. The hypothesis that minds are brains is part of a highly successful and rapidly expanding research program that has been generating neural explanations for a wide range of mental phenomena. Experimental methods used by this research program include not only brain scans that can identify correlations between thinking and neural activity, but also transcranial magnetic stimulation that can cause changes in thinking by noninvasive alteration of the electrical activity of neurons. In this technique, electromagnetic pulses are used to disrupt neural firing, causing changes in cognitive processes such as vision and memory.

Later in this book I will provide more evidence supporting mind-brain identity. Chapters 4–6 will provide fuller accounts of how brains know the world, have emotional experiences, and make decisions. Proponents of the soul hypothesis cannot avoid the evidence that links such aspects of mind with brain processes, but they have to say that the brain hypothesis is not by itself sufficient to explain everything about thinking. Dualism maintains that people consist of both minds and bodies, or more specifically souls and brains. Let us now consider some evidence that might support dualism over the simpler identification of minds with brains.

Evidence for Dualism?

Survival after Death

Despite my current confidence that minds are brains, I could be convinced otherwise by evidence that is best explained by the supposition that minds are nonmaterial substances. By far the most powerful kind of evidence would be observations showing that minds survive the loss of their bodies. Christians, Muslims, Jews, Hindus, and proponents of most other religions firmly believe that our mortal lives are only a small part of our existence. What would show that they are right?

Communication from the dead would certainly be compelling evidence that people survive the destruction of their bodies. My parents are long departed, but if I were able to have conversations with them that showed they were familiar with my activities since they died, I would have to consider the hypothesis that their souls had survived their deaths. Of course, I would also need to rule out alternative hypotheses, such as that the apparent conversations were fraudulently contrived, or that I had succumbed to a mental illness that made me prone to hallucinations. But if communication with the dead were a common part of many people's lives without the occurrence of fraud or psychosis, it would be convincing evidence supporting dualism over the mind-brain identity theory. In the nineteenth century, it was common for people to attend séances in which communication with the dead was arranged by mediums, and there are psychics today, such as Sylvia Browne who appears on television and tells people how their departed loved ones are doing. Many mediums and psychics have been exposed as frauds, however, so the mind-brain identity theory can explain sporadic reports of communication with the dead as resulting from a combination of fraud and wishful thinking.

Another possible source of evidence for the mind's surviving the brain is the occurrence of near-death experiences. People who have come close to death because of medical emergencies often report that they experience going off into a tunnel with a bright light at the end, only somehow to be pulled back. Even the famous atheistic philosopher A. J. Ayer reported a near-death experience that temporarily weakened his conviction that death would be the end of him. However, reports of near-death experiences are only very weak evidence for the existence of souls, because science provides plausible alternative explanations. Heart attacks and other medical conditions can cause shortage of oxygen in the brain with cognitive effects that are heightened by people's expectations: many people have heard about walking down a tunnel toward a light. Out-of-body experiences can be induced by laboratory experiments that produce confusion between the senses, and may be due to neural disruptions at the boundary between the temporal and parietal regions. Hence reports of near-death experiences are like reports of communications with the dead in that we can explain them without supposing that minds survive death.

If there is scant evidence for survival after death, why do so many people believe in their own immortality? I think the two main reasons are religious faith and motivated inference. People acquire belief in life after death (and, for Hindus, in life before birth) from their religious teachers, especially their parents. As I remarked in the previous chapter, it is natural for children to acquire beliefs from their parents and other seeming authorities, and these beliefs are often reliable. Life after death is a part of a whole package of beliefs that includes God and the soul. Immortality is a particularly attractive part of the package, as it provides a way of reducing fear of death and separation from loved ones. Illness and the other difficulties of life are of small significance if you have the prospect of eternal happiness in heaven, united with God and all the people you care about who have died before you. Some religions, however, make survival after death less clearly attractive because of the prospect of eternal punishment in some version of hell. The Greek philosopher Epicurus maintained that the expectation that your existence will end should eliminate the fear of death because you will then have no awareness of anything. Nevertheless, for most people the prospect of immortality is positive. As Woody Allen remarked: "I don't want to achieve immortality through my work. I want to achieve it through not dying." Unfortunately, the belief in a soul that survives death is faith based rather than evidence based.

Parapsychology

Another possible source of evidence for the soul is parapsychology, the study of such unusual phenomena as extrasensory perception (mind reading, remote viewing, or precognition) and telekinesis (mind over matter). Such phenomena would be very difficult to explain from the perspective of mind-brain identity, because they seem to violate basic principles of physics. For example, telekinesis would require that brains somehow have the ability to influence external objects through means other than the forces currently recognized by physics. Precognition would require some way in which events in the future could cause changes in present brains. If parapsychological phenomena are real, they would indeed provide empirical support for the hypothesis that there is more to mind than brain.

Historically, efforts to validate parapsychology have not been even moderately successful. Informal studies of extrasensory perception and telekinesis, such as performers who seem to bend spoons just by looking at them, are worthless because of their lack of controls that rule out fraud and self-deception. When attempts have been made to conduct carefully controlled experimental tests of extrasensory perception, the results have been at best very weak and open to many methodological criticisms, such as sloppy design or statistical errors. Hence parapsychology provides no more support for the existence of the soul than do séances and near-death experiences.

Consciousness

The real psychological phenomena that most seriously might support dualism concern conscious experience. Your consciousness includes perceptual experiences such as colors, shapes, sounds, tastes, smells, and touches. You are also often aware of emotional states (e.g., being happy or sad), bodily feelings (pain, fullness after a meal), and thoughts (I am now reading this chapter). One of the biggest remaining challenges for neuropsychology is to come up with a plausible explanation of how such experiences arise from brain processes. Some materialist philosophers and behaviorist scientists have attempted to stave off the challenge of consciousness by denying its existence, but for most people the conscious aspect of perceiving, feeling, and thinking is undeniable. To ignore consciousness would amount to admitting that it provides insurmountable evidence supporting the soul hypothesis over mind-brain identity.

My strategy for dealing with the problem of explaining consciousness is first to refute arguments that it cannot possibly be dealt with scientifically, a task pursued in the next section. The more positive task of sketching what a neuropsychological explanation of consciousness might look like is pursued in chapter 5, on how brains feel. There I offer not a general theory of consciousness but rather a neural model of one important kind of experience, emotional feeling. This model is still highly provisional but at least suggests one plausible route that neuroscience can take to bring conscious experience within the scope of causal explanation. The difficulty of accounting for consciousness is the major obstacle to my more general claim that mind-brain identity is part of the best explanation of all the available evidence about mental phenomena, but I will try to show how progress in overcoming it can be made. Other mental phenomena that are sometimes taken to show the limitations of neural explanations will also be discussed in later chapters, including intuition (chapters 5 and 9) and free will (chapter 6).

If consciousness can be explained by psychology and neuroscience, then the case for mind-brain identity is overwhelming. I argued that we already have excellent starts on neural explanations for perception, learning, memory, and other mental processes, such as reading. The main phenomena that might support the alternative hypothesis that minds are souls, including reports of communication with the dead, near-death experiences, and parapsychology, can be explained away as incidents of fraud and error. Consciousness cannot be explained away, but chapter 5 will point to paths that take it seriously but suggest how scientific advances might occur.

If minds are brains, we just do not need the hypothesis that they are souls too. Dualist explanations are inherently less simple than materialist ones, as they posit the existence of two kinds of things rather than one. Simplicity is not a virtue all by itself, as we see in the hypothesis of the first great philosopher-scientist, Thales, that everything is water. Einstein said that everything should be as simple as possible but not simpler, and Thales' hypothesis is just too simple, as was Aristotle's somewhat more complicated story that the four fundamental elements include earth, air, and fire as well as water. Modern chemistry sees the need to consider more than a hundred elements, including hydrogen and oxygen, which combine to produce water. Similarly, it is possible that there could be phenomena that require explanations invoking soul or spirit in addition to matter and energy. However, the rapidly progressing development of neuroscientific explanations of many mental phenomena suggests that souls are no more part of our best general explanatory account than is caloric, which was thought to be the substance of heat before the advent of the theory that heat is just molecular motion.

Sufficient evidence has been presented in this chapter to justify using mind-brain identity as the basis for the rest of the book's discussion of the nature of knowledge, reality, morality, and meaning. Figure 3.3 shows the overall structure of the inference to the best explanation that minds are

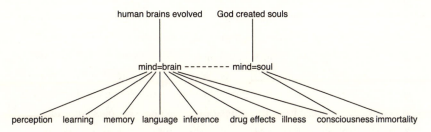

3.3 Structure of the inference that mind-body identity is the best available explanation
of many psychological phenomena. Explanations are indicated by solid lines, and
competition between hypotheses by dotted lines.

brains, including the kinds of evidence that are increasingly being accounted
for in terms of neural mechanisms. The hypothesis that minds are brains
competes with the hypothesis that minds are souls, whose explanatory successes are few. The figure also shows competition between the higher-level
hypothesis that minds evolved naturally and the hypothesis that minds arise
from divine creation. If you are convinced by my argument that minds are
brains, then proceed to chapter 4. For the sake, however, of philosophical
skeptics about mind-brain identity, I will close this chapter with a discussion of some of the most influential objections to it.

Objections to Mind-Brain Identity

For most people, the immediate objection to the claim that minds are brains
is that it conflicts with their religious beliefs about immortality. Their faith
says that God created souls that can survive the death of their bodies. But I
argued earlier in this chapter that there is no good evidence for immortality,
and in the previous chapter I showed why evidence provides a better way
of justifying beliefs than does faith. Another sweeping rejection of my approach would be the postmodernist charge that I dogmatically ignore the
philosophical view currently dominant in cultural studies that the world is
just a text and that science is just one of many equally good ways of talking about it. My defense of evidence over faith in chapter 2 is one part of
a response to this view, and a further response will be found in chapter 4's
discussion of the nature of reality and its independence of mind.

Mind-brain identity often seems intuitively implausible even to nonreligious people, because the conceptual schemes that we acquire from our cultures are inherently dualist. Languages from Hebrew to Greek to English have terms for mind and spirit that seem to designate nonphysical entities. Children learn from their parents to see their thoughts and feelings as intrinsically different from the states of their bodies. People's conscious experiences strongly suggest to them that their minds are making free choices independent of biological causes. The Brain Revolution requires a major conceptual shift to reclassify states of mind as neural.

Some philosophers have used such dualist intuitions to challenge mind-brain identity through thought experiments. The most prevalent is the "zombie" argument, which goes like this. Imagine people who are just like us in all physical respects but differ only in that they lack consciousness. Call them zombies, although they are not like the fearsome zombies of horror movies. Such people are clearly conceivable—just think of anyone you know and imagine that he or she is not really conscious but only seems to be. Because we can imagine beings that are physically identical to us but lack conscious experience, conscious minds are not necessarily identical to brains. But for an identity statement to be true, it has to be necessarily true, true in all possible worlds, like any identity statement, such as A = A. Hence the possibility of zombies shows that it is not necessarily true that minds are brains, so it is not true at all. There must be more to consciousness than brain states.

There are several things wrong with the zombie argument. First, it is obviously too strong, for it rules out many theoretical identifications that have been highly successful in the history of science. Examples mentioned earlier in this chapter included water is H_2O, combustion is rapid oxidation, heat is motion of molecules, light is electromagnetic energy, and lightning is atmospheric electrical discharge. I can easily imagine that lightning is not electrical—maybe the ancient Greeks were right that it's just the God Zeus showing his powers. But the conceivability of lightning's not being electrical does nothing to undermine the mass of evidence, accumulated since the eighteenth century, that it is. By far the best explanation of this evidence includes the identity hypothesis that lightning actually is electrical discharge in the atmosphere. As I argued in chapter 2, thought experiments are fine for suggesting and clarifying hypotheses, but it is folly to use them to try to justify the acceptance of beliefs.

Second, the zombie argument assumes the philosophical idea of necessary truths as statements that *must* be true, in contrast to ones that are true only of our world. As I argued in chapter 2, the concept of necessity is inherently problematic. We cannot simply say that necessity is truth in all possible worlds, since necessity and possibility are interdefinable: something is possible if its negation is not necessarily false. Nor can we define possibility in terms of conceivability, since what is conceivable at any time is not absolute, but merely a contingent function of the available concepts and beliefs. It is also not effective to say that something is possible if it is consistent with the laws of logic, since there is much debate concerning what the laws of logic are. I described in chapter 2 how even the principle of noncontradiction, that no statement can be both true and false, has been disputed. Hence the claim that such identity statements as "minds are brains" must be necessarily true is ill specified and should not be used to challenge a claim for which there is substantial evidence. Chapter 5 will provide more specific evidence that emotional conscious experiences are brain processes, along with a theory that makes it clear why philosophical intuitions should not be mistaken for evidence.

Some philosophers think that ascription to the brain of psychological properties such as consciousness is incoherent—it simply makes no sense. Well, it may not make sense if your conceptual scheme is mired in dualism, but understanding the mind requires willingness to develop and consider the evidence for new conceptual schemes. Just as the Copernican, Darwinian, and other scientific revolutions required gradual appreciation of the explanatory force of new conceptual schemes, so the Brain Revolution requires recognition of the explanatory gains that become available when the neural mechanisms for mental processes such as perception are identified. The best response to people who say that they just can't imagine how the mind could be the brain is: try harder. Overcoming the compelling illusion that the mind is nonmaterial is not easy, but one can succeed in doing so by acquiring sufficient understanding of neural mechanisms for thought and behavior.

Mind-brain identity is also challenged by nondualists who think that the development of computers reveals the hypothesis that minds are brains to be much too narrow. The possibility of artificial intelligence, which is the construction of computers capable of reasoning and learning, suggests that we should identify mental processes more generally with computational processes that can occur, not just in brains, but also in machines made out of silicon chips or other kinds of hardware. This view is called functionalism, because it says that mental states are inherently functional, providing causal connections between inputs and outputs in ways that produce intelligent behaviors. Computers and other machines, or maybe even extraterrestrial organisms, can have such functional states without having brains, so identification of mind and brain is a mistake. It is mental software that makes minds work, and the particular hardware on which it runs is not very important. I found this computational view appealing when I first got interested in cognitive science in 1978, but came to doubt it in the late 1980s when I began to work on neural network models, and even more in the 1990s when I started research on emotion.

My first response to functionalism is that the mere possibility of intelligence supported by physical systems other than brains is not sufficient to undercut the mind-brain identity hypothesis. Despite decades of search for extraterrestrial intelligence, we have no evidence that there are minds anywhere in the universe except on our meager planet. If such evidence arises and we can discern anything at all about the nature of intelligent beings other than humans, I will be eager to see what can be learned about their thinking processes. If their intelligence derives from physical systems very different from our brains, I will be happy to retreat to the more modest hypothesis that *human* minds are brains.

Similarly, if artificial intelligence substantially surpasses its rather modest accomplishments of the past five decades, I would be willing to consider the possibility that there are multiple kinds of minds, including the human variant that we can identify with brains and whatever machine mentalities arise. Computer intelligence has had some remarkable successes in areas such as game playing, robotics, and planning, but still falls far short of full human-level intelligence. Hence the idea that a full range of mental processes can be implemented in many different kinds of physical processes is still more a thought experiment than a piece of evidence that undermines the identification of mind and brain.

In the first few decades of modern research in cognitive science, from the 1950s to the 1970s, it seemed that progress in explaining the mind would come primarily from describing thought in terms of computational processes independent of their neural underpinnings. But as I sketched earlier in this chapter and will show in more detail in chapters 4–8, much of the most exciting current progress in cognitive science combines experimental studies of the brain with computational models of how it works. This research suggests that mental processes are both neural *and* computational, combining the basic insight of functionalism with the mind-brain identity theory.

Some current critics of mainstream cognitive science argue that its computational understanding of mental processes has been fundamentally wrong because it ignores the nature of mind as embodied, extended, and situated. Minds are embodied in that our thinking depends heavily on the ways our bodies enable us to perceive and act in particular ways, not on abstract information-processing capabilities. Thinking is extended and situated in that it occurs in ways heavily dependent on interactions with our physical and social environments. Minds are part of the physical and social worlds, not disembodied entities like desktop digital computers that just sit and crunch numbers. I agree that minds are embodied, extended, and situated, but these claims pose no problem for mind-brain identity, as brains are obviously embodied, extended, and situated too, in ways that will be made clear in the chapters that follow. Particular ways that our bodies enable our brains to know reality and to use emotion to appreciate its significance and relevance will be discussed in chapters 4 and 5. We will see that the embodied and situated aspects of brains are compatible with an understanding of their processes as representational and computational.

Who Are You?

If minds are brains, we need to rethink common conceptions of the nature of persons and the self. The religious idea of the immortal soul provided an appealing picture of the self as a spiritual entity, but overcoming the soul illusion requires a dramatic shift in how we view ourselves. The empiricist philosopher David Hume argued that there is nothing more to the self than a bundle of perceptions, but our thinking seems more unified than just a series of sensory experiences. Immanuel Kant sought such unity in transcendental selves that make all experience possible, but there is no more evidence for such entities than there is for souls. Can understanding the brain tell us anything about the nature of persons and start to answer the troubling question of who you are?

The Brain Revolution requires a major conceptual shift about the self, from viewing our selves as things to viewing them as complex processes. The neuroscientist Joseph LeDoux eloquently writes:

> In my view, the self is the totality of what an organism is physically, biologically, psychologically, socially, and culturally. Though it is a unit, it is not unitary. It includes things that we know and things that we do not know, things that others know about us that we do not realize. It includes features that we express and hide, and some that we simply don't call upon. It includes what we would like to be as well as what we hope to never become.

LeDoux describes how the brain employs both parallel plasticity, which is learning occurring in diverse brain systems, and convergence zones, which are regions where information from diverse systems can be integrated. This combination explains how the self can possess a unity in diversity.

Thinking of the self as a complex neural system takes us far from common sense, and further departures are required. A full theory of the self remains to be developed, drawing not only on neuroscience but also on social psychology, which discusses such topics as self-regulation, self-esteem, and cultural variations in self-concepts. In chapter 5, I will argue that full understanding of emotions and other aspects of the self requires attention to mechanisms that operate at four different levels, including the molecular, psychological, and social as well as the neural. The discussion of moral responsibility in chapter 9 will treat persons as inherently part of their social worlds, requiring attention to social relations as well as neural mechanisms. Claiming that minds are brains is compatible with the social character of persons and the self.

Conclusion

I may be wrong that minds are brains. Perhaps I will be amazed after my final, fatal heart attack to discover that I can still think without my body, and will realize that this whole book has been a mistake. Less drastically, new evidence may arise in the form of many well-controlled experiments concerning communications from the dead or paranormal powers that cannot be explained by any hypothesis assuming that only matter and energy exist. Then the Brain Revolution that overturns our dualist conceptual scheme would not need to proceed, and people would be able to feel secure in their view that there is more to us than our bodies. Religion and commonsense dualism could legitimately survive. We would not have to give up the highly appealing conceptual scheme that offers us immortality, a caring God, free will, and our experienced centrality to the universe.

But currently available evidence suggests otherwise. This chapter gave a quick sketch of why the best explanation of mental processes such as perception, memory, learning, and drug experiences is that they are processes of the brain. I refrained from going into a lot more detail about how the brain supports these kinds of thinking because I wanted the reader to grasp the overall structure of the argument that minds are brains. Much more detailed explanations can be found in chapters that follow and in the extensive literature in cognitive neuroscience.

In contrast, I described the dubious nature of proposed evidence for dualism based on communications from the dead, near-death experiences, and parapsychological capacities such as extrasensory perception. The one serious psychological phenomenon that might seem to require dualist explanation is consciousness, but we will see in chapter 5 that neuroscience is beginning to understand how brains can have conscious experiences. Thought experiments about zombies provide no impediment to adopting the hypothesis that mental processes are brain process, nor do concerns with the computational and embodied nature of thinking.

The Brain Revolution requires a substantial change in widely accepted theories and concepts. Our beliefs and other representations need to be reconceived as patterns of activation in neural populations, which requires understanding them as processes rather than things. Inference is a neural process involving parallel interactions among neural populations, not just a step-by-step linguistic procedure. Most generally, minds and selves need to be conceived as processes operating in relation to the world and other minds, not just as things. Shifting to understanding the world in terms of relational processes rather than things and simple properties has been a major part of the development of science, as in Newton's recognition that weight is a relation between objects, and the recognition of thermodynamic theory that heat is a process of motion of molecules.

More difficult even than such reclassifications are the emotional conceptual changes we must embrace to shift from the attractive picture of minds as immortal souls central to the universe to the biological picture of minds as neural processes of no apparent cosmic significance. I hope that chapter 7 will ease such emotional transitions by showing how understanding brains can help us to appreciate how minds nevertheless can find and create meaning through the pursuit of love, work, and play, reducing the lure of dualism. This biological picture need not be at all dismal and can suggest effective means of increasing human well-being.

All the evidence that minds are brains justifies pursuing wisdom, meaning, and other philosophical questions from a neuroscientific perspective. Let us now see what attention to brains can tell us about reality.

how brains know reality

Reality and Its Discontents

The comedian Lily Tomlin said that reality is a crutch for people who can't handle drugs. Some philosophers also have a low opinion of reality, seeing it as a mere construction of people's minds or social contexts. In contrast, this chapter argues that the things investigated by science exist independently of our minds, construed as brains. Using perception and inference, brains can develop objective knowledge of reality, including knowledge relevant to assessing the meaning of life.

The previous chapter's conclusion that minds are brains has major implications for two central philosophical questions: what is reality, and how do we know it? These questions are interrelated, as consideration of what things exist needs to fit with discussion of what it takes to gain knowledge about those things. For example, an empiricist who believes that knowledge can come only through the senses might conclude that physical objects such as lions and mountains are not real, because we sense only features of them, not the things themselves. At the other extreme, an idealist who believes that reality is inherently mental might also conclude that lions and mountains cannot be said to be real apart from how we think about them.

I think that lions and mountains are real, and so are clouds and electrons. But the hypothesis that minds are brains does not support a kind of naive realism according to which things are just as we perceive or conceive them to be. We know enough about how brains work to show that both perceiving and theorizing are highly constructive processes involving complex inferences. Nevertheless, there are good reasons to believe that, when the brain is working well, it achieves knowledge about the reality of both everyday objects like mountains and theoretical scientific entities like electrons. This chapter shows how brain science and philosophical reflection together support a kind of *constructive realism*, the view that reality exists independently of minds, but that our knowledge of it is constructed by brain processes.

I aim to show that constructive realism is superior to alternative theories of knowledge and reality offered by different variants of skepticism, empiricism, and idealism. Skepticism is the view that we have no knowledge at all, so that any talk of the nature of reality is pointless. Some ancient Greek philosophers advocated an extreme form of skepticism according to which neither sensation nor opinion could give us any grounds for separating truth from falsehood. An influential current form of skepticism is found in postmodernist philosophers and literary theorists who view the world as a text open to many kinds of interpretations, none of them demonstrably better than the others. In fields such as history, anthropology, and cultural studies, it has become fashionable to claim that reality is just a social construction, so that the idea of objective knowledge is only a myth. I will try to show how objectivity is possible through the complex perceptual and theoretical abilities of our brains. Brains are not mirrors of nature, but they are powerful instruments for representing it.

Empiricism tries to avoid skeptical problems by restricting knowledge to what can be perceived by the senses. From early modern philosophers such as John Locke and David Hume to later thinkers such as Rudolf Carnap and Bas van Fraassen, the restriction of knowledge to sense experience has had strong appeal. I will show, however, that strict empiricism is incompatible both with the neuropsychology of perception and with the practice of science. Our brain processes are, fortunately, capable of reliably taking us well beyond what is presented to us by our senses.

Another approach to understanding knowledge of reality is idealism, which views reality as dependent on or even constituted by minds. This view is more compatible than is empiricism with the constructive nature of perception and inference, but grossly overestimates the contributions that minds make to the world. It leaps from the insight that there is no knowledge of things without construction of mental representations of them to the conclusion that entities are mental constructions. The philosopher Immanuel Kant thought that he had accomplished a kind of Copernican revolution by placing mind at the center of knowledge and reality. But idealism is actually attempting a kind of Ptolemaic counterrevolution, as implausible as reactionary attempts to return the earth to the center of the solar system or to deny human evolution. To develop my alternative, brain-based approach to constructive realism, I will first discuss perception of objects and then move on to how inference enables us to go beyond perception.

Knowing Objects

There is an old baseball story about three umpires calling balls and strikes. One says, "I call them as I see them." The second says, "I call them as they are." The third insists, "They ain't nothing until I call them." These attitudes correspond to the philosophical positions of empiricism, realism, and idealism. For neuroscience to support realism about objects, I need to show that the structures and processes used by the brain enable it to represent things in the world as they are, at least approximately.

It is tempting to think about mental representations of the world by analogy to the linguistic representations that we use to communicate with each other in speech and writing. The philosopher Jerry Fodor claimed that there is a language of thought with the same kinds of structures as a natural language such as English or Chinese. Many contemporary philosophers assume that knowing is a propositional attitude, which is a relation between a person and some kind of sentencelike entity. But understanding minds as brains requires us to take a much broader view of representations, with linguistic structures such as sentences serving as only one way that the brain knows the world. You do not have to be a linguistically sophisticated adult human to have knowledge of objects. Other language-limited animals such as rats and lizards have perceptions too, as do human infants well before they have learned to talk. In the previous chapter, I described how we can think of brains as functioning by using patterns of activity of firing by interconnected neurons. Now I will go into a bit more detail about how visual perception of objects works in the brain.

When you see an object—say, a duck—light in the form of wavelike particles called photons is reflected off the object into your eyes. At the back of your eyes, your retina has photoreceptor cells that convert light energy into chemical signals that travel to your brain via the firing activity of cells in the optic nerves. These signals are carried to the back of the brain where multiple areas of the visual cortex are engaged. Cells in the area called V1 respond to basic features such as color, motion, and orientation, while other areas contain neural populations that are specialized for more elaborate representations, such as faces. Different neural populations interact to determine what features can be grouped together, as when you perceive both the color of the duck and the shape of its bill. These neural interactions can also fill in gaps in your visual information, as when you can see that the object is a duck even though you can see only part of its bill. The brain manages to tie various features together, so that you don't perceive separately the duck's bill, its color, and its motion, but rather you see together a white duck with a yellow bill moving down the road.

These processes driven by sensory information from the physical world are called *bottom-up,* in contrast to *top-down* processes that are driven by knowledge, expectations, and goals. The importance of top-down processes in visual perception is evident from failures of object recognition caused by brain damage, called *agnosia.* People with agnosia can accurately detect features such as edges and shapes, but cannot put them together to see an object. Such recognition is difficult because a duck or other object can be presented to us from many different viewpoints, and there are many different kinds of duck. The initial pattern of firing in the retina is two-dimensional, but somehow we recognize a duck as a three-dimensional object. The brain is able simultaneously to match features, components, and configurations to its previous experience through the dynamic interaction of billions of neurons in several different brain areas. If you suffer damage to parts of the brain that have neurons with connections constituting your learned knowledge about ducks, then you will not be able to put all the features and configurations together to recognize an object as a duck. People with damage to the fusiform face area in the brain may suffer from *prosopagnosia*, the inability to recognize faces.

The top-down nature of visual processing is also evident in Gestalt figures such as the reversing duck-rabbit (figure 4.1). If you are expecting to see a duck, then you will see the lines on the left as constituting a bill, whereas if you shift your focus and look for a rabbit, they will appear as ears. This kind of inference consists not of serial linguistic steps but rather of the parallel dynamic interaction of neurons that encode sensory information with neurons that encode expectations and knowledge of what ducks and rabbits look like.

4.1 Duck-rabbit reversing figure.

Perception is a kind of inference, but it is very different from the kind familiar from our use of language. When we speak or write, we encounter one sentence at a time, and seem to infer the next sentence from the ones that came before, just as with a proof in mathematics. But inference in the brain does not operate in this serial, step-by-step way. Each neuron is connected synaptically with thousands of others, so its firing pattern is affected by all the neurons that excite or inhibit it, and it in turn affects the firing of all the neurons that it excites or inhibits. Thus inference is parallel, in that many neurons are firing at around the same time, and asynchronous, in that there is no central clock that coordinates the waves of firing that spread through the neural populations. Hence perception is very different from the kind of serial steps of linguistic inference that have served as models of reasoning since Aristotle identified such syllogisms as *A is B, and B is C, so A is C*. Because brains perform inferences using parallel activity of millions of neurons, perception can elegantly integrate both bottom-up and top-down information. We will see in chapter 5 that emotional feelings involve a similar kind of dynamic integration of multiple kinds of information.

Our sense of smell also requires a combination of bottom-up and top-down processing. When you inhale, odorants excite subsets of the millions of cellular receptors in your nose, sending patterns of neural activity to the olfactory bulb on the bottom of your brain. The olfactory bulb also receives inputs from other brain areas, such as the hippocampus and the neocortex, so that the signals it sends to the rest of the brain are already a combination of bottom-up sensory information and top-down processing. Hence when you smell something, like a live duck in a barnyard or a cooked one in a restaurant, the smell is the result of dynamic interactions of different brain areas involving both sensory inputs and previous knowledge and expectations.

The complexity of perceptual processing in the brain shows the implausibility of the traditional empiricist view that our sense experiences are copies of objects in the world. Without previously acquired or inherited concepts, we would have a very difficult time dealing with the vast number of sensory signals that our eyes, ears, and other sensors send to our brains. Perception requires brains to be able to relate inputs from sensory organs with information they have already stored in the form of synaptic connections between neurons. Ambiguous examples like the duck-rabbit show that perception is not just the bottom-up processing of sensory inputs; it also involves top-down interpretation based on what is already known. Because the brain is a parallel processor capable of assessing many aspects simultaneously, we do not have to choose between hypotheses that perception is primarily driven by input to sensory receptors or that it is primarily driven by top-down interpretation. Rather, brains can perform inferences that simultaneously use both kinds of information.

Appearance and Reality

The essential top-down contribution of previous knowledge to perception has tempted some philosophers and psychologists to conclude that the senses do not enable us to know what objects are, only what they appear to be. Some worry that the gap between appearance and reality cannot be bridged, as when Kant said that we cannot know things in themselves. Some psychologists writing on hallucinations have claimed that support for Kant's idealism comes from the brain's capability of generating illusory perceptions that have no connection with reality. A few micrograms of a drug like LSD can disengage your brain's perceptual apparatus from the usual sensory inputs and generate fantastic images that have no correspondence to anything in the world. You do not have to take drugs to hallucinate, as a similar process takes place every night when you dream. Your brain generates complex and often compelling sensory experiences that are not directly caused by anything in the world. Last night I dreamed that I was shopping in a supermarket and bought some delicious bread, but morning brought the realization that the market and the bread were unreal.

Nevertheless, we should not infer from the complexity of perceptual processing and phenomena like hallucinations and dreams that the senses fail to provide us with knowledge about how the world actually is. Support for the reality of objects is based on inference to the best explanation, as defended in chapter 2. There is abundant evidence that the bread I ate for lunch today exists and has the properties I attribute to it.

First, I do not have to rely exclusively on a single sense. I see the color and shape of the loaf of bread, but I can cross-check the shape using my sense of touch, confirming that it feels the same way that it looks. I can also use hearing to investigate the bread by banging the loaf against a pot and hearing the ding. Further, the bread produces pleasurable stimulation of my senses of taste and smell. The brain has different sensory systems but can combine them to form unified perceptions. In contrast to hallucinations and dreams, which are hard to control, systematic experiments are possible: I can generate integrated and coherent sensations of the bread— for example, by simultaneously looking at it, scratching it, and eating it. Because I can make the bread cause these experiences, and because there is no evidence to support alternative hypotheses (e.g., I am hallucinating or dreaming), it is reasonable to conclude that the bread exists. Its reality is the best explanation of my diverse experience of it.

Second, evidence for the reality of objects does not have to rely only on my own specific sensory experiences of them, as I can also often rely on the testimony of others. Any doubts I have about the bread's causing my experiences can be reduced if I share it with other people, who will generally report similar experiences. You may not like this whole-grain bread as much as I do, but I would be very surprised if your reports of its color, shape, texture, smell, and taste turned out to be much different from mine. We can make a party of it and have a bread tasting in which we all compare our sensory experiences. I predict that reports of the sight, feel, taste, smell, and sound of the bread will be remarkably convergent. The best explanation of this convergence across the sensory experiences of multiple people is that there really is a loaf of bread that is causing all of our brains to generate similar experiences. The reports of similar experiences by me and other people all result from a combination of physical mechanisms by which the bread affects our senses and neural mechanisms by which our brains interpret sensory inputs.

But should we rely on the testimony of other people as part of our inference to the best explanation of sensory reports? After all, they might be lying or joking, rather than actually reporting their experience of the bread. Once again, our assessment of the truth of what people say to us is a matter of inference to the best explanation. You are justified in believing that someone is telling the truth if that is the best available explanation of all the available evidence. People are usually motivated to describe things as they think they are, so you are justified in taking what they say as relevant evidence, as long as there isn't evidence supporting alternative hypotheses such as deception or hallucination. Testimony justified by inference to the best explanation allows me to reasonably believe many things observed by others. I have never been to Mount Everest myself but do not doubt its existence, because the observational reports of many others are better explained by the hypothesis that the mountain exists than by alternative hypotheses such as mass deception.

But how do we know that the experiences reported by other people are at all the same as ours? Maybe when you say you are experiencing brown, chewy bread, you are really having the same experience I have when I experience white, soggy bread. There are two reasons for doubting that there is sufficient variability in experience to undermine the usefulness of testimony. First, the general pattern of experiences that people usually report has a great deal of overall coherence with my pattern of experience, which makes it implausible that we differ in just one kind of experience such as brown or chewy. Second, there is much evidence from anatomy and brain-scanning experiments to suggest that people's brains are very similar for sensory processing. Hence there is good reason to take the testimonial reports of other people at face value, in the absence of evidence that they are lying or demented.

In addition to multisensory coherence and the testimony of other people, there is a third reason for inferring that our perceptions of objects are approximately true: we can often corroborate them with measurements taken by instruments. People don't usually subject a loaf of bread to instrumental inspection, but a physicist could use calipers to measure its height and width, a spectrometer to measure the color reflectance of the loaf, an artificial odor detector to measure molecules near the loaf, and so on. Such measurements carried out by people or possibly even by robots provide further evidence best explained by the supposition that the loaf of bread exists. Similar arguments support inference to the existence of many other kinds of objects, from lions to mountains. Contrary to empiricism, scientific knowledge does not come just from our senses, but goes beyond them via a multitude of reliable instruments from telescopes and microscopes to Geiger counters (used to measure radiation) and particle colliders (used to detect the behavior of subatomic particles). The efficacy of scientific instruments is incompatible with idealism, because their measurements do not depend on mental activity, but it fits well with constructive realism.

You might think that even if pieces of bread are real, their properties (color, taste, smell, and texture) are not, because these are so heavily dependent on our minds. Many philosophers have thought that nothing in the external world corresponds to people's experiences of colors, eliminating them as real. Their arguments rely on the fact that there is no simple mapping between the space of colors that people experience and the properties of objects that affect how they reflect light of different wavelengths. Paul Churchland has found, however, a way of construing the physical properties of objects that reveals a correspondence between their reflectance efficiencies and people's experiences of colors like red, green, and blue. He describes how the human visual system successfully tracks approximations of the reflectance profiles of objects at a low level of resolution, so that colors can be viewed as objectively real properties of objects even if color vision is highly context sensitive.

The correspondence between reflection properties and color experience makes sense given current theories of how the brain processes color information, from stimulation of cells in the retina that code for specific wavelengths of light to interpretations generated in the visual cortex. I like the conclusion that colors are real properties of objects, and it does seem to fit with the best available understanding of how the brain interacts with objects. But realism about objects could be true even if realism about colors is not, as long as we have good reason to believe that objects and at least some of their properties exist independently of mental representations of them.

I have tried to show in this section that the best explanation of the convergence of experiences from the multiple senses of many people and instruments is that there really are physical objects that cause these experiences. Moreover, the observable properties of these objects are much as we perceive them to be. Of course, they have other nonobservable properties, such as their atomic structure, that we can learn about only from scientific theorizing.

In sum, attention to how the brain functions in perception supports constructive realism over empiricism and idealism. The constructive nature of perception with both top-down and bottom-up processing shows the implausibility of a narrow empiricism that ties knowledge too closely to sensory input. On the other hand, the robustness of sensory inputs of different kinds counts by inference to the best explanation against the idealist view that the existence of objects is mind dependent. Our perceptual knowledge is both constructed and about real things. Such constructive realism is also the best approach to theoretical knowledge that uses concepts and hypotheses to go well beyond perception.

Concepts

There is much more to knowledge of reality than sensory experience. Human discourse is full of concepts, including *knowledge* and *reality,* that are not directly tied to what we can see, touch, taste, smell, or hear. Philosophers, psychologists, and now neuroscientists attempt to figure out the nature of such concepts. For Plato, concepts were abstract entities he called the forms, existing in some heavenly realm graspable by souls. In contemporary cognitive science, concepts are mental representations, which the previous chapter implies are brain representations. A major current research problem is to figure out how patterns of neural firing play all the roles needed to explain the many cognitive uses of concepts.

Greg Murphy's *Big Book of Concepts* provides a thorough review of current psychological theories. According to the *classical* theory, still assumed by many philosophers and nonacademics, we can strictly define concepts by giving their necessary and sufficient conditions. For example, the concept of a triangle consists of the definition that a figure is a triangle if and only if it has exactly three sides. Unfortunately, few concepts outside mathematics are amenable to such strict definitions. This difficulty applies not only to abstract concepts like *reality,* but also to many everyday concepts such as *chair* and *cat.* If you don't believe this, try to give a rigorous definition of a chair that includes everything you want without arbitrary exclusions: must it have a back, legs, or what? Nevertheless, a full theory of concepts would require room for the existence of those rare concepts such as mathematical ones that are actually definable.

In the 1970s, some philosophers, psychologists, and computer scientists advocated a more relaxed view of concepts as *prototypes*, which are mental representations that specify typical rather than defining properties. Whereas a definition attempts to list those properties possessed by all and only chairs, a prototype just includes features that are typical of chairs. Prototypes are more flexible than definitions, and there are experimental reasons to think that they give a better account of the psychology of concepts. However, they may not be flexible enough, so some psychologists have claimed that people actually store concepts, not as prototypes but as sets of examples, so that your concept of a chair consists of a stored representation of many different chairs. This claim is called the *exemplar* theory of concepts.

The other major account of concepts currently discussed by psychologists is called the *knowledge* view or sometimes the theory-theory. This view points to the large role that concepts play in providing explanations. For example, your concept *drunk* helps in explaining the behavior of people who have had too much alcohol, as when you say that Fred crashed his car because he was drunk. Then a major part of a concept is not just its defining characteristics or its typical conditions or its set of associated examples, but the causal relations it identifies between things. Another complication in recent experimental work on concepts is the suggestion that many concepts are inherently multimodal, having a large sensory component such as visual, tactile, or auditory, not just a verbal one. For example, your concept of a chair may be highly visual if it involves pictorial representations derived from previous perceptions of chairs. Your concept of a drunk may be partly olfactory if it includes the smell of alcohol on a person's breath.

Although psychological evidence counts against the classical account of concepts as strictly definable, it does not suffice to enable us to choose definitively among prototype, exemplar, knowledge, and multimodal theories.

But I see no reason to take these as competing views; rather I prefer to interpret them as capturing various aspects of how concepts are represented in the brain. Some concepts like mathematical ones may even be definable. In chapter 3 I suggested that concepts and other mental representations are patterns of neural activity. What I need to show now is that the brain-based view of concepts can support all these diverse aspects of concepts.

It is not hard to see how multimodal, exemplar, and prototype characteristics of concepts can be supported by neural populations. A concept does not have to involve activation in just one neural population in an isolated area of the brain restricted to language processing. A concept can be multimodal in that it involves multiple neural populations, including ones dedicated to sensory representations. The psychologist Larry Barsalou reviews evidence that your concept of a *car,* for example, is distributed across areas of the brain that include ones primarily concerned with visual representations. Hence the mental pictures that you can make of cars may be part of your concept, as may be the sounds and smells that you associate with cars. Concepts are patterns of activation in neural populations that can include ones that are produced by, and maintain some of the structure of, perceptual inputs.

Simulations with artificial neural networks enable us to see how concepts can have properties associated with sets of exemplars and prototypes. When a neural network is trained with multiple examples, it forms connections between its neurons that enable it to store the features of those examples implicitly. These same connections also enable the population of connected neurons to behave like a prototype, recognizing instances of a concept in accord with their ability to match various typical features rather than having to satisfy a strict set of conditions. Thus even simulated populations of artificial neurons much simpler than real ones in the brain can capture the exemplar and prototype aspects of concepts.

It is much harder to understand how concepts as patterns of neural activation can play the explanatory role required by the view that a crucial role of concepts like *drunk* is their contribution to causal explanations. Perhaps the brain manages to use concepts in explanations by embedding them in rules, such as: If X is drunk, then X stumbles. But what is the neural representation of the connection between the concepts *drunk* and *stumbles*? This structure requires also some kind of neural representation of *if-then,* which in this explanatory context involves some understanding of causality:

drunkenness causes stumbling. I will deal with the representation of causality later in this chapter, but for now the main concern is to try to see how the brain could use neural populations to represent that there is a relation between the concepts of *drunk* and *stumbles*.

The philosopher and theoretical neuroscientist Chris Eliasmith has been developing interesting ideas about how brains can deal with such relations. I will omit the technical details, but will try to give you the flavor of how this works in his computer simulations and how it might work in the brain. Eliasmith has developed a general method for representing vectors, which are strings of numbers, in neural populations. We can associate a concept with such a string—for example, in a simple way by thinking of the numbers as the firing rates (number of electrical discharges per second) of the many neurons the brain uses for the concept. (Eliasmith's method is more complicated.) Similarly, relations such as *cause* and *if-then* can also have associated vectors. Now for the neat trick: there are techniques for building vectors out of vectors, so that *drunk causes stumbles* can get a vector built out of the vectors for *drunk*, *causes*, and *stumbles*. Crucially, the new vector retains structural information, maintaining the distinction between "drunk causes stumbles" and "stumbles causes drunk." Once this whole relational structure is captured by a vector, we can use Eliasmith's method to represent it in a population of thousands of neurons. Such neural representations can be transformed in ways that support complex inferences such as if-then reasoning.

It is too early to say whether the brain uses anything like Eliasmith's mathematical technique to build structure into vectors and then translate them into neural activity. But his work suggests one possible mechanism whereby the brain might combine concepts into more complicated kinds of relational representations. Hence we have a start at seeing how concepts can function in the explanatory way suggested by the knowledge view: explanations are built out of complexes of relations that can be represented in brain patterns. Moreover, because concepts on this view have the same underlying nature as patterns of activation in neural populations, the knowledge view remains compatible with prototype, exemplar, and multimodal views of concepts. In those rare cases where strict definitions of concepts are available, as in *a triangle is a figure with three sides*, the necessary and sufficient conditions can be represented by relations between concepts that can be captured by vectors of vectors and then modeled as neural activity.

From my simplified account, one might worry that the account of concepts as patterns of neural activation is so vague and general that it would be compatible with any view of concepts at all, thus lacking any content. We can overcome this worry first by looking at the detailed mathematical analyses and computational simulations that are already available to show how artificial neural populations can have the desired properties required for modeling exemplars, prototypes, and relations among concepts. Second, the account I have been offering is strongly incompatible with at least one currently prominent view of concepts, the conceptual atomism of Jerry Fodor. According to atomism, lexical concepts (ones for which we have words) have no semantic structure at all and get their meaning only from their relation with the world. This view is psychologically implausible in that it cannot explain the mass of evidence available that supports prototype, exemplar, and knowledge views of concepts. I mention it here because of its incompatibility with the view of concepts as patterns of neural activation: such patterns are clearly affected not only by perceptual interactions with the world, but also by interactions with many other neural populations.

The meaning of concepts is relational and multidimensional, and should not be understood in terms of some thing that constitutes *the* content of a concept. For example, the concept *chair* construed as a pattern of neural activation has meaning in part because that pattern has causal correlations with the world through various kinds of perceptual and motor interactions. Chairs have causal effects on neural activity through sensory processes, and neural activity has causal effects on chairs through brains' ability to direct bodily movements. But it is equally important that the pattern has correlations with other neural patterns, some of which may have little direct connection with perception. For example, it is part of the meaning of the concept of a chair that it is a kind of furniture and can be bought in stores.

In chapter 3, I argued for the conceptual shift away from thinking of minds as things to thinking of them as relational processes. Similarly, a difficult but explanatorily valuable part of the Brain Revolution is its shift away from thinking of concepts and their meaning as entities and toward understanding them as processes with relations along multiple dimensions, involving both the world and other concepts.

We will see in chapter 7 that the meaning of life is also multidimensional, concerning relations between persons and various aspects of their lives, especially love, work, and play. Because the meaning of a concept does not depend simply on perceptual experience, concepts can constitute knowledge about things that our senses are too crude to perceive. Let us now look at how we can have knowledge about things that goes well beyond our rather limited sensory capacities.

Knowledge beyond Perception

In science and in everyday life, many of our concepts go beyond sensory experience. For example, our talk about the minds of other people frequently refers to their beliefs, wants, and emotions even though we cannot directly experience them. Scientific theories evoke many kinds of entities that cannot be directly observed—among them, atoms, electrons, quarks, black holes, genes, biochemical pathways, viruses, personalities, and mental representations. Our knowledge of the world would be desperately limited if we had to follow the injunction of strict empiricists that our knowledge be confined to what human senses can experience. Other animals have superior senses: birds can see ultraviolet light, dogs have more sensitive noses, bats can use echolocation, and so on. The particular range of sensory experience open to humans is a coincidence of biological evolution, not a perfect guide to the nature of reality. Where humans far exceed other animals is in our ability to construct and evaluate brain representations that transcend our sensory limitations.

Allowing knowledge that goes beyond the information given in sense experience raises two difficult philosophical questions. The first concerns how concepts can be meaningful if they go beyond experience, which empiricists take to be the source of meaning. The answer arises from the recognition that the meaning of concepts, construed as patterns of neural activation, is relational and multidimensional. Theoretical concepts like *atom* and *virus* are only indirectly related to sense experience, but that is neither a philosophical nor a psychological problem because such concepts are richly related to other concepts by virtue of the theories of which they are a part. For example, the concept *atom* is related to other concepts, such as *element*, *molecule*, *electron*, and *proton*, all of which contribute to the atomic theory of matter that explains a vast number of experimental findings in physics, chemistry, and molecular biology. The meaningfulness of such concepts is a puzzle only if one assumes a narrowly empiricist view of how concepts depend on sense experience.

The second question is much more serious: if concepts can go beyond sense experience, how do we know which of them have anything to do with reality? There are many concepts that may be meaningful because of their relation to other concepts, but which fail to refer to anything in the world. Children readily acquire concepts such as *elf* and *unicorn,* but eventually learn that these are mythical. If my critique in chapter 2 of faith-based thinking is right, then concepts like *god* and *angel* are equally mythical.

The same problem arises in the history of science, where concepts that are crucial parts of once-dominant theories become abandoned. For example, in eighteenth-century chemistry, before Lavoisier developed the oxygen theory, most chemists accepted the phlogiston theory of combustion. They thought that burning consisted of an object's giving off an element called phlogiston, which we no longer think exists. Why today do we assume that the concept of oxygen refers to reality but the concept of phlogiston does not? Other concepts that have been rejected with the theories that contained them include the caloric (heat element) of eighteenth-century chemistry, the vital force of nineteenth-century biology, and the luminiferous ether of pre-relativity physics. Like our favorite concepts today, these were constructed in such a way that they seemed meaningful to those who used them; yet we now see them as having nothing to do with reality. Perhaps all our current scientific concepts are like that, temporary ways of thinking that will eventually be retired along with the superseded theories that contain them.

I doubt, however, that most of our current scientific concepts will go the way of phlogiston. The reason that concepts like *oxygen* and *atom* are still around is evidence based, in line with the principles of inference to the best explanation described in chapter 2. The oxygen theory of combustion superseded the phlogiston theory because Lavoisier showed that it provides a better explanation of the available chemical experiments. For example, when objects are burned in jars that prevent matter from escaping, objects gain weight, as predicted by the theory that combustion involves combination with oxygen, rather than losing weight, as assumed by the theory that combustion involves release of phlogiston. But inference to the best explanation is more complicated than just counting the number of facts that a theory explains, because a theory can sneakily make extra assumptions allowing it to apply to experimental results that ordinarily it has trouble with. For example, some defenders of the phlogiston theory desperately suggested that phlogiston has negative weight, in an attempt to explain why objects gained weight while burning and supposedly losing phlogiston. Hence we want to evaluate the best explanation not only by considering how many facts each theory explains, but also by considering how many extra assumptions it makes in order to generate these explanations. Also relevant is how compatible those assumptions are with other accepted theories: physics had no room for negative weight. A theory such as Lavoisier's oxygen theory has both explanatory breadth and simplicity, in that it explains a lot with a small set of assumptions.

Another crucial aspect of inference to the best explanation is that we sometimes evaluate hypotheses not only by how much they explain, but also by how they are themselves explained by higher-level hypotheses. In chapter 2, I gave the example of how a criminal hypothesis that someone committed a murder becomes more plausible if there is a motive that provides an explanation of why the murderer wanted the victim dead. Similarly, over time, the best scientific hypotheses are themselves explained. Lavoisier hypothesized that oxygen combines with objects when they burn, but he had no idea of why this happened. In the twentieth century, the theory of chemical bonding was developed that explains at the subatomic level how oxygen atoms combine with carbon atoms to form carbon dioxide and carbon monoxide. Hence the oxygen theory of combustion is even stronger now than it was at the end of the eighteenth century, because it is coherent with subatomic physics as well as with the many facts that it still explains. Over more than two centuries, the oxygen theory has not only broadened to explain many facts besides combustion; it has deepened through discovery of the underlying mechanisms that make oxygen contribute to burning, rusting, and respiration.

Another good example of a theory that has both broadened and deepened is the germ theory of disease proposed in the nineteenth century to explain why people get such diseases as tuberculosis, cholera, and influenza. Today we not only use the germ theory to explain how people get many different diseases as the result of infection by bacteria, viruses, and other infectious agents; we can also explain mechanistically how these agents disrupt cells and organs by describing their operations in terms of the underlying genes and biochemical pathways.

These two aspects of highly developed science, involving progressive broadening and deepening of explanations over time, allow us to overcome the pessimistic view that current science is likely just as transient as old, superseded theories and concepts, such as phlogiston. I don't know of a single broadened and deepened scientific theory that has turned out to be false. Of course, inference to the best explanation and any other kind of evidence-based thinking is fallible. There is always the possibility that new evidence will be gathered or new hypotheses will be generated showing that our current ideas are wrong. But the coherence of the atomic theory of matter and the germ theory of disease, not only with what they explain but also with underlying mechanisms that explain them, makes me confident that they will be not be superseded. Such theories not only have constructed concepts and hypotheses; they also seem to capture important aspects of reality.

Hence scientific thinking, like perceptual knowledge, exemplifies the view I called constructive realism, as opposed to empiricism or idealism. We have good reason to believe that both perception and scientific thinking, despite their fallibility, can often be reliable sources of knowledge about the world. Concepts such as *electron* and *gene* that go well beyond sensory experience can nevertheless be judged to refer to real objects, as long as they are parts of theories that provide the best explanation of the available evidence.

It has become common in some areas of the humanities and social sciences to claim that science is socially constructed. As a modest claim that science is a social enterprise carried out by groups of people interacting with each other, social construction is obviously a significant aspect of the development of scientific knowledge. Unfortunately, social construction is often used aggressively to imply that science has nothing to do with a reality independent of human groups, so that all scientific development is just a matter of social negotiation and power.

These contentions conflict with much of what we know about perception and the practice of science. Our perceptual apparatus has the capacity to observe objects approximately as they are. As a result, scientists cannot get just the experimental results that they want, but have to work with what their observations and instruments tell them. Hypothesizing about mechanisms produces the progressive deepening as well as broadening of scientific theories. The technological applications of scientific theories make no sense without some connection between theories and the world. My cognitive and neural explanations of perception and scientific thinking are highly compatible with there being many social factors in the development of everyday and scientific knowledge, but rule out the imperialistic claim that the only legitimate explanations are social ones.

Thus thinking in science and everyday life can go far beyond perception yet still gain knowledge of reality. To do so, minds need to use evidence that depends on the general reliability of our perceptions to provide observations and experimental results, but they also need effective use of inferences to the best explanation of those observations. Such inference evaluates theories in comparison with competing theories, based on how coherent they all are with evidence that they explain and with theories that explain them. Then we get good reason to believe that the hypotheses and concepts in the theory have some approximate grip on reality, constituting knowledge about objects and processes that goes well beyond what we can perceive. Let us now look more deeply at how the brain can accomplish such coherence.

Coherence in the Brain

In discussing perception, I contrasted the step-by-step, language-based inferences that occur in speaking or writing with the parallel, often non-linguistic kinds of inference performed by brains. Because people argue about the best explanation of crimes or scientific experiments, it seems at first that inferences to hypotheses are made serially and linguistically. But the brain does it differently, with multimodal representations of hypotheses and causality, and with parallel assessments of coherence.

As common sense suggests, language is an important part of how minds represent hypotheses, but other sensory modalities can also contribute. You can represent your conjecture that O. J. Simpson killed his ex-wife by the sentence "O. J. killed Nicole." But if you have seen pictures of Simpson, you can also represent this hypothesis by the dynamic mental image of him slashing Nicole with a knife, a kind of moving picture in your head. Similarly, scientists can represent the simplified structure of the atom with the words "The electron revolves around the proton," but they can also use diagrams or mental pictures to represent this hypothesis visually. Other sensory images can also help constitute hypotheses—for example, if you imagine the sound of Nicole screaming.

Whether hypotheses are expressed in words or in sensory images, in the brain they still amount to the same thing: patterns of activation in neural populations. I already gave an idea of how this might work when I discussed how concepts like *drunk* can contribute to explanations. If your brain has neural populations for representing Simpson, Nicole, and *killed*, then it can also have patterns of neural activity that represent the hypothesis that Simpson killed Nicole. Your mental representation of Simpson can include both verbal information, such as that he used to be a football player, and visual information, such as your memory of his face; so the patterns of neural activity that represent the murder hypothesis can combine verbal and visual aspects. How the brain combines patterns of activity in this way is still poorly understood. But the Eliasmith method of translating concepts and relations into vectors, and vectors into activities of neural populations, shows the computational feasibility of representing explanatory hypotheses using the behavior of large numbers of neurons.

With hypotheses and evidence represented by patterns of neural activity, we can build up even higher-level relational assertions, such as: That Simpson killed Nicole explains why Nicole is dead. But how shall we understand *explains*? Much philosophical discussion of explanation tries to elucidate it in terms of logical relations such as deduction or mathematical ones such as probability, but there are good philosophical and psychological reasons to maintain that explanations are causal. That Nicole is dead is explained by Simpson's having killed her in that her death was (hypothetically) caused by his actions. That combustion is oxidation explains why burning matter gains weight in that oxidation causes weight gain. But now we have the problem of trying to understand causality.

I propose the hypothesis that much of our appreciation of causal relations is preverbal and multimodal, shared with infants and nonhuman animals that lack language. Even at 2½ months, human babies act surprised when colliding objects do not behave in normal ways, which suggests that they already possess some elementary understanding of causality. The linguistic and mathematical limitations of infants require us to look elsewhere for ideas about how they represent causality, which I conjecture is mainly based on sensory-motor patterns. Babies have patterns of neural activation for sensory experiences such as seeing a toy or hearing a bell, and they also have neural patterns corresponding to sequences of motor behaviors such as reaching out and grabbing the toy. It would be fascinating to work out an account of how neural populations can combine sensory and motor patterns. For example, when a baby sees a rattle, grabs it, moves it, and then sees the toy in a different place while hearing it make a sound, there is a repeated pattern of experience that is sensory-motor-sensory.

Within a few months of birth, babies have an extensive history of such sensory-motor interactions that provide them with a good idea of what it is to manipulate the world, not just observing it but constantly intervening to make things happen in it. Much later, when, as children, they have acquired language, they can use the word "cause," but its meaning still depends on the earlier preverbal experience of perceiving a situation, acting, and perceiving the results of the action. Much later still, people can acquire a richer understanding of causality by education in statistical inference, but that still depends on an intuitive notion of causality as intervention that began with sensory-motor experience.

Even very sophisticated ideas about causality, such as Bayesian networks, require an intuitive notion of causality to provide a scaffolding for how variables are related to each other. Brains meld this preverbal sensory-motor notion with later linguistic representations to provide a highly useful, neurally encoded concept of causality that supplies the basis for the explanatory relation that holds between hypotheses and evidence. Thus we are beginning to glimpse the neural mechanisms that allow brains to represent hypotheses and concepts, including explanation and causality, using patterns of neural activity that constitute both verbal and multimodal representations. I suspect that human understanding of time, like that of space and causality, is often difficult to put into words because its neural encoding is partly dependent on physiological rather than verbal representations.

But we still need an account of how brains integrate many competing claims about explanations to make an inference to the best explanation, which requires figuring out the most coherent way of accepting some hypotheses and rejecting others. Hypotheses and evidence are related to each other by both positive constraints that concern how they fit together, and negative constraints between representations that resist fitting together. The most important kind of positive constraint is that when a hypothesis explains a piece of evidence, they cohere with each other. For example, the hypothesis that Simpson killed Nicole fits with the evidence that Nicole is dead because the killing causally explains the death. The most important kind of negative constraint is between hypotheses that contradict each other or that compete more loosely to explain some piece of evidence. For example, the hypothesis that Simpson killed Nicole competes with the defense's hypothesis that she was killed by drug dealers.

To see how this might work in the brain, begin with a highly simplified view of elements such as hypotheses and evidence as represented by single neuronlike units rather than by patterns of activation in neural populations. We can then build an artificial neural network that represents constraints among elements by links between the units that stand for them. Figure 4.2 shows a simple network that has units representing competing hypotheses in the Simpson case. Positive constraints based on what explains what are captured by excitatory links between units, roughly analogous to the synaptic connections that enable one neuron to excite another. Note that figure 4.2 allows levels of explanatory hypotheses, with the hypothesis that Simpson was angry at his ex-wife explaining why he killed her, which explains why she is dead. Negative constraints are captured by inhibitory links between units. Another positive constraint that affects the network is that we should tend to accept what we have observed with our senses, in this case that Nicole is dead.

In order to figure out the best explanation of the evidence, we need to figure out how to maximize satisfaction of positive and negative constraints, where we satisfy a positive constraint between elements by accepting both of them, and a negative constraint by rejecting one and accepting the other. Fortunately, there are various computational algorithms available for maximizing constraint satisfaction. The most psychologically natural one uses a number called activation to represent the high or low acceptability of a unit, where activation is roughly analogous to the firing rate of a neuron. Then we can use simple algorithms to spread activation in parallel among the units in a network until some are accepted and others are rejected. For example, when activation is spread among all the units in the network in figure 4.2, the result is that the unit for the hypothesis that Simpson is a murderer gets activated, and the competing unit about drug dealers gets deactivated. In

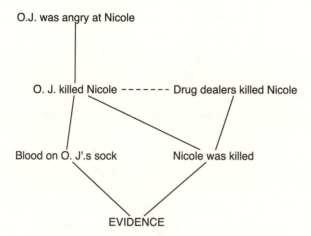

4.2. Structure of the inference concerning who killed Nicole Simpson.

this way, a highly simplified neural network can make a complex coherence judgment using parallel constraint satisfaction. This method of maximizing explanatory coherence has been used to model a great many examples from law and science, including the theory revisions that occurred in the major scientific revolutions wrought by Copernicus and Einstein.

From a brain science perspective, the method just described is unsatisfactory because it is obvious that complex hypotheses such as crime explanations and scientific claims are not represented in the brain by single neurons. Another problem is that constraints in figure 4.2 are symmetric, allowing two elements to mutually constrain each other, so that excitatory and inhibitory links between units are also symmetric. But in real neural networks it never happens that two neurons both excite or inhibit each other. Fortunately, it is possible to model the calculation of explanatory coherence in a much more neurologically realistic way.

First, we represent each element by a population of neurons rather than by a single unit. Second, we represent a link by a whole complex of links between neurons in multiple populations. At this level, there is no problem in having symmetrical connections because some of the neurons in one population excite neurons in the other, while others in the second population excite other neurons in the first one. The resulting neural networks with thousands of artificial neurons are much larger than the few dozen units that suffice for modeling the Simpson trial and other legal and scientific cases. But your brain has approximately one hundred billion neurons to work with, so this scale does not seem to be a problem. Our computer simulations show that more biologically realistic neural networks can accomplish the same kind of parallel constraint satisfaction as can the simpler ones that use one unit for each element.

Thus we are beginning to understand how inference to the best explanation might occur in the brain. As we saw with perception, inference is the result of the dynamic parallel interaction of neural patterns, not of serial linguistic steps. Attention to brain mechanisms shows how inference can nonmysteriously be holistic and multimodal. Later chapters will show how similar neural mechanisms tie inference with emotions and actions.

Coherence and Truth

Brains know reality through a combination of perception and inference to the best explanation of what is observed. Such inference attempts to maximize explanatory coherence, which sometimes requires rejection of what the senses tell us. Rejection of observations occurs both in everyday life, as when a drunk decides that a double image of a person cannot be right, and in science, as when a researcher throws out some experimental data that conflict with a well-supported theory. Hence gaining knowledge is a matter of seeking coherence among many hypotheses and pieces of evidence, not of starting with some indubitable foundation in sense experience or a priori knowledge and trying to base everything else on that.

There are no foundations for knowledge, even though the overall reliability of perception justifies recognizing that the results of observation should have a degree of priority in the maximization of coherence. Knowledge is not a matter of pure coherence, because observational evidence does get some priority and provides some constraint on utterly fanciful speculation. Nevertheless, I advocate a kind of coherentism, the view that beliefs are justified by how well they fit with other beliefs and with sensory experience. This coherentist view of knowledge meshes well with constructive realism to provide an answer to the two questions that began this chapter:

what is reality, and how do we know it? Reality consists of objects and their properties that we can learn about through perception and inference to the best explanation.

In chapter 2, I described how inference to the best explanation in science differs from everyday inference in employing mechanistic explanations and more thorough assessment of a broader range of evidence gained from careful experiments. Hence well-supported scientific theories are usually a more reliable guide to reality than is common sense, which is often derived from tradition rather than systematic evaluation of alternative hypotheses with respect to evidence. So at any particular time, we should accept what the best available scientific theories tell us, while acknowledging that the collection of new evidence and the development of novel hypotheses may well lead to the eventual conclusion that some current theories are not adequate representations of reality. Based on current evidence, we should be content to recognize as real various forms of matter and energy, from atoms, electrons, and quarks to human minds construed as brains.

Perception and inference to the best explanation are both fallible and require complex mental processes, but there are nevertheless good reasons to resist idealism, the view that reality is somehow dependent on mind. Evidence suggests that our universe is more than thirteen billions of years old, but human minds have been around for only, at most, a few million. According to the fossil record, the first mammals, whose brains were larger and more advanced than those of the reptiles they evolved from, came along only around two hundred million years ago. Hence we have abundant evidence that reality existed long before minds came along, and presumably will continue long after all minds are extinct. Accordingly we must resist the Ptolemaic counterrevolutionary attempts to reassuringly make human minds the center of reality. As chapter 7 will show, life can be meaningful even if minds are brains rather than supernatural entities.

Because we have good grounds for asserting the existence of mind-independent reality, we can construe truth as correspondence between mental representations and aspects of reality. The relevant representations include not only linguistic sentences, but also sensory images and extensions of them, such as mental pictures we construct. The correspondence relation between representations and reality need not simply be the binary true/false relation, but can involve approximations. A set of representations such as a theory is approximately true if most of its claims are quantitatively close to actual conditions in the world. Truth is then a legitimate aim of scientific and everyday theorizing, along with explanation and prediction.

Conclusion

I said at the beginning of this chapter that accepting the mind-brain identity theory has major implications for questions about reality and knowledge, and I have tried to show how neural processes such as perception and inference enable brains to have knowledge of reality. Implication, like inference, is not a simple relation, as it requires looking at the most fully coherent system of hypotheses, assessed through the dynamic interaction of representations operating in parallel. Hence my argument is not some simple deduction: minds are brains, so constructive realism is true. Rather, like all inferences, my conclusions are justified by overall coherence: given that minds are brains, and given everything else we know, the most coherent conclusion is that people use perception and inference to the best explanation to construct knowledge about reality. This process of justification will seem circular if you think that knowledge should have a foundation of indubitable truths from which other truths are derived. But no one has ever succeeded in identifying such a foundation in either sense experience or a priori reasoning, so we have to strive instead to construct the most coherent systems of representations that we can.

Fortunately, in realms such as everyday perception and theories in the natural sciences, our brains frequently succeed in producing such systems that approximate how the world really is. For perception, the reason for this success is evolutionary, in that human perceptual systems and their forerunners in primates and other predecessors underwent selection for organisms that function well in their environments. The explanation for scientific success is much more cultural, as powerful methods such as controlled experimentation, statistical inference, and computer modeling have been devised only in recent centuries. With such methods, it becomes possible to develop knowledge that goes well beyond perception without succumbing to supernatural fantasies.

However, to possess wisdom and appreciate the meaning of life, it is not sufficient simply to know reality. You need to know what aspects of reality matter, and why they matter. Wisdom without knowledge is empty, but knowledge without wisdom is blind. The capacities of brains to gain knowledge by perception and inference to the best explanation are required for the acquisition of wisdom, but also required are capacities for assigning positive and negative values to what is represented, including aspects of love, work, and play. We can understand this more deeply by investigating how brains have emotions.

how brains feel emotions

Emotions Matter

Here is a story that may have an emotional effect on you. Mother Superior calls all the nuns together and says to them: "I must tell you all something. We have a case of gonorrhea in the convent." "Thank God," says an elderly nun at the back of the room, "I'm so tired of chardonnay." Most people react to this joke with pleasurable surprise, including laughter. This chapter will try to explain the neural basis of this and other emotional reactions that are integral to appreciating the meaning of life.

Here are some facts you probably didn't know. Tirana is the capital of Albania. Sarcoidosis is an immune system disease characterized by small nodules in various organs. Flatworms lack endocrine glands. If the rest of this chapter were so boring, you would probably stop reading soon. People generally use perception and inference to acquire knowledge that matters to them, not just isolated pieces of information that are irrelevant to their lives. But if you are excited about a trip to the Balkans, or worried about a lump in your lymph nodes, or fascinated by invertebrate anatomy, then you may well become interested in Albania, sarcoidosis, or flatworms. Emotions such as excitement and worry shape our knowledge of reality by guiding us to acquire information that matters to us. Although there are destructive emotions like deep depression that sometimes suck all meaning out of people's lives, without emotion there would be no sense of what matters, and hence no wisdom.

This chapter describes brain mechanisms that constitute emotional feelings and thereby make possible valued experiences, wisdom about what matters, and meaningful lives. Basic emotions like happiness, sadness, fear, anger, disgust, and surprise can all be understood as brain processes, as can more complex social emotions such as shame, guilt, contempt, envy, pride, and gratitude. Psychologists and philosophers have long debated whether emotions should be understood as (1) cognitive appraisals that people make about the degree of satisfaction of their goals, or (2) perceptions of their physiological states. We will see how the brain can accomplish such appraisals and perceptions simultaneously, dynamically integrating them with cognitive representations like concepts and beliefs. Such integration is crucial for the accounts presented in subsequent chapters about decision and action, what makes life worth living, and moral judgments.

People are often told to be rational *instead* of emotional. The view that emotions conflict with reason goes back at least to Plato, who said that the intellect needs to control passions as a charioteer controls a horse. There are indeed many ways in which emotional states can interfere with making good inferences, ranging from psychiatric problems such as mania and depression to more everyday afflictions such as wishful thinking, motivated inference, weakness of will, and self-deception. Understanding emotional brain processes can help us to deal with these problems, but it can also help us to appreciate how emotions are essential for effective thinking in all domains, from practical decision making to scientific discovery.

Valuations in the Brain

The mind does not just have concepts and beliefs, but also attaches values to them. How do you feel about the following kinds of things: babies, dogs, chocolate, beef, basketball, beer, television, cockroaches, and broccoli? Your mental representations of many of these probably involve definite emotional attitudes, positive or negative, although you may be indifferent to some of them. Different facts about these things are also accompanied by emotional attitudes—for example, the positive thought that chocolate tastes good and the negative thought that it can be fattening. When our brains represent things using concepts and beliefs, they connect these representations with positive and negative valuations.

Suppose, as the last two chapters argued, that your concept of chocolate is a pattern of activation in a population of neurons. These neurons do not need to be confined to brain areas devoted to thinking with words, but could also include neurons in areas for sensory processes such as sight, smell, and taste. Hence the look, feel, and taste of chocolate are as much a part of your concept of chocolate as is the verbal information that it is made out of cocoa beans. The activity of neurons in different regions of the brain is temporally coordinated through the interactions that take place via synaptic interconnections, produced by long axons that enable neurons in one part of the brain to excite or inhibit neurons in other parts. Such multimodal activity makes it possible for you to recognize a morsel as chocolate because it has the sensory properties, such as taste, smell, and mouth feel, of your previous experiences of chocolate. For concepts and beliefs, similar kinds of coordination occur with brain areas important for emotions.

There are many relevant brain areas, but I will focus on just two that are known to affect emotional processes. First consider the amygdala, a small almond-shaped area located in the lower middle part of the brain, below the cortex (figure 5.1). Recordings of neuron firings in animals and brain-scanning experiments in humans show the amygdala is important for emotions, especially fear. For example, when people are shown a picture of a scary face, brain scans show an increase of blood flow to the amygdala, indicating that the neurons in it are firing more rapidly and need renourishing. Hence it is plausible that the experience of being afraid of a gruesome face requires an association between the firing of neurons that visually represent the face and the firing of neurons in the amygdala. We may say or think that the face is scary, but this is only a verbal description of the emotional experience of fear of the face. All mammals have an amygdala, and there are analogous regions in fish and reptiles. The amygdala has reciprocal connections with many other brain areas, including the prefrontal cortex, so that neural populations in the amygdala can increase the firing of neurons in the cortex, and vice versa.

Another brain area important for emotions is the nucleus accumbens, located above the amygdala. If you like eating chocolate, doing so probably increases activation in this region of your brain, which has been extensively studied because of its role in addiction to drugs such as alcohol and cocaine. Both of these drugs increase firing of neurons in the nucleus accumbens and related areas. Feelings of pleasure and anticipation of desirable outcomes are associated with a circuit of neurons that employ the neurotransmitter dopamine, running from the ventral tegmental area through the nucleus accumbens to the prefrontal cortex. Such brain circuits are reciprocal, with many feedback loops. Hence for people like me, who love chocolate, the pattern of neural firing associated with eating it includes neurons in the nucleus accumbens as well as parts of the brain involved in verbal, visual, and other sensory representations.

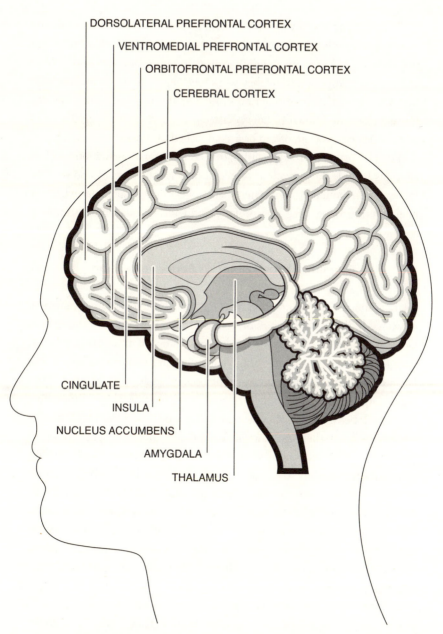

DORSOLATERAL PREFRONTAL CORTEX

VENTROMEDIAL PREFRONTAL CORTEX

ORBITOFRONTAL PREFRONTAL CORTEX

CEREBRAL CORTEX

CINGULATE

INSULA

NUCLEUS ACCUMBENS

AMYGDALA

THALAMUS

5.1 Location of the amygdala and some other brain areas important for emotion. Locations are only approximate because of the difficulty of portraying the three-dimensional structure of the brain.

I won't try now to review all the brain regions that contribute to human emotions, a long list that includes the orbitofrontal cortex (behind the eyes), the ventromedial (bottom middle) prefrontal cortex, and the insula. More will be said below about how they work together to produce emotions. The key point is that definite brain areas such as the nucleus accumbens and the amygdala are known to be associated with positive and negative emotions, and such associations can be accomplished through coordinated neural firings. The patterns of neural firing that constitute representations such as concepts include the operations of neural populations in areas known to be involved in emotional processing. Such associations ensure that when the brain is representing some aspects of the world, it is simultaneously valuing it.

Cognitive Appraisal versus Bodily Perception

There is much more to emotion than just positive and negative valuation, as we see in the many varieties of feelings, such as happiness, elation, contentedness, fear, anger, disgust, and horror. Philosophers and psychologists have long debated the nature of the emotions, and their proposed theories fall into two main camps: cognitive appraisal and bodily perception. According to cognitive appraisal theories, emotions are judgments about the extent to which a perceived situation accomplishes a person's goals. According to bodily perception theories, however, emotions are not judgments but rather perceptions of physiological states. I will briefly review these historically competing theories, and then offer a synthesis of them in the form of a model of how the brain combines both cognitive appraisal and bodily perception.

When something happens to you, you naturally evaluate how it affects your life. When you get a good job offer, it usually makes you happy because it contributes to your goals of having a successful career and making money. According to the cognitive appraisal approach to emotions, a situation makes you happy when it contributes to your goals, with greater contributions leading to greater happiness. Sadness is the opposite, indicating that a situation impedes accomplishment of your goals, as when you do not get a job you want or get a puny raise. Anger occurs when someone blocks the accomplishment of your goals—for example, when a fellow worker keeps you from being successful at your work. Fear arises in situations that threaten your survival goals, such as when a car cuts you off on the freeway and almost makes you crash. Disgust is basically a violation of your eating goals and desire for bodily integrity, as when someone tries to feed you something repulsive like fried worms, but can also extend to noneating situations such as sexual acts you consider depraved. In all these cases, you experience different emotions because your appraisal of the situation produces a judgment about its relevance to your goals.

Complex social emotions such as shame and pride seem to involve a kind of cognitive appraisal with respect to goals connected with relations to other people. If you perform an act, such as theft, that goes against the expectations of people you care about, or that contravenes the moral code you have been brought up with, then you will feel shame or guilt. These reactions arise in part from a judgment that you have violated your goal of receiving the approval of others. On the other hand, if you accomplish something like winning an award that fits with the values you share with your social group, then you can feel pride. Gratitude is the positive feeling you have toward someone who has helped you accomplish your own goals. Envy is the negative feeling toward someone who has something you want. Social emotions require a recognition of your place in a social network and a judgment about how a particular situation is affecting other people in that network.

Nevertheless, some psychologists and philosophers reject the cognitive appraisal approach in favor of the claim that emotions consist merely of bodily perceptions. The body is undeniably an important part of people's emotions, as is especially evident in negative emotions such as fear. Suppose you suddenly hear that someone you care about has been in a serious car accident. Your body will undergo dramatic changes, including increases in heartbeat, breathing rates, blood pressure, and circulating levels of the stress hormone cortisol. Such physiological changes are sensed by the body and communicated to brain areas such as the amygdala and the insula.

According to bodily perception theories, your emotion is your brain's response to such physiological changes, as expressed in a famous quote from the American psychologist/philosopher William James:

> The more rational statement is that we feel sorry because we cry, angry because we strike, afraid because we tremble, and not that we cry, strike, or tremble, because we are sorry, angry, or fearful, as the case

may be. Without the bodily states following on the perception, the latter would be purely cognitive in form, pale, colourless, destitute of emotional warmth. We might then see the bear, and judge it best to run, receive the insult and deem it right to strike, but we could not actually *feel* afraid or angry.

Which is right, the view that emotions are bodily perception, or the view that they are cognitive appraisals?

We needn't choose. I think that the debate between cognitive appraisal and bodily perception theories is similar to two other classical debates about the mind: genetic versus environmental explanations of behavior, and top-down versus bottom-up accounts of perception. In each of these debates, both sides are partly right, in ways that start to become clear with the development of a rich theory of how dynamic interactions produce the full range of phenomena to be explained. I won't get into nature versus nurture here, but I have already sketched in chapter 4 how perception involves simultaneous, parallel processing that combines top-down knowledge with bottom-up perceptual input. Analogously, emotions can be understood as the dynamic interactions of brain areas that perform both bodily perception and cognitive appraisal.

Synthesis: The EMOCON Model

In an attempt to explain emotional consciousness, I developed the EMOCON model shown in figure 5.2, which depicts relations among many of the most important brain areas. The arrows indicate that activity of neural populations in one area causes neural activity in other connected areas. The figure shows perceptual information coming from sensory processes on the left, which is then simultaneously communicated via the thalamus to cortical areas such as the dorsolateral prefrontal cortex that make cognitive judgments, and to areas involved in bodily perception such as the amygdala and the insula. Moreover, the thalamus also affects bodily processes such as heart rate via the hypothalamus, not shown in the figure. If the brain were a serial processor like most computers, it would have to alternate between processing the sensory inputs cognitively and doing so bodily, but the power of parallel processing allows it to do both simultaneously.

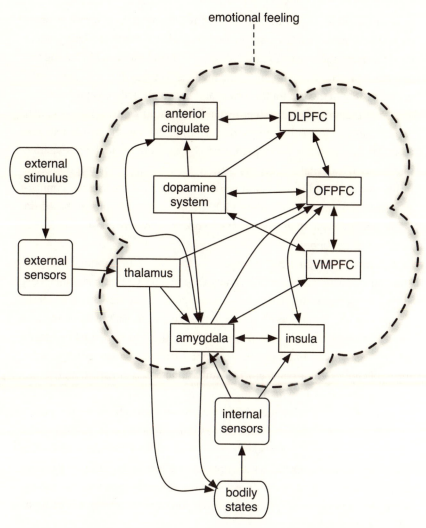

5.2 The EMOCON model of how different brain areas interact to produce emotions as the result of both cognitive appraisal and bodily perception. Abbreviations: DLPFC is dorsolateral prefrontal cortex; OFPFC is orbitofrontal prefrontal cortex; VMPFC is ventromedial prefrontal cortex. The dotted line is intended to indicate that emotional consciousness emerges from activity in the whole system. See figure 5.1 for the relevant brain anatomy.

Because of the large numbers of reciprocal connections between brain areas, the results of processing in one part of the brain can easily affect processing in other parts. Figure 5.2 displays many interactions among the dopamine system, which includes the nucleus accumbens, the cognitive appraisal system in the prefrontal cortex, and the emotional perception system involving the amygdala and the insula. There is no central processor that coordinates all the results and yields a decision. Rather, the brain's reaction to a scary face or other sensory stimulus comes about through the dynamic interaction of external sensory perception, internal sensory perception, cognitive appraisal, and positive and negative valuation. Note that the connections between brain areas in the EMOCON model are reciprocal, based on neural evidence that there is extensive feedback between neural populations in each pair of regions.

The model in figure 5.2 incorporates the bodily perception theory of emotion by virtue of the role played by the amygdala and the insula in collecting input from internal sensors that respond to bodily changes. These changes are the result of both sensory input conveyed via the thalamus and the feedback relations between physiological processes such as heartbeat and respiration and brain processes in areas such as the amygdala and the insula. People have a penchant for simple linear causal explanations: factor A causes factor B, which causes factor C. But biological systems often involve extensive causal interactions based on feedback, so that A and B interact to cause C, which then has a causal influence on A. For example, your liver function and diet both increase your cholesterol level, which then induces your liver to produce less cholesterol. Understanding how the brain produces emotions requires appreciating the complex of reciprocal connections shown in figure 5.2, producing highly nonlinear processes because of all the feedback that occurs.

Although bodily perception theories of emotion have become popular in recent years, they fail to account for the full range of emotional phenomena. There are only weak correlations between emotions such as anger and fear and physiological states such as facial behavior and autonomic arousal. The subtle differences between diverse emotions have not been found to be closely related to distinct physiological states, their magnitudes, or particular neurotransmitters. Surgical disruption of bodily signals does not eliminate emotional reactions. Manipulations of physiology by injection of epinephrine can produce different emotional reactions depending on how people interpret their social situations. Social emotions such as guilt and pride require an appreciation of one's location in a social network. Hence cognitive appraisal is needed to complement bodily perception to generate a full range of emotional reactions. However, bodily perception remains a crucial part of the EMOCON model, which assumes that appraisal alone would not produce the kinds of feelings that occur in emotional consciousness.

Figure 5.2 shows how integration of cognitive appraisal and bodily perception might work by virtue of the interactions among the amydgala, the insula, and several parts of the prefrontal cortex. The dorsolateral prefrontal cortex, at the top and sides of the brain, is important for verbal processing and working memory. The orbitofrontal prefrontal cortex, at the bottom of the brain behind your eyes, contributes to assessment of value, in concert with the dopamine system. Positive and negative valuations that are central to emotions occur because of coordination of the activity of neural populations in these areas with neural activity in other areas supporting verbal or sensory representations. The ventromedial part of the prefrontal cortex is important for communication between the cortex and the amygdala. People with damage to this area have great difficulty making good decisions.

Psychological and philosophical theories that take emotions to be based on cognitive appraisal have had little to say about the brain mechanisms needed to evaluate the relevance of a situation to a person's many goals. Evaluation of a simple sensory stimulus (a man with a gun aimed at you) may be relatively simple, but reflection on a complex situation (a job offer in a far-off city) may require an assessment with respect to many goals. In chapter 4, I described theory evaluation as involving a kind of parallel evaluation of multiple constraints, and cognitive appraisal is also naturally conceived as parallel constraint satisfaction. Hence the brain can accomplish cognitive appraisal of a situation with respect to multiple goals using the same kind of mechanism described in chapter 4 for inference to the best explanation.

For appraisal, different aspects of the situation and different goals are represented by different neural populations. Positive and negative constraints between the aspects and the goals are captured by excitatory and inhibitory synaptic connections between the neurons in the different populations. Overall appraisal of how a situation fits or fails to fit with your goals comes about because of parallel processing through the firing activity of the neural populations as they interact. Value naturally enters the picture because the neural populations involved in the representation of the situation and personal goals include ones in areas such as the amygdala, the nucleus accumbens, and the orbitofrontal prefrontal cortex that help to encode positive and negative features. An overall assessment of value comes about when parallel constraint satisfaction combines the features of the situation, goals, and values to compute the overall emotional coherence of the situation.

Figure 5.2 shows how bodily perceptions can contribute to cognitive appraisal and assessment of value through the interactions of the amygdala and the insula with cortical areas. Hence the parallel constraint satisfaction that assesses the relevance of situations to goals includes bodily perception as an important part. Emotions are not just gut reactions, because they also involve cognitive judgments. But contrary to purely cognitive theories of emotions, gut reactions are a part of appraisal. This combination would be very puzzling if you tried to think of the brain as operating in a series of steps, and had to decide what it does first: cognitive appraisal or bodily perception? But the kinds of dynamic interactions depicted in figure 5.2 show how emotion can be both representational and embodied.

Like all models, EMOCON is oversimplified in many ways. There are many other relevant brain areas—for example, the hippocampus, which plays a major role in memory and interpreting situations in the context of previous experience. Figure 5.2 might be taken to suggest that the brain is a kind of passive observer, waiting for sensory information to come in to be interpreted. But brains are much more active, anticipating situations in ways that can lead to action. Chapter 6 will say much more about how emotions contribute to decisions about how to act. We have already seen, in chapter 4, that perception is a top-down as well as bottom-up process, so even processing of sensory information in the thalamus is affected by expectations stored in the prefrontal cortex. Hence figure 5.2 should not be interpreted as maintaining that emotions are just responses to stimuli, but rather as showing a simplified part of more complex thought processes that include expectations and actions.

Emotional Consciousness

Something important is missing so far in all this talk of interacting brain areas. People don't just have emotions, they *feel* emotions, and the title of this chapter proposed that brains actually feel emotions. Every human knows what it is like to feel happy, sad, angry, afraid, disgusted, surprised, and so on. Where is the feeling in the EMOCON model in figure 5.2? The name "EMOCON" is supposed to indicate that it is a model of emotional consciousness, but this would be bogus if it did not tell us something about conscious experience, about what it is like to feel happy or sad. I suggested in chapter 3 that finding mechanisms for consciousness is the major barrier to acceptance of the inference to the best explanation that minds are brains. I will not offer a full theory of consciousness in this book, but I will sketch how the EMOCON model suggests a mechanistic explanation of emotional consciousness. My goal is not just to describe aspects of emotional experiences, but to sketch how the interactions of neural populations can generate and indeed constitute such experiences.

Think of a recent time when you were happy, perhaps because you enjoyed the convent joke at the start of this chapter, or more intensely because you got an invitation to visit a good friend in an exciting city. Such experiences are not raw wholes incapable of further interpretation; they have identifiable aspects. First, your happiness was not free-floating, but was connected with cognitive representations of the world, such as your friend and the city. You were happy *that* you were invited to make the visit. Second, conscious emotional experiences have a positive or negative character, in this case not just a feeling, but a good feeling. Third, conscious emotional experiences have an intensity, in this case a high degree in contrast to other situations that may make you only a little happy. Fourth, this emotional experience is differentiated from other emotions, including negative ones such as sadness and more or less intense versions of happiness. Fifth, emotional experiences begin and end: you start feeling happy as you first get the invitation and stop feeling happy when you get distracted by some annoying work task that must be completed. It would be pointless to try to give a mechanistic explanation of anything so vague as "what it feels like" to be happy, but the EMOCON model has much to say about the five aspects of conscious experience just described.

Concerning the first aspect, I have already shown how emotions such as happiness and cognitive representations such as visiting a friend can be integrated, through the coordinated activity of neural populations in different brain areas. Hence the EMOCON model shows how emotional experiences are not just feelings but feelings about things. Second, the positive and negative character of emotional experience has been explained by the role of particular brain areas such as the nucleus accumbens and the amygdala, well known to be associated with feeling good or bad. The reason that it feels good to be happy is neural, related to activity in particular brain regions associated with both bodily perceptions and cognitive appraisals.

Third, the varying intensity of emotional experience seen in greater and lesser bouts of happiness can naturally be explained in terms of degree of activity in the relevant neural populations. There is research showing that being *more* hateful involves *more* activity in areas such as the insula, and that anticipation of greater rewards correlates with increased activity in the nucleus accumbens. It is possible to test the hypothesis that increased degree of intensity of an emotional experience correlates with increased rapidity of neural firing in the relevant brain areas as measured by brain scanners that detect increased blood flow. For example, people's preference for Coke over Pepsi correlates with increased activation in the ventromedial prefrontal cortex. The link between preference and activation could be shown to be more than correlational, if some technique like electrostimulation of neurons or transcranial magnetic stimulation could be used to send varying degrees of excitation or inhibition to the appropriate brain areas.

Fourth, unlike the narrow account of emotions as bodily perceptions, my combined model of emotions can explain how emotional experience can be so finely differentiated. It is not just that emotions come with many different combinations of positive/negative valuations and degrees of intensity, but also that they involve an unlimited number of different cognitive appraisals with respect to multiple goals. There is a vast number of possible brain states with different combinations of firing patterns of billions of neurons in brain areas that cover external sensing, internal sensing, valuing, and assessing of coherence with goals. So it is not surprising that we have such a variety of emotional experiences. Mixed emotions, such as a parent's feeling both proud and worried when a child leaves home, are easily explained by the complexity of neural constraint satisfaction involving representations of multiple goals.

Fifth, changes in emotional experience are naturally explained by the sensitivity of the EMOCON model to perceptual experience, which frequently changes and thereby provides new inputs to the whole process depicted in figure 5.2. The starting and stopping of emotional experiences can also be prompted by internal cognitive processes, as when you suddenly remember an overdue project and worry about it. In this case, activity in the prefrontal cortex initiates the bodily reactions and cognitive appraisals that generate emotional experience.

Because the EMOCON model can explain all these characteristics of emotional experience, it becomes plausible to identify emotional feelings with brain states. Your feeling happy is a complex pattern of neural processing of the sort sketched in figure 5.2. Emotions are patterns of activity in multiple brain areas that integrate cognitive appraisal and bodily perception, producing conscious experiences and guiding action. Some philosophers will respond that they just can't imagine how feelings could be brain processes, and that they can easily imagine having brains exactly like ours without having any feelings. But I argued in chapter 2 that such capacities and incapacities for understanding the mind as brain should not be taken seriously, because what we manage to conceive is an indicator not of reality, but only of our current limited understanding of it. I predict that progress in neuroscience will continue to make it easier for us to think of mind as brain, and we will only get better at imagining how brains can feel emotions.

It should now be clear how religious faith can be a kind of emotional consciousness. When people maintain that their faith assures them of the existence and goodness of God, their certainty derives from an intense feeling based on emotional coherence of those beliefs with their personal goals, not from an inference to the best explanation based on evidence. Feelings that come from the heart or from the gut may be compelling because they strongly combine cognitive appraisal of goal relevance with bodily perceptions, both of which are performed unconsciously and come to consciousness only as part of the integrated process tied to working memory displayed in the EMOCON model. But emotional consciousness justifies belief only when it is based on full evaluation of alternative hypotheses with respect to all the relevant evidence. Spiritual experiences and philosophical intuitions are products of interacting brain processes, not sources of special evidence about the nature of mind and reality.

My concern in this chapter has been only with emotion, but mechanistic explanations are starting to emerge for other kinds of consciousness, especially visual experience. In contrast, dualist explanations of consciousness as resulting from ineffable spiritual powers remain mysterious. Hence phenomena of consciousness are not barriers to the conclusion that minds are brains. There are, of course, many questions that remain to be answered, such as why and how consciousness evolved.

It is easy to appreciate the evolutionary advantages that animals gain from the evaluative aspects of emotions, guiding organisms toward more effective strategies of surviving and reproducing. But why should feeling be part of the process? One possibility is that emotional and other kinds of consciousness are just by-products of the organizational complexity of the brain, without any special evolutionary contribution. But it is also possible that brains evolved to have feelings as complex representations because of their contribution to the effectiveness of both individuals and groups. A feeling such as happiness or fear can provide a concise summary of the complex unconscious evaluation by constraint satisfaction of the advantages and dangers of a situation. Feelings provide succinct information about anticipated benefits and risks, and thereby foster quick and effective action. Other likely advantages of emotional consciousness are social, providing a more direct way of understanding the emotional states of others (see the discussion of empathy in chapter 9). Perhaps we will be in a better position to figure out the evolutionary significance of emotional consciousness when more is known about the neural mechanisms that support it.

Multilevel Explanations

That emotions such as happiness and sadness are neural processes does not rule out other kinds of mechanisms as also relevant to explaining events like becoming sad or falling in love. When hearing some good news makes you happy, this change is the result of your brain's undergoing the neural processes I have described, such as activation of your nucleus accumbens. But a full explanation of your happiness can legitimately operate at four different levels: molecular, psychological, and social, as well as neural.

The molecular level is important for understanding how neurons work. I have already mentioned the neurotransmitter dopamine used by neurons that cause feelings of pleasure. When one of these neurons fires, it does not send an electrical charge directly to the other neurons that it excites, but instead releases molecules of dopamine that cross the synaptic gap between the end of the axon of one neuron and the dendrites of the receiving neurons. Dozens of other neurotransmitters play similar roles in making neural processes chemical as well as electrical. The most important include glutamate, which contributes to excitation, and GABA, which contributes to inhibition. I described in chapter 3 how such neurotransmitters can be manipulated by recreational and therapeutic drugs. Besides neurotransmitters, other kinds of molecules are important for explaining emotional changes—for example, cortisol produced by the adrenal glands in reaction to stressful situations, and hormones such as estrogen and testosterone. Hence neural explanations of emotions like the ones provided by the EMOCON model have a molecular underpinning.

But that does not mean that we can replace descriptions of neural mechanisms with descriptions of molecular ones, for two reasons. First, the molecular mechanisms are far too complex to permit us to describe completely how they make even a single neuron work. The internal operations of a neuron are controlled by thousands of genes affecting the chemical interactions of thousands of proteins and other molecules. Much is known about these molecular workings, but the complexity of interactions is so enormous that science may never be able to give a full mechanistic account of the firing of individual neurons, just as explanatory and predictive models of the weather may never be complete. Fortunately, we do not have to wait for the full story about how cells such as neurons work, but can build an approximate account based on the crucial properties of neurons: their ability to accumulate and pass on electric charges.

Second, even if we could have a complete molecular account of how a single neuron works, we would still need mechanisms that show how networks of billions of neurons interact to produce complex effects such as emotional feelings. Currently, we can best approach the emotional phenomena we want to explain by looking at interactions among entire brain regions, not at single neurons or even populations of neurons. Even when much more comes to be known about the operations of single neurons and neural populations, it will still be useful to consider how aggregates of neural populations such as brain regions interact to produce psychological effects. Hence neural and molecular mechanistic explanations complement rather than compete with each other.

Similarly, accepting the claim that emotions are brain processes does not eliminate the value of psychological explanations. I don't mean the simple explanations of ordinary people who rely on folk ideas about beliefs and desires, but rather the theoretical ideas of cognitive psychologists, who often find it useful to talk about mental representations such as concepts, rules, images, and analogies. Saying that concepts are patterns of neural activity enhances rather than eliminates the explanatory value of such representations. When you become happy because of your winning a lottery, we cannot probe into your brain to determine exactly what is happening to your neural populations, so the best explanation available may rely on such descriptions as this: you are happy that you won the lottery because you need the money.

Part of such psychological explanations requires noting the positive valuation you attach to such concepts as *winning* and *money*. Even though these valuations have a neural basis, through coordination between neural populations for verbal representations and ones for positive value, the psychological level of explanation remains important because of our lack of knowledge about the neural details and the direct relevance of concepts like *money* to our practical interests. Hence psychological explanations of emotions can coexist with and complement neural ones, just as molecular explanations can.

Social levels of explanation are also highly relevant to emotions. When you win the lottery, the event is highly social, from the interaction with the ticket seller who can confirm your win to the joy of telling your friends and family about your luck. Many of the goals that generate happiness, sadness, and other emotions are inherently social, tied to your relationships with the people who are important in your life. Your happiness about winning the lottery may derive from your considering not only what the money can do for you, but also what it can do to further the goals of your family. Social emotions such as guilt and pride can be understood only through consideration of your place in social networks such as your family, friends, and people you work or play with. In chapter 7, I will discuss the importance of emotions for love, work, and play, all of which are best understood in terms of interactions among neural, molecular, psychological, and social levels of explanation.

Hence my defense of the claim that mental processes such as emotions are brain processes does not diminish the relevance of social, psychological, and molecular explanations. We should be neither reductionist, claiming that explanation ought to be at just one fundamental level, nor antireductionist, claiming that levels of explanation are independent of each other. The best approach to explaining mental events requires attention to multiple levels, from the social to the molecular, with a focus on how they interact. Neural processes such as the ones that constitute emotions are clearly affected both by underlying biochemical reactions involving neurotransmitters and by social relations among people.

To take one vivid example, consider what happens when you have a friend who suddenly becomes insulting and threatening. We can best understand your emotional reaction of fear and anger by considering all of the following: (1) firing of neural populations in brain areas such as the amygdala; (2) increased operation in your brain of such molecules as adrenaline and cortisol; (3) application of concepts such as *insult* and *danger*; and (4) the social interaction with your friend that prompted the emotional reaction in the first place. The full explanation of fear notes the relevance of molecular changes to neural changes, and of psychological changes to social changes; but it also appreciates how mechanisms are related in the other direction. For example, the social interaction of being threatened causes the molecular change of increased cortisol. Levels of explanation are intertwined, not simply reductive. But in rejecting a ruthless reductionism, we should not embrace a blind antireductionism that ignores how social groups consist of persons, who consist of organs such as brains, which consist of neurons, which consist of proteins and other molecules.

Rationality and Affective Afflictions

That thinking is generally emotional is shown by many kinds of evidence, from psychological studies concerning the general attachment of valuations to concepts, to neural studies of the interconnections among cortical regions and emotional centers such as the amygdala. But my aim in this book is not just to describe psychological phenomena but also to address normative, philosophical questions concerning the meaning of life. So I have to ask: is it good or bad that thinking is emotional?

Emotions are widely thought to be bad for you. We saw this in Plato's metaphor of the charioteer and the frequent opposition of "emotional" and "rational." Many people believe that children and women are emotional, but real men don't cry. Perhaps we should view emotions as annoying intrusions into rational thinking, like hunger, thirst, and the need to go to the toilet. Then wise thinking should aim to minimize the role of emotions, overcoming their irritating interference with proper thinking based on logic. Although I want to reject such complete removal of emotions from rational thought, I will review some of the ways in which emotions can indeed obstruct people's attempts to develop wise pursuit of highly meaningful lives. There are at least five affective afflictions, ways our emotions can seriously skew our thinking away from rationality: motivated inference, self-deception, weakness of will, depression, and manic exuberance.

In chapter 2, I described how motivated inference can interfere with the objective evaluation of evidence. Inferences are motivated when they are affected by our personal goals, as when people try unverified medical treatments in the hope of improving their physical conditions. Such motivated inferences are clearly emotional, because the belief that a treatment will work is based on the valuation attached to the goal of getting better rather than on evidence of efficacy. Most of us are prone to believe things that make us happy. Such inferences are not usually pure wishful thinking, because people make them not by completely ignoring evidence, but rather by selectively considering evidence that supports the view they want to hold. For example, if a friend tells you that the herbal drug echinacea helped with a cold, then your emotional desire not to be sick may incline you to elevate this small piece of evidence over large studies finding that the substance is ineffective.

Motivated inference can contribute to self-deception, which occurs when you form a belief even though you have evidence against it. For example, you might think of yourself as a conscientious person, even though you know that you often fail to meet your obligations. Some philosophers have puzzled about how self-deception could be possible, since they assume that people have the ability to rationally examine their full set of beliefs. But our thinking has no direct access to our huge numbers of neural representations and processes, so it is not surprising that we can deceive ourselves by making motivated inferences to some conclusions that available evidence should lead us to reject. Motivated inference can contribute to bad decisions arising from conflicts of interest, as when a medical expert gives distorted testimony in favor of the efficacy of a drug even though the expert suspects the evidence for the drug is flawed.

An even more common affective affliction is weakness of will, which occurs when you find yourself doing something that you know is not in your best interests. Familiar cases are eating fattening foods, drinking too much alcohol, gambling more than you can afford, having inappropriate sex, or lazily watching television instead of completing some overdue work. Such failings occur frequently because of the strong emotional pull of activities such as eating, drinking, gambling, sex, and avoiding chores. Even though our conscious thought may place a higher value on goals such as health, morality, and productivity, the brain's emotional mechanisms may send us in a direction that we would prefer not to pursue, all things considered.

Weakness of will is fostered by the operation of separate neural systems for immediate and delayed rewards. The midbrain dopamine system is preferentially activated by decisions involving immediately available rewards, whereas regions of the lateral prefrontal cortex and the posterior parietal cortex are engaged uniformly by long- and short-term choices. People are particularly prone to make bad choices when they are tired, stressed, and presented with tempting sensory stimuli. The prefrontal cortex says no, but the nucleus accumbens says yes, yes, yes!

Many people suffer occasionally or chronically from depression, a state of pervasive sadness in which one finds it hard to see how anything can have any value at all. A depressed person may lose the ability to find any enjoyment in previously pleasant activities and may slump into inactivity. Depression can lead to bad decisions based on beliefs inconsistent with the evidence you already possess—for example, that you have a history of successful and enjoyable pursuit of valuable goals. Cognitive therapy is often effective by helping people to change their beliefs about the hopelessness of their conditions. It can complement drug therapy that changes the brain by affecting levels of neurotransmitters such as serotonin and increasing the generation of new neurons in the hippocampus.

At the other extreme, some people have bouts of mania, a state of great excitement in which anything seems possible. In extreme cases, people suffering from the manic side of bipolar disorder may take crazy risks such as wild driving or dangerous sex. A more moderate form of mania is irrational exuberance, when people become so excited about a financial or romantic prospect that they ignore cautions about perilous ventures. Financial bubbles such as the dot.com stock market boom of the late 1990s and the American housing bubble of the 2000s are fueled by irrational exuberance, when people become convinced that what goes up can only keep going up.

The negative effects of motivated inference, self-deception, weakness of will, conflicts of interest, depression, and manic exuberance—and additional affective afflictions, including fears not based on evidence—do indeed make it tempting to embrace the classical view that emotions just get in the way of rational thinking. These affective afflictions make implausible the romantic view that our feelings are inherently good and just need to be let loose. I certainly do not endorse the view "If it feels good, believe it."

But there are strong reasons why the classical path to wisdom based on relinquishing or overcoming emotions is not feasible. First, you cannot simply turn off the emotional mechanisms that link your neural processes of inference with processes of valuation that employ interconnections with brain areas such as the nucleus accumbens and the amygdala. You can no more decide to operate in a fully nonemotional mode than you can decide to cut your left hemisphere off from your right hemisphere without highly destructive neurosurgery.

Second, if you could give yourself an emotionectomy, the costs of doing so would be enormous. While greatly reducing your susceptibility to the various afflictions, you would also lose most of what gives you a reason for doing anything at all. Even intellectual work would become pointless without the joy of discovery, the fear of failure, and the satisfaction of modest progress. Without emotional processes in the brain that tie representations of concepts, beliefs, and goals to assessments of value, you would lose the continuous assessment of situations and options that provides guidance about what to pursue. All facts and theories would be equally trivial, and all courses of action would be equally pointless. Thought and action would become equally bereft of motivation. Like a computer that lacks the capacity to care about whether it is turned on or off, your brain would have no way of determining what is worth thinking about or doing. All the reasons that chapter 7 presents to explain why life is worth living would vanish. Hence the classical strategy of relinquishing or dominating emotion is no route to wisdom.

So what are we to do if we want to be *both* rational and emotional? Compare eating, which can be a highly rational enterprise if you consume healthy foods and avoid ones that will hurt your body. Just as you cannot eliminate emotional thinking, you are not physiologically capable of abandoning eating, whose metabolic value is great despite the negative results of consuming too many things that are bad for you. Nutritional science enables us to learn how to eat moderately in ways that enhance rather than limit our health. The simplest but nevertheless valuable rule I have heard is Michael Pollan's suggestion: eat food, not too much, mostly plants.

By analogy, I propose this rule: feel emotions, not too strongly, mostly happy. We need emotions to motivate and guide our inferences, but emotional intensity should be proportionate to their relevance to our goals, which must be coherent with our overall interests and evidence-based beliefs. Chapter 6 describes decision making in terms of the coherence of goals and actions. Although negative emotions such as fear, anger, and sadness are occasionally unavoidable, far more effective and pleasant motivations come from positive emotions such as the many variants of happiness.

My rule about emotions would be useless if emotions were forces entirely out of our control, as often seems to be the case. How can you keep yourself from feeling the full strength of emotions and tilt yourself toward feeling more positive than negative emotions? Answers to these questions are more a matter for clinical psychology than for my own philosophical inquiry, but the EMOCON model points in some useful directions. The bodily perception component of the model suggests that we should be able to modify emotions by changing our physical states, and there are effective ways of accomplishing this. Meditation and other relaxation techniques can be used to calm breathing and heart rates, helping to reduce negative emotions such as anxiety. Exercise is another excellent way to relieve stress by changing bodily states.

Emotions can also be adjusted through alterations to cognitive appraisals, and psychological techniques such as cognitive therapy and rational-emotive therapy help people critically examine their beliefs and goals in ways that can markedly improve their mood. Drugs used to treat anxiety such as Valium and Xanax change neural processing but can also alter bodily processes such as heartbeat. Hence emotions construed as a combination of bodily perception and cognitive appraisal can be altered by behaviors and treatments that affect one or both of these. We can sometimes avoid the affective affliction of weakness of will by activating the amygdala to side with the prefrontal cortex against the nucleus accumbens, as when fear of bad health helps to overcome tendencies to eat or drink too much.

On the more philosophical side, we can ask normatively how people should work to reduce the impact of affective afflictions in their lives by striving to be rationally emotional. First, people can be aware of the impact of emotions on themselves and others, looking for the frequent occurrences of motivated inference, weakness of will, and self-deception. Often it is easier to recognize such errors in others than in yourself, so it is important to have family and friends who can help you spot your own emotional deviations.

Second, people need to adopt normative models of good inference that are psychologically natural—for example, inference to the best explanation, as described in chapter 2. With such models, they can easily ask the relevant questions concerning the full range of evidence and the alternative explanations. Technical tools of rationality such as probability theory can be very useful in situations where the data are amenable to statistical inference, but need to be embedded in a broader understanding of evidence-based thinking.

Third, people need to be aware of how to optimize emotional cognition in social contexts, looking to positive emotions such as enthusiasm to motivate people rather than to negative ones such as anger and fear. I hope that these three strategies, along with alterations to bodily perception and cognitive appraisal, can help people to become more rationally emotional as well as more emotionally rational.

Conclusion

In the past two decades, neuropsychology has made great progress in enabling us to understand emotions such as happiness and fear as neural processes. Mental representations are multimodal not only in including the various kinds of sensory ones described in chapter 4, but also in including aspects of emotional value. The brain integrates bodily perceptions with cognitive appraisals to experience a wide range of emotions that are crucial for action, and that also heavily influence what inferences we make and how we make them, for good and ill. The good emotional influences are the values that emotions attach to what we know and what we want to know, enabling us to acquire beliefs that can be relevant to our goals, rather than the unlimited number of boring and irrelevant beliefs that we might acquire by observation and inference. Unfortunately, emotions can also lead us to neglect good principles of evidence and to acquire beliefs primarily because they fit with our personal goals and prejudices. To overcome such afflictions as motivated inference, we need to be aware of how good canons of reasoning such as inference to the best explanation can be undermined by emotional distortions. In addition, we need to manage our emotions in positive directions, in ways described in chapter 8.

Neuropsychology is beginning to provide explanations of the most puzzling aspect of emotional and other kinds of thinking, conscious experience. A brain model such as EMOCON uses neural mechanisms to explain how emotional experiences are integrated with cognitions, have positive and negative valuations, vary in intensity, have broad diversity, and begin and end. A full account of emotions needs to pay attention not only to neural mechanisms involving interactions of brain areas and other bodily processes, but also to mechanisms that operate at complementary levels of explanation. Neural processes are increasingly coming to be understood at the biochemical level that includes genes and molecules operating within and between neurons. The psychological level of explanation in terms of mental representations such as goals, concepts, and beliefs remains useful for describing the aggregate effects of neural processes. The causes of emotions are often social, heavily influenced by our interactions with other people. Claiming that emotions are brain processes does not neglect the value of intertwined social, psychological, and molecular levels of explanation for accounting for emotional behavior.

The neuropsychological account of emotions provided in this chapter is pivotal for what follows. If my account is correct, emotions are not just supplemental to thinking but an integral part of all kinds of evaluative thinking. They play a crucial role in decision making and action, the topic of the next chapter, which explores the neural mechanisms underlying human choices. In chapter 9 I will describe the contributions that these mechanisms make to moral thinking, enabling us to care about others and make ethical decisions about them.

Emotional thinking is also integral to wisdom, which I described as knowing what matters, why it matters, and how to achieve it. The way that things matter to us is via our emotions, including both the positive things we want and the negative things we don't. In chapter 7 I will describe how three major realms of human life—love, work, and play—make life worth living. Like mattering, perceptions of *worth* are inherently emotional, and I will show how neural mechanisms make possible the kinds of enjoyment (and sometimes distress) that arise from social relationships, productive activity, and amusements. Pursuits such as marriage, employment, sports, and the arts are all heavily dependent on the kinds of emotional experiences that this chapter has described.

I argued in chapter 2 that thinking should be evidence based, but it should now be clear that it is inevitably emotion based as well. One of the central problems of rationality is how to combine these two essential facets of human thought. Shakespeare asked in *The Merchant of Venice*: "Tell me where is fancy bred, Or in the heart or in the head?" My answer is that thinking needs to integrate cognition and emotion to be fully effective, and we have the brain mechanisms that perform such integration well, at least much of the time. Let us now see how such integration occurs when people make decisions.

Chapter Six

how brains decide

Big Decisions

The hardest decisions that people face during their lifetimes include choosing a career, changing jobs, retiring, getting married, getting divorced, and having a baby. Mathematical decision theory ought to help with such difficult choices, but here is a story about Howard Raiffa, one of the founders of the field. It concerns a conversation he had with Ernest Nagel, a distinguished philosopher of science and expert on probability theory. I can't remember who first told me this story, but when I recounted it at Tel Aviv University years ago, a member of the audience said afterward that he had been a student of Nagel's and had heard it from him.

Nagel encountered Raiffa one day outside his office at Columbia University, muttering, "What shall I do?" When Nagel asked him what the problem was, Raiffa said that he had a job offer and couldn't decide whether to take it. Trying to be helpful, Nagel said to Raiffa: "Howard, you're one of the world's experts on decision making. Why don't you draw up the decision tree of all the possible actions and outcomes, use probabilities to calculate expected utilities, and decide?" Raiffa replied with annoyance: "Ernest, this is serious!" If you have ever tried to make an important decision about careers or relationships using such quantitative methods, you have probably experienced the same kind of frustration.

Important decisions such as career changes are inherently emotional, in several ways. First, when you make a decision, the way you evaluate the attractiveness of different outcomes is rarely quantitative but rather involves a kind of emotional imagination. If you have a job offer that requires moving to California, you can pleasantly imagine the fine weather, but worry about the high cost of housing and traffic congestion. Sunny weather for most people has positive emotional value, whereas spending a lot of money and being stuck in traffic has negative value. In the brain, such valuations are represented by the kinds of brain activity described in the previous chapter, not by easily accessible numbers.

Second, the decision-making process often generates emotions such as anxiety and excitement. Making decisions requires balancing costs and benefits, but it is rarely possible to pull up a spreadsheet that can do the calculations for you. One of the many paradoxes in the empirical study of decision making is that people who have a choice between two excellent options, such as two highly attractive job offers, may feel intense distress about the conflict instead of the happiness of knowing that the outcome should be fine in either case. Getting a decision out of the way can bring peace.

Third, the result of a decision is often a positive emotional value attached to the action or actions that have been judged to be the best. If Raiffa finally managed to decide to move, then he probably felt good about this action, and bad about the conflicting action of staying at Columbia. The deliberation about the pluses and minuses of moving should eventually resolve into a set of positive emotional feelings about chosen outcomes. Thus emotions are (1) inputs to decisions through the valuation of their components, (2) accompaniments to the process of decision making, and (3) outputs of the process that include feelings about the actions chosen as well as an overall feeling of satisfaction or dissatisfaction about the choices that have been made.

This chapter will extend the discussion of emotions in chapter 5 to provide a general account of how brains make decisions that can lead to action. I will first propose an account of decision making as inference to the best plan, analogous to the account of inference to the best explanation given in chapter 2. I will then describe how the brain can accomplish such inferences using the mechanisms for emotional valuation previously described. Evaluating actions requires assessing how they contribute to one's goals, but what are goals and where do they come from? I will sketch an account of how goals are acquired and revised in the course of decision making, and will then discuss the relation between decision and action, arguing that free will is an illusion we can do without.

This chapter is concerned not only with the descriptive question of how people make decisions, but also with the normative question of how people ought to make decisions. In particular, I explore the question of how goals sometimes ought to be changed in ways that contribute to greater wisdom and more meaningful lives.

Inference to the Best Plan

Suppose you are trying to decide what to do for dinner tonight. Your choices might include cooking at home or going out to a variety of restaurants such as fast food, casual dining, or gourmet. Then your decision requires you to choose among at least these four possible actions, taking into account a variety of goals such as getting tasty food, eating healthily, spending money sensibly, and not wasting too much time or effort. Your decision is not, however, just an inference to the best action, because it usually requires a complex of actions to be carried out. For example, if you decide to cook at home, you may have to go to the grocery store to shop for food—an option requiring two or more actions, which constitute a plan. You need to somehow choose the best overall plan, taking into account the full range of relevant options and goals. Such choices can become more complex when they involve other people, as when you want to eat with a group and so have to take into account their goals as well as your own.

Chapter 2 presented the view that beliefs are accepted or rejected on the basis of inference to the best explanation, which we achieve by evaluating competing hypotheses with respect to how well they explain all the available evidence. Analogously, I propose that decisions are made on the basis of inference to the best plan, which we achieve by evaluating competing actions with respect to how well they accomplish all the relevant goals. In theory evaluation, you want to figure out which package of hypotheses provides the most explanatory power, whereas in decision making you need to find out which package of actions provides the most goal accomplishment.

Neither assessment can be performed by simply counting pieces of evidence or number of goals, because of the complex interactions among the elements to be assessed. Chapter 2 described how the acceptability of a hypothesis depends on its overall coherence, not only with what it explains but also with hypotheses that explain it. Further, coherence needs to take into account how a hypothesis combines with other hypotheses to accomplish explanations, and how it competes with alternative explanations of the evidence. Similarly, the acceptability of an action depends on its overall coherence with a whole set of actions and goals, all of which are under evaluation too. If you decide to cook at home, it may be because of multiple hierarchies of goals. For example, you may want to eat healthy food to satisfy the goal of avoiding illness, which contributes to the goal of living longer. Moreover, you may want to eat cheaply to satisfy the goal of saving money toward a foreign trip, which contributes to the goal of having fun. Alternatively, you may just go out to a restaurant because these goals are dominated by more immediate ones of getting fed quickly and avoiding the effort of shopping and cooking.

Inference to the best plan at its simplest is just accepting an action because it is the best means of accomplishing your goals. But usually it requires evaluating together whole competing systems of actions and goals. Described in words, this all sounds rather mysterious, but there are computer algorithms available for assessing just such highly connected kinds of coherence. The algorithms include ones that use simple neural networks to assess coherence, and these can be adapted to work in more biologically realistic kinds of networks.

Although inference to the best explanation and inference to the best plan are structurally similar, the major psychological difference concerns the role of emotion. Evaluation of hypotheses is in part an emotional process, in that we need emotions to guide us to what inferences are worth making, and accepting a highly coherent theory can generate pleasure. But the basic assessment of how coherent a set of hypotheses are with respect to evidence and alternative explanations should not be skewed by the kinds of motivated inference discussed in the previous chapter. Hypotheses and evidence need to be assessed according to how well they correspond to reality, not on the basis of how happy they make you. In contrast, the main point of inference to the best plan is to contribute positively to happiness and other emotions. There is psychological evidence that successful goal pursuit has a positive effect on well-being.

To a large extent, inference to the best plan depends on the kind of assessment of evidence that is integral to inference to the best explanation. Good decisions require reliable information about how well particular actions will serve to help us accomplish particular goals. For example, if you decide to go to an expensive restaurant because you think it has the best food, you ought to have accumulated reliable evidence that the food really is good. An advertisement claiming that the restaurant has superb food should not be trusted, because the best explanation of this report may be that the restaurant wants to lure you into eating there. On the other hand, if you read a newspaper report by a restaurant critic with a track record of identifying fine establishments, then the best explanation of this report may well be that the restaurant really does have good food. Thus inferences to the best plan need to be based on a complex of inferences to the best explanation concerning projected causal relations between options and outcomes with respect to goals. How does the brain carry out such inferences?

Decisions in the Brain

First, we need to consider how the brain represents actions and goals. You have verbal representations of actions such as cooking at home and goals such as saving money. You use words for actions and goals when you talk with other people about what to do, as when you say, "Let's go to that Italian restaurant that has great lasagna." But the brain's representations of actions are usually multimodal in that they can include different kinds of sensory, motor, and emotional information. When you think of cooking, your sensory representations might include a pictorial image of you at the stove or an olfactory image of how the dish you make might smell. Thinking of yourself making an omelet may well also involve a motor image of what you do with your arms when you shake the pan. Your representation of going out to a restaurant may include an image of the motions required to walk or drive to it. When you first start to think about what to do for dinner, various actions may not have much emotional information attached to them, but as you deliberate, you may find yourself becoming increasingly enthusiastic about one option while feeling negative about the others.

Goals are inherently emotional from the start. The importance to you of saving money is captured by the positive or negative value that you attach to verbal or multimodal representations of spending cash or banking it. The mere thought of saving money may make you feel good if you are frugal, or it may seem repugnant if you enjoy spending. Some goals may be visual, as when you imagine yourself lounging on a beautiful beach; tactile, as when you think of being caressed by a lover; or linked with taste and smell, as when you imagine eating a favorite food. Representation of goals that include the beach, the lover, or the food all require the brain to combine representations that involve words, sensory experiences, and emotions. Humans differ from other animals in that our representations are not confined to immediate situations but can portray complex future scenarios involving relations that we have never observed. For example, you can imagine yourself in Tahiti being caressed by a native who is feeding you breadfruit, even if you have never been to Tahiti or eaten breadfruit. In sum, goals are emotionally valued mental representations of imagined states of the world and self.

Chapters 4 and 5 described how such multimodal combinations can work for concepts and beliefs, and the same mechanisms apply to actions and goals understood as patterns of neural firing activity in multiple brain regions. Different regions are required to capture the various verbal, sensory, motor, and emotional components of representations of what to do and why to do it. Dynamic integration of neural activities in these regions is accomplished through synaptic connections that generate temporal coordination among the millions or billions of neurons involved in the representation. For example, when you consider a plan that includes the actions of going to a Chinese restaurant and eating shrimp, the brain represents these actions using activities in regions that range from Broca's area (verbal) to the occipital cortex (visual) to the nucleus accumbens (pleasure). In addition to actions and goals, the brain needs to represent causal relations, such as the understanding that if you go to a particular restaurant, then you will get good food.

A crucial part of the brain's representation of goals is their association with rewards and punishments. When you accomplish a goal, you experience a pleasurable reward through the activity of neural populations in areas such as the orbitofrontal cortex and the nucleus accumbens. Even the anticipation of such accomplishment can produce a reward, as when you imagine yourself completing a major project. Goal accomplishment is thus like other rewarding experiences that offer pleasure in expectation as well as in realization. For example, thinking of the piece of chocolate cake you will have for dessert is not as rewarding as actually having the cake, but it is pleasurable nevertheless. Such anticipation of reward serves to motivate people to perform the actions that are required to accomplish the desired goal. Motivation can also come from desire to avoid negative emotions that come from failures to accomplish goals. Brain scans of people making purchasing decisions have found that product preferences correlate with activation of regions associated with anticipating gain, such as the nucleus accumbens. On the other hand, excessive prices correlate with regions associated with anticipating loss, such as the insula.

Given such encodings of relations among actions and goals, the brain is equipped to make inferences to the best plan. The process of deliberation is not like the step-by-step verbal expressions that we use when we talk to people or write things down, but rather like the parallel constraint satisfaction that I described in chapter 4 for inference to the best explanation, and in chapter 5 for cognitive appraisal of emotions. The major positive constraints consist of relations between actions and goals, so that if an action accomplishes a goal, then they are coherent with each other. The major negative constraints consist of incompatibility relations between actions—for example, that you cannot both cook at home and go out to a restaurant to eat. When actions and goals are represented by patterns of activity in neural populations, the constraints among them can be captured by excitatory and inhibitory links between the relevant neurons. To oversimplify, if the action of cooking at home is represented by neural population A, and the goal of saving money is represented by neural population B, then the information that cooking saves money can be captured by synaptic connections running in both directions between neurons in the two populations. Then the complex computation of what combination of actions produces the best overall plan can be accomplished by the parallel firing of all the relevant neurons produced by the connections among them.

Viewed this way, decision making is not the kind of serial inference suggested by verbal arguments, nor the kind of mathematical calculation required by decision theory, but rather a process of parallel constraint satisfaction performed through the coordination of multiple brain areas. Because representations of value are a crucial part of goals, the brain areas will include the ones that chapter 5 described as important for emotions. For example, the dopamine system operating in the nucleus accumbens and connected regions is important for attaching positive value to goals and to chosen actions, whereas the amygdala, the insula, and other regions associated with negative emotions are important for producing the rejection of actions that are not part of the inferred best plan.

We saw that a similar process of parallel constraint satisfaction in inference to the best explanation can occasionally lead to the rejection of pieces of evidence on the basis of their incompatibility with good hypotheses. Similarly, the brain's evaluation of actions with respect to goals can also lead to reevaluation of the importance of goals. You may discover in the course of deciding what to do for dinner that you don't much care that day about saving money, or that when you start thinking about eating a favorite restaurant dish, you really want it a lot. We need to investigate now in much more detail where goals come from, and how they can be established and adjusted in the brain.

Changing Goals

Economic theory says that people do and should make decisions by maximizing expected utility. For nineteenth-century theorists such as Bentham and Mill, utility was a psychological entity akin to happiness or pleasure. Twentieth-century economists devised a less mentalistic conception of utility as a mathematical construction from people's preferences as revealed by their choice behavior. This construction was elegant, but useless as an explanation of decision making: economists abandoned the attempt to say where preferences come from. This abandonment was consistent with the behaviorist prejudices that dominated psychology in the 1940s and 1950s, but the cognitive revolution of the 1960s should have allowed economists to return to the idea of explaining preferences in terms of mental processes that included utility as an emotional state or process. Yet economists have resisted the return to explanations based on mental representations, despite the numerous experiments that have been performed to show that traditional expected utility theory often fails to account for human choice behavior.

Acquiring Goals

My view of decision making is intended to be much more psychologically and neurologically realistic. People's choice behavior is caused by their preferences, where preferences between particular options are derived from people's goals. But where do goals come from? Some goals are intrinsically biological in origin, such as wanting food when you're hungry, liquids when you're thirsty, sleep when you're tired, and so on. Other goals are easily understood as subordinate to more basic goals. For example, if you are hungry and so have the goal of eating, you can set the subgoal of going to the store to buy food because that would help accomplish the goal of not being hungry. But many of the goals that drive people's behavior in modern society are not physiological ones or subordinate to them. Goals such as having a good career are related to biological ones in that having money lets you buy food, but the decisions made by young people planning their educations and futures are not tied to immediate physical needs. The decisions may, however, depend on deep psychological needs to act effectively and to be related to other people (the biological basis of such needs is discussed in chapter 8). Still, some goals are acquired as people go through life, so we need to look for additional mechanisms.

The artificial intelligence pioneer Marvin Minsky has an intriguing idea about how early goals can arise because of what he calls attachment-based learning. Children naturally develop strong emotional attachments to their caregivers, usually parents. Caregivers transmit to children not only factual information but also emotional values, including ones that become attached to goals. If a parent cares strongly about a goal—for example, that the child do well in school—then the child may acquire this goal as well. Acquisition is not simply a matter of instrumental subgoaling in which the child wants parental approval and therefore adopts school performance as a way of achieving it. Rather, the emotional value that motivates accomplishment of a goal can come about more directly through emotional contagion in which the child actually acquires some of the emotional experiences of the parent by physical mimicking. This process is furthered by the operation of mirror neurons that can put the child in approximately the same brain state as the parent experiencing positive or negative emotions (see the discussion of mirror neurons in chapter 9). Thus children and even adults in closely attached relationships can acquire goals from other people. Such emotional transfer of goals is likely to be more effective than merely telling people what they ought to want.

A related way of acquiring goals can come about through analogical thinking using role models. You may not be sure about what you want to do with your life, but someone you admire may suggest a set of goals that you can adopt as your own. For example, if you hold Mahatma Gandhi in high esteem because of his political and moral accomplishments, you may adopt some of his goals as your own, perhaps by becoming a pacifist and vegetarian. Such analogical role modeling involves not biologically intrinsic goals, instrumental subgoals to your other goals, or close personal attachment, but rather a kind of emotional analogical thinking in which you acquire emotional values for goals by comparing yourself to another person. Moreover, negative role models can be a way of suggesting what goals *not* to have, as when you know you don't want to end up like Britney Spears.

Other important goals arise naturally just because we care for other people, including family members, friends, and, at times, a broader range of people in need. Economists sometimes assume that rationality is inherently self-interested, but there is abundant evidence that people are often altruistic, acquiring goals because of their relevance to the welfare of others. For example, the goals that lead me to do things for my children and to contribute to charity are in place not just because they are subordinate to other goals that I have for myself, but because, like most people, I care about my children and about people in need. Not everyone does, but I will discuss the nature of psychopaths in chapter 9.

On most days of your life, you don't need to think much about adopting new major goals, as most of your decisions concern choosing actions or subgoals to the major goals you already have in place. In fact, most of what you do requires little decision making at all, as your actions follow familiar habits. But there are times, such as young adulthood, when selection of life goals is unavoidable. Choice of careers and family patterns requires not only calculating the best means to established ends, but also figuring out what ends to pursue. Another time of major goal change is when people approach retirement, facing not only important decisions about when and how to retire, but also fundamental questions about the point of the remaining years of their lives. In such times as young adulthood and retirement, people adopt new goals driven by their biological needs, attachment-based motivations, and role models. How they *ought* normatively to form new goals is a philosophical issue that I will explore briefly later in this chapter and more thoroughly in chapter 8, concerning the question of what people need to be fully human. A rare but potentially powerful method of goal acquisition is the creative generation of novel goals, discussed in chapter 10's section on brain mechanisms for change.

Abandoning Goals

Biological goals such as eating, drinking, and sleeping are with us through our entire lives, but many other goals are abandoned as we age. For example, a child may rate playing sports as a top priority and even fantasize about a professional career. Such goals usually wane in importance as other activities arise, and as the realization sets in of how rare and difficult it is to make the big leagues. There are several kinds of situation that can lead to the abandonment of a goal, including realizing that its attainment is impossible, discovering conflicts with other goals, and changes in circumstances and information.

First, you may realize that achieving a goal is factually impossible given your abilities and situation—for example, if you are a violinist not quite good enough to play professionally. The realization of impossibility can generate intense emotions preceded by great frustration in attempting to achieve the goal but followed by relief in abandoning it. William James eloquently remarked: "To give up pretensions is as blessed a relief as to get them gratified; and where disappointment is incessant and the struggle unending, this is what men will always do." Aging necessitates the gradual abandonment of various goals, as physical and mental abilities decline after peaking in people's twenties or thirties. For most people, it is physically impossible to run as fast or work as hard at sixty as they could at twenty.

Abandoning unachievable goals is difficult, but it is an inevitable part of rational development. W. C. Fields supposedly advised: "If at first you don't succeed, try again. Then quit; there's no use being a damn fool about it." Relinquishing some goals that have proven to be impossible is much less extreme than the *New Yorker* cartoon in which one alcoholic bum says to another: "Then, I thought, Hey, hold on a minute—maybe failure is an option." Clinical psychologists have found that disengagement from unattainable goals has benefits for health and general well-being.

Goals may be relinquished for less extreme reasons than impossibility. You may discover that a goal conflicts with another goal that deserves higher priority. For example, if you want to become a partner in a leading law firm, you may need to work eighty hours per week, which might conflict with your desire to spend time with your family or your athletic buddies. Reconciling these conflicts may require you to abandon a whole package of goals, such as becoming rich and powerful.

Changes in circumstances and information may lead to the abandonment of subgoals. Most simply, if you are pursuing a subgoal because it contributes to a goal that you abandon, it makes sense to abandon the subgoal as well. For example, if you want to be an Olympic athlete and must therefore train forty hours per week, you can quit training once you abandon the goal of making it to the Olympics. Another reason for abandoning a subgoal is a realization that in fact the subgoal does not lead to the accomplishment of the goal that inspired it. People often think that money buys happiness, but empirical results show that extremely rich people are not markedly happier than people who are financially comfortable (see chapter 7). Hence if your financial goals are linked to happiness, then you can abandon them if you realize that making a huge amount of money will probably not accomplish your higher-level goal of being happy. Of course, if making money has become an independent goal for you, then it will survive your realization that being rich won't make you happy.

Revaluing Goals

I have described four ways of acquiring goals, through biological drives, subgoaling, attachment-based learning, and role modeling. In the other direction, I have identified four reasons for abandoning goals: they are impossible to achieve; they are incompatible with other goals; they are obsolete owing to their being subgoals to abandoned goals; or they are ineffective because they cannot accomplish the goals that they were supposed to help with. In addition to acquiring whole new goals or abandoning them, we can make more minor adjustments to goals by revising their priority upward or downward. For example, you may realize that you still want to play sports, but not as much as you used to, in part because you now care more about doing well in your schoolwork or career. We need both a psychological theory of how such adjustments are made, and a normative philosophical theory of how they can best be made.

For now, I can sketch a descriptive theory based on the ideas about parallel constraint satisfaction already mentioned. When actions and goals are represented by neural populations, the process of adjusting activations of neurons in order to satisfy constraints favors actions that accomplish goals. But selection of actions can also adjust goals, downgrading their importance if the most coherent set of actions does not fit with them. For example, if you are planning a trip to Europe and realize that you won't have time to get to Barcelona, you may reduce the emotional importance of going to that city. All this happens well below the level of consciousness because of the parallel processes that link different brain areas: importance is represented by coordination between the neural representation of situations such as being in Barcelona with activities in brain regions tied to emotions. Then the synaptic connections that link the neural populations for Barcelona to populations that attach emotional value to it will be weakened, perhaps by the reverse of Hebbian learning in which neurons that no longer fire together no longer wire together. There is experimental evidence that when people make decisions, they alter judgments about goals as well as judgments about actions. These alterations are not just sour grapes as in Aesop's fable about the fox who couldn't reach the grapes and then muttered that he didn't want them anyway because they're sour. Rather, revaluing goals such as going to Barcelona is the result of a rational process of balancing incompatible goals against each other.

In addition to adjustments made by parallel constraint satisfaction, goal revaluing may happen through simple Hebbian learning. If the neurons that together represent a goal are steadily firing when rewards are achieved, then synaptic connections between neurons representing goals and neurons in the dopamine-based reward system will be strengthened, so that the goals will have higher valuation than before. Neuroscientist Read Montague's *Why Choose This Book* provides a good introduction to the role of the dopamine system in decision making.

Telic Rationality

As a philosopher, I cannot avoid addressing normative questions about how we ought to go about adopting, abandoning, and revaluing our goals. The ancient Greek word for goal or end is "telos," so I will call the consideration of how we should change goals *telic rationality*. Aristotle said that deliberation is of means, not ends, but we have seen that the evaluation of basic ends is unavoidable.

One question that naturally arises is why we should have any more than the basic set of biological goals needed to keep us alive. The cognitive appraisal theory of emotions raises the possibility that you could be happy and avoid sadness by having only a few simple goals that are easy to accomplish. If all I aim to do is get up and feed myself, then my goals for the day are accomplished and I should be happy. Similarly, according to the cartoon characters Calvin and Hobbes, the secret to self-esteem is to lower your expectations to the point where they're already met. Sheryl Crow sings that life is not about having what you want, but wanting what you've got. Some ascetics such as Buddhist monks set out to renounce all worldly desires.

Telic rationality cannot completely rule out minimalism about goals, but there are powerful psychological reasons that resist the kind of slacker serenity that it might promote. We do not get autonomously to choose our goals, because some are handed to us by our biological needs and others are transmitted socially, through mechanisms such as attachment-based learning, role modeling, and altruism. From such basic goals, many other subordinate goals naturally arise through acquisition of information about what changes can lead to what outcomes. In chapter 7, I will discuss in much more detail some of the major goals in human lives concerned with love, work, and play, and then return to the question of why goal minimalism is undesirable. Chapter 9 considers how basic human needs give rise to ethical goals that everyone is morally obliged to pursue.

Compare goal minimalism to evidence minimalism, which would be the view that we should collect as little as evidence as possible so that we don't need to go through the work of finding hypotheses that explain them. We advance knowledge by collecting as much interesting evidence as possible and explaining it with an economical set of explanatory hypotheses. Similarly, we advance practical life by having a rich set of goals and devising coherent plans for accomplishing them.

Telic rationality is crucial for developing the social innovations needed to deal with major world problems such as climate change, energy shortages, and global inequities. For social change to take place, politicians and other people have to be convinced to adopt new goals, such as caring more about the state of the environment. Some of the changes required are in factual beliefs—for example, accepting the large amount of scientific evidence that global warming is a growing threat to human welfare. But additional changes require adopting or increasing the valuation of goals such as reducing energy consumption. As we saw in chapter 5, our brains operate with an integrated package of beliefs, emotions, and goals that change together. So social innovation requires changes in goals and emotions as well as in belief. Goal change and emotion change are tightly coupled, because new goals generate different cognitive appraisals and hence new emotions in accord with the mechanism described in chapter 5.

How to Make Bad Decisions

Psychology is largely concerned with the descriptive task of saying how people *do* make decisions, whereas philosophy is mostly concerned with the normative task of prescribing how people *ought* to make decisions. But applications of psychology to areas such as education and organizational behavior naturally raise prescriptive questions concerning how people in schools, businesses, or government can make better decisions. Conversely, philosophy requires attention to empirical results of decision making in order to develop normative models that are not so abstract that they are useless for helping people make better decisions.

One important question that is both descriptive and normative concerns how people make objectively bad decisions, choosing actions that can be recognized by others and even themselves as not best for accomplishing the relevant goals. Everyone makes bad decisions some of the time, many of them small, such as buying a sweater that you should have recognized as ugly. But some decisions can have horrible consequences, as when a president pursues a war that costs hundreds of thousands of lives, or an ordinary person chooses an unsuitable career or an incompatible spouse. I don't mark a decision as bad when there are unforeseeable consequences that ruin a plan, such as a vacation interrupted by a hurricane. Rather, bad decisions are ones that could have been avoided by careful attention to all the relevant actions and goals. The theory of decision making as inference to the best plan based on emotional brain mechanisms ought to provide some guidance about how to reduce such mistakes.

Here are some ways to really screw up your decisions. First, make them very rapidly, so that you do not have time to consider all the relevant actions and goals. Instead of considering a range of possible actions, fixate on one set of actions and ignore others that might accomplish your goals better. For example, if you are a high school student planning your education and career, try to think about only one university and one course of study. To simplify your decision even more, concentrate on only one or two goals, such as your desire to make a lot of money, and forget about other things you care about, such as having a family or time to play. If you use analogies in your decision making, restrict yourself to a single comparison—for example, considering a military situation as akin to one with a successful outcome, such as the Second World War, rather than a debacle like the American intervention in Vietnam.

By working quickly and restricting the range of factors you consider, you can rely on the brain's limited capacity for short-term memory to ensure that when it comes time to make the decision, you will have only a small number of actions and a small number of goals in mind. Your emotional consciousness will then generate an inferior answer that you can trust like any other intuitive judgment. Trust your gut, as George W. Bush recommended. Ignore Maureen Dowd's comment on him: "Every gut instinct he had was wildly off the mark and hideously damaging to all concerned. It seems that if you trust your gut without ever feeding your gut any facts or news or contrary opinions, if you keep your gut on a steady diet of grandiosity, ignorance, sycophants, and peanut butter and jelly sandwiches, those snap decisions can be ruinous."

Second, avoid collecting reliable information about the extent to which different actions facilitate different goals. Such information can be very hard to find, whether you are just an ordinary person making routine decisions or a political leader affecting the lives of millions. Gathering all the relevant evidence in order to make inferences to the best explanation about how different actions affect different goals takes a lot of time and effort, so you are better off just going with what you've already been told by whatever people or media you happen to have encountered.

As we saw in chapter 2, evidence-based thinking takes a lot of effort, so just go on faith that the action you first think of will be the best. Motivated inference will help you ignore evidence that does not fit with your goals, so you can ignore whether or not various actions actually will accomplish the goals. Emotionally salient analogies and metaphors can help distract you from the annoying complexities of a situation. Do not keep track of what decisions you have made and whether or not they worked, so you will not have to learn from your mistakes. Think seriously about the costs you have already sunk into a course of action rather than thinking about its future effects. Don't try to forecast the effects of plans on your future emotions, relying on the psychological finding that people are often not very good about emotional forecasting anyway. Even if there are data available that might enable you to use the potentially effective quantitative tools of statistics and decision theory, don't bother.

Third, neglect to carefully evaluate the importance of different goals. Your brain assesses the priority of goals using the combined activity of neural populations involving multimodal representations of situations, including populations in areas such as the amygdala required for emotional interpretations. In principle, the brain can carry out an effective process of parallel constraint satisfaction considering all the relevant actions, goals, and relations among them. But in practice, thinking is often skewed by stimuli with powerful emotional influences. For example, you may be trying carefully to weigh different options and be distracted by some unduly influential piece of information, such as the interjection of a friend that what you're wanting is crazy.

A good way to emotionally skew your decisions is to make them under the influence of drugs such as alcohol. According to Herodotus, the ancient Persians recommended deliberating on important matters while drunk and then reviewing the decision while sober. Perhaps this method has the advantage of granting increased access to emotionally relevant factors in the drunken phase, but it risks elevating some emotionally powerful goals beyond what is appropriate. At the extreme, addiction to a drug such as crack cocaine can completely hijack the process of goal evaluation, so that all that matters is getting more of the drug, rather than trivial concerns such as health, work, and relationships.

Follow the natural brain tendency to place more weight on short-term goals such as eating than on long-term goals such as being healthy. By focusing on short-term rewards, your brain can primarily employ the midbrain dopamine system rather than frontal and parietal regions needed for assessing long-term implications of your actions. Avoid the ugly philosophical enterprise of trying to evaluate whether your current goals are appropriate.

Ignore the horribly difficult problem of how to reconcile the goals of future generations with those of current ones, which can make problems such as dealing with global warming overwhelming.

Fourth, once you have a made a decision, be completely confident in your choice and ignore any new information about developing situations that might make you inclined to change your plan. The world is annoyingly variable, hence the saying that people plan and God laughs. But you were comfortable in your initial decision made on limited information, so there is no point in changing your mind if new evidence comes along.

Fifth, make the decision on your own without consulting other people who might have a broader idea of the full range of possible actions, goals, and factual connections between them. If you must rely on a group of people to help you with your decisions and assure you that you are doing the right thing, be sure to choose associates who share your prejudices. Then your faith-based decision making can proceed uncomplicated by evidence.

Sixth and finally, make your decisions in line with only your own goals, and ignore the goals and needs of other people. This restriction fits with economic prescriptions about rational *self*-interest and avoids the messy ethical complications that are discussed in chapter 9.

If you follow these six suggestions, you can be assured of frequently making bad decisions. On the other hand, if you monitor your process of decision making and enlist the help of others who are aware of psychological pitfalls, then you may find it possible to improve your choices by following these positive rules when making decisions:

1. Carefully consider all the relevant actions and goals.
2. Collect reliable information about how well different actions facilitate different goals.
3. Evaluate the importance of different goals.
4. Remain flexible and open to new information.
5. Consult other people about actions and goals.
6. Altruistically take into account the goals of other people.

Always keep in mind that a subjective feeling that you are making a good decision is likely to be useless, because most of the processes of decision making described in this chapter are unconscious. We have little access to the activity of neural populations in different brain areas needed to

represent actions, goals, and their relations, nor to parallel constraint satisfaction computation of the best plan. Usually, we don't know what we're
doing when we make a decision. We can hope to do better only through
conscious monitoring that includes watching for such ways of making bad
decisions as neglecting relevant actions and goals, failing to evaluate goals,
and using bad information about how actions affect goals. Howard Raiffa
may not have been able to use mathematical decision theory to tell him
whether to accept his job offer, but he could still have benefited from deliberation based on multiple goals and actions.

Intuitions can be reasonable when they are based on unconscious parallel
satisfaction of all the relevant constraints concerning all the relevant actions
and goals. But intuitions are just as likely to arise from faulty unconscious
processing of limited information, so they should not be trusted without
conscious deliberation of a full range of factors. Like choice of explanatory
hypotheses, decision making should be evidence based.

Living without Free Will

If this chapter is right about how minds work, then decisions are brain processes, and all our actions are caused by brains interacting with physical and
social environments. Psychologists such as Daniel Wegner have compiled
substantial evidence against the everyday view of conscious action. Behaviors such as getting up and walking occur because of activity in multiple
brain regions, especially prefrontal areas that seem to be particularly important for executive functioning and working memory, as well as motor areas
such as the cerebellum, the basal ganglia, and the primary motor cortex
that send signals via the spinal cord to muscles that move the body. Many
behaviors result not from decisions but from established habits, which are
acquired through neural learning mechanisms. Even our most important
decisions are causally constituted by brain processes. By now you may be
aghast: does this mean that we don't have free will?

In many years of teaching undergraduate courses in the philosophy of
mind, I have often witnessed students become distressed at the suggestion
that free will might be an illusion. Their religion and general culture have
raised them to believe that they make their choices freely, which is why they

are responsible for them. If choices are caused, then freedom and responsibility seem to go out the window. If your thinking is just a brain process, then you may seem no better than a toaster as far as concerns your ability to control your own actions. Hence the evidence-based, materialist view I have been defending looks triply cursed. Not only have I worried you about losing access to a comforting God and the prospect of immortality; now I've hit you with the threat that you lack free will. To complete the massacre, you might expect that morality will be dispensed with too.

Don't worry: at least ethics can survive, as I will argue in chapter 9. But the biological approach I support as part of a general scientific understanding of the world does require us to give up a lot, including theology and immortality. That is why the Brain Revolution, like the Copernican and Darwinian ones, requires conceptual change that is heavily emotional, not only reorganizing our system of concepts and beliefs but also adjusting the values that we attach to them.

Philosophers such as Daniel Dennett and Owen Flanagan have shown that giving up free will in the absolute sense provided by the view of mind as nonmaterial soul is not so bad as you might think. We can still have many of the desirable attributes of free will, including self-control, self-expression, individuality, sensitivity to reasons, rational deliberation, accountability, and an important kind of autonomy discussed in chapter 8. Chapter 3 argued that the Brain Revolution requires shifting from thinking of the self as a nonmaterial soul to considering it as a complex neural system embedded in its social environment. From this perspective, self-control amounts to the pervasive ability of individuals to determine their behaviors by their own normal brain processes. In the absence of social coercion and mental disorders such as schizophrenia, most people are capable of self-control in a way that will be better understood when a theory of the self as a system of multilevel mechanisms has been developed.

It would be misleading, however, to attempt to redefine free will as this kind of control of behavior by thought, if thought is recognized as a neural process. We should not underestimate the attractiveness of full-blown, brain-independent free will, which like immortality is something that is naturally desired. Both are part of the powerful lure of dualism. The thought that your life need not end with death has great appeal, and so does the vision that you are, in the words of Tennyson, the master of your fate and the captain of your soul.

However, the approach to knowledge defended in chapter 2 requires abandoning beliefs incompatible with the available evidence. All the evidence that actions are caused by brain processes puts free will as performed by a conscious soul in the same boat as immortality. The account of telic rationality I proposed earlier in this chapter advocated abandoning goals that are impossible to accomplish, so we need to stop wanting absolute free will and immortality. These supernatural benefits would certainly be nice, but you just can't have them, given the material nature of minds. The evidence-based view that the brain works by dynamic interactions among multiple areas requires abandonment of the commonsense notion of a central, conscious controller in charge of decisions.

The assertion that you lack free will does not imply that you are a mindless robot condemned to a meaningless life predetermined to unfold as fate intended no matter what you try to do. You are obviously not mindless, as your brain is fully capable of carrying out a broad range of mental processes such as perception, memory, learning, and inference. Your brain is far more intelligent and flexible than any current robot, although it is possible that some far-off day there might be robots that can make decisions as complex as the ones we have been discussing. Your life may lack the meaning promised by the eternal company of a divine being, but you can still thrive in the pursuits of love, work, and play discussed in chapter 7. Ideas about predetermination and fate are essentially religious; they pose no scientific threat to the reduced kind of freedom consistent with viewing the brain as a collection of causal processes.

There are even some advantages to recognizing immortality and free will as illusions. As chapter 3 pointed out, death is much less scary if it just means you cease to be. If immortality is a possibility and you may have latched onto the wrong religion as the unlucky result of being born into the wrong family, then you ought to be worried about an eternity of suffering at the hands of a wrathful god. Doesn't the void sound a lot better than that? Similarly, if your actions are caused by brain processes including ones highly susceptible to the kinds of cognitive and emotional distortions that can result in bad decisions, then you have more reason to be tolerant of yourself when you sometimes make mistakes. You also have an excellent reason to be more tolerant of others, appreciating that their mistakes are the result not of willful sins but of a multiplicity of causal forces.

Emotions such as guilt, shame, and remorse can still be appropriate, as long as they serve to prevent mistakes in the future. But there is no point to the overwhelming sense of sinfulness, fear, and trembling that afflicts some religious people. The concept of free will is part of a theological package that includes the ugly trio of sin, guilt, and eternal punishment; so the emotional conceptual change required to recognize it as an illusion can be positive as well as negative. In sum, you can have a meaningful life without believing in free will, as chapter 7 argues. Chapter 9 will argue that you can even have a moral life in which you can be held responsible for your actions.

Conclusion

Decision making is usually not a step-by-step verbal argument or a mathematical calculation, but rather a mental parallel process of inference to the best plan. This process involves assessment of competing actions to determine which combination of them best accomplishes a person's goals. Goals are emotionally valued mental representations of imagined states of the world and self. The brain performs such representations by patterns of firing in neural populations in multiple brain areas, including ones that encode verbal and sensory information. Emotional value is part of the representation of goals and actions by virtue of coordination with brain areas such as the nucleus accumbens and the amygdala, which encode positive and negative aspects of the world. The overall assessment of the coherence of actions and goals is the result of parallel constraint satisfaction carried out by firing of neurons in all the relevant populations based on the synaptic connections among them. You don't tell your brain what to do, and your brain doesn't tell you what to do: you *are* your brain deciding what to do in your physical and social environment.

Because of the centrality of goals to decision making, a major part of rationality is the adoption, abandonment, and revaluing of goals. We adopt new goals because of biological needs and because they are subsidiary to goals we already have, but also through emotional social processes such as having people who care for us, role models, and people we care about. When we recognize that achievement of a goal is not possible or that situations have changed to make it no longer subsidiary to a higher goal, then it is rational to abandon the goal. The process of decision making, in which parallel constraint satisfaction is used to assess the coherence of actions and goals, can lead to the downgrading of the importance of some goals. Wisdom—knowing what matters—requires the adaptive capability of acquiring, abandoning, and revaluing goals.

The inherently emotional nature of decision making has important implications for many areas of human activity, including politics. The psychologist Drew Westen pointed out in 2007 the repeated failures of American political strategists who tried to approach voters through dispassionate, issue-oriented campaigns. He says that voters' decisions are based on answers to four questions. How do I feel about the candidate's party and its principles? How does this candidate make me feel? How do I feel about this candidate's personal characteristics, particularly his or her integrity, leadership, and compassion? How do I feel about this candidate's stands on issues that matter to me? Westen does not infer from the substantial evidence about the impact of emotions on voting the view that the Democratic Party he supports should ruthlessly exploit people's hopes and fears. Rather, he urges the party to select leaders who have the wisdom, integrity, and emotional appeal to convince voters to accept them based on their values and the best available evidence. The triumphant 2008 U.S. presidential campaign of Barack Obama showed the power of combining strong arguments with emotional magnetism.

The psychological and neural complexities of decision making allow many ways in which people can make bad decisions, such as neglecting relevant goals, alternative actions, and relations among them. Decision making is ineliminably emotional, with its input valuations of relevant representations, accompanying feelings such as excitement or anxiety, and outputs such as satisfaction or disappointment. Understanding decisions as brain processes has the distressing consequence that the traditional dualistic idea of free will must be abandoned, but life can still be meaningful and moral, as the next three chapters will show.

Chapter Seven

why life is worth living

The Meaning of Life

Albert Camus did not kill himself. I started chapter 1 with his startling statement that suicide is a philosophical problem, part of the question of why life is worth living. Camus wrote that statement in his late twenties, but he never attempted suicide and died in his mid-forties when a car driven by a friend crashed into a tree. His wife, however, did try to kill herself, suffering from depression caused in part by his infidelities. Camus himself led a rich life, with a family that included two children, strong friendships, affairs with young actresses, and great professional success as a novelist, dramatist, and journalist. His youthful claims that life is absurd were contradicted by the many sources of meaning in his life, from his activities in the French resistance against the Nazi occupation to his abundant and successful writings.

Less famous people also find many kinds of meaning in their lives, through their families or friends, workplace or hobbies, and enjoyable activities that range from playing sports to reading books to listening to music. The meaning of life for human beings embraces love, work, and play. Each of these needs to be construed broadly, so that love includes friendship and compassion for others as well as romantic and family attachments. Work ranges from manual labor such as carpentry to intellectual work such as writing a book. Play is not just children fooling around, but includes many kinds of entertainment for adults such as music, reading, sports, and travel.

I will draw on the psychology and sociology of these activities, but also examine the emerging understanding of how brain processes make love, work, and play sources of meaning. My descriptive aim is to show that people seem to find meaning through such pursuits, but my normative aim is to show that love, work, and play really do make life worth living. The normative leap to what ought to be requires connecting these realms with people's vital needs, via an account of how brains work. I will relate what is known about the neurophysiology of love, work, and play to the neural models of emotions and goals presented earlier. A review and analysis of how brains function in love, work, and play will tell us much about how and why people lead their lives, although the full normative story about why these activities ought to matter to people will have to wait for the discussions of needs and morals in chapters 8 and 9.

The study of brains does not tell us what to value, but it reveals how we value, as chapter 5 described. Neural activity that combines representation of situations and activities with embodied appraisal of them attaches value to those situations and activities. Something matters to you if your brain representation of it includes associations that generate positive emotions. I will discuss how an aggregate of meaning can develop in a person's life through coherence of goals and actions.

I do not have an irresistible, a priori argument that the meaning of life is love, work, and play. My defense of this claim relies on three kinds of reasoning. First, there are serious problems with alternative answers, including the nihilistic one that life has no meaning, the theological one that meaning is furnished by God or some other spiritual source, and the monolithic one that the meaning of life is just happiness. Second, there is abundant psychological and sociological evidence that love, work, and play are in fact sources of valued goals in people's lives. Third, there is emerging neurological evidence that indicates how goals and needs related to love, work, and play operate as part of human cognition and emotion to motivate human activities.

Nihilism

Nihilism is the view that life has no meaning at all. In Camus' novel *L'Etranger*, the narrator, Meursault, has been accused of murder. The examining magistrate is outraged by Meursault's assertion that he does not believe in God: "[The magistrate] told me that it was impossible, that all men believed in God, even those who wouldn't face up to Him. That was his belief, and if he should ever doubt it, his life would become meaningless." The magistrate's view is not just that the nonexistence of God would make his life meaningless, but that the mere belief in the nonexistence of God by someone such as Meursault would render life meaningless. What would it take for someone's life to be totally devoid of meaning?

At the most extreme, your life would be meaningless if you had no mental representations at all. This state would require you to have no conscious beliefs and experience, and no prospect of having any. Temporarily you might have no conscious experience because of deep sleep or a medical condition that puts you into a coma, but in these cases you have the potential of having conscious representations when you wake up. People who suffer extensive brain damage may enter a persistent vegetative state from which recovery is impossible. At this point, life is meaningless for them, although it may still have some meaning for people who care about them. For example, when the parents of Terri Schiavo resisted her husband's decision to remove her feeding tube in 2005, she was still important to them, despite her extensive brain damage, which an autopsy revealed was as serious as doctors had advised. Nevertheless, given her apparent inability to form any representation of anything, it seems to me that Terri Schiavo's life really had become meaningless.

Without such severe brain damage, your life would be lacking in meaning if nothing at all was important to you, as seems to be the case with Camus' character Meursault, who asserts: "Nothing, nothing mattered." It is hard to imagine someone totally lacking in goals, as even severely depressed people usually take minimal steps to feed themselves and protect themselves from harm. But Meursault and severe depressives lack more ambitious goals, which chapter 6 described as brain states that combine representations of situations with emotional valuations of them. Meursault says he had no regrets about anything, suggesting a woeful incapacity to attach emotional significance to important events, including both his arrest for murder and the death of his mother. Unlike the state of a temporarily depressed person whose life will be enjoyable again when things improve, Meursault's condition appears to be chronic. Perhaps it is fair to conclude that his life really is meaningless and that he lost little by being executed. In modern popular culture, the character who comes closest to having a meaningless life is probably George Costanza from the television show *Seinfeld*, although even he did much better than Meursault at love, work, and play.

The American essayist Roger Rosenblatt expresses nihilism in amusing form in the first of his rules for aging:

Rule #1: It doesn't matter

Whatever you think matters–doesn't. Follow this rule, and it will add decades to your life. It does not matter if you are late, or early; if you are here, or if you are there; if you said it, or did not say it; if you were clever, or if you were stupid; if you are having a bad hair day, or a no hair day; if your boss looks at you cockeyed; if your girlfriend or boyfriend looks at you cockeyed; if you don't get that promotion, or prize, or house, or if you do. It doesn't matter.

Like Rosenblatt's second rule, "Nobody is thinking about you," his first rule is a useful antidote to excessive worrying about small or medium-sized matters. But no one should take it as a literal suggestion that personal relationships and work do not matter at all. Nihilism can take the form of despair, the intensely negative emotional attitude that life is nothing but a boulevard of broken dreams. Another, culturally popular form is ironic detachment, in which people present themselves as not caring much about anything, even though they have deep, unmet needs.

Counting against nihilism is the empirical finding that most people are happy. On average, across many cultures, when people are asked to rate their life satisfaction on a zero-to-ten scale, people rate themselves around 7. Thus Camus' Meursault, Rosenblatt's rule 1, and severe depressives are exceptional in their inability to find aspects of life that matter. Using depressives as the standard for human meaning would be like using schizophrenics as the standard for human knowledge: in both cases neurochemical disturbances seriously diminish brain functioning. According to Kay Jamison, an expert on manic-depressive illness, 90 percent of people who commit suicide have a diagnosable psychiatric illness.

Of course, the fact that most people are happy does not in itself refute nihilists, who could argue that the common pursuit of enjoyment is no more convincing than is the prevalent endorsement of dualism. Perhaps only depressives have an accurate view of the worthlessness of life. But the discussion to come of how love, work, and play furnish meaning by contributing to vital human needs will show that happy people are not delusional.

Historically, the main alternative to nihilism has been the theological view that God created the universe and established a purpose for it. In fact, people who are religious are on average happier than those who are not. But I argued in chapter 2 that there is no evidence for the existence of a deity who could make life meaningful, so we must look elsewhere. Contrary to Meursault's magistrate, the abandonment of theology does not imply nihilism without a thorough search for other sources of significance. Few people, fortunately, have Meursault's emotional incapacity, and we can reject Camus' suggestion that everyone's life is as absurd as that of his main character. Perhaps the meaning of life is just happiness.

Happiness

An extensive body of research has developed in the past decade using surveys to identify the extent and the sources of human happiness. Various studies discuss how happy people are, how much life satisfaction they have, and the extent to which they experience "well-being." Happiness, life satisfaction, and well-being are not exactly the same, but I see no sharp differences among them. Obviously, people would rather be happy than not, so why not just identify the meaning of life with happiness? There are several reasons for adopting a less monolithic view of the meaning of life.

Meaning is provided by more local goals than happiness. Recall the understanding of happiness gained from the cognitive appraisal component of emotional consciousness described in chapter 5. As proponents of the cognitive theory of emotions have long urged, people are happy when they accomplish their goals. But this implies that what people are aiming for, what gives meaning to their lives, is in fact their goals: happiness is a product of goal satisfaction. It is unclear how people could actually set themselves a reasonably achievable goal of being happy. Nathaniel Hawthorne wrote: "Happiness is as a butterfly which, when pursued, is always beyond our grasp, but which if you will sit down quietly, may alight upon you." The only way you can set out to make yourself happy is to adopt goals whose satisfaction could then make you happy, in line with the cognitive appraisal component of emotional consciousness. Of course, someone could argue that goals such as love, work, and play are important only to the extent that their satisfaction makes you happy, but this argument is undercut by closer attention to the dynamics of happiness.

Research on the dynamics of life satisfaction show that different factors contribute to happiness at different stages of life. The American economist Richard Easterlin described a study that looked at life cycle patterns for overall happiness. It found that happiness on average is fairly stable through the life span, with a very mild peak around age 51. This result is consistent with the view of some psychologists that each person has a "set point," a level of happiness that is only mildly perturbed by life events. But the same study also measured reported satisfaction in four more specific domains of life: family, job, finances, and health. Except for family satisfaction, which also peaked around 50, these showed very different patterns from overall happiness. Financial satisfaction tended to rise steadily after 40, but job satisfaction tended to peak around age 62. Satisfaction with health, on the other hand, fell steadily from age 18 on. Easterlin argues against the view that happiness is relatively constant as the result of personality and genetic makeup, and uses statistical analyses to show that the life situations of family relations, financial situation, job, and health all contribute to happiness. Thus the relatively stable pattern of people's happiness over their lifetimes is the result of other factors balancing out. Taken together, the four domain satisfaction variables predict fairly closely the actual pattern of life cycle happiness.

Additional evidence that happiness is an effect of satisfaction in other domains rather than an end in itself comes from a study of marital status. Widowhood and divorce both produce strong drops in life satisfaction, requiring years of recovery. Widows and widowers in particular require on average seven years to regain the level of life satisfaction they had a year before the death of their spouse, a level that was already lower than where they were a few years before. Similarly, unemployment produces a strong drop in life satisfaction that lasts for years. These findings undercut the view that each individual has a happiness set point, as well as the view that happiness is a single factor not determined by other key factors such as relationships and work. Of course, if the set point theory of happiness were true, it would strongly count against the view that happiness is the major goal in life: it would imply that there is little you can do about it, because you cannot change your genetically determined personality!

Another study, conducted by the Pew Research Center, provides additional evidence for decomposing happiness into its constituents. A survey of Americans in 2004 found that 34 percent described themselves as very happy, 50 percent as pretty happy, and only 15 percent as not too happy. These percentages have been fairly constant since 1972. The study also looked at various factors that correlated with being very happy or not too happy. People with incomes over $100,000 were twice as likely to be very happy as those with incomes under $30,000, and they were significantly happier than those with incomes between $75,000 and $100,000 (49 percent versus 38 percent). Other correlations also stand out. Married people are happier than unmarrieds, although having children makes little additional difference. People who attend religious services frequently are happier. Republicans are happier than Democrats, an effect not accounted for solely by the fact that rich people are happier than poor ones. The largest factor that predicts differences in happiness is being in good health, as 55 percent of people who say their health is poor describe themselves as not too happy. Another demographic group with happiness deficits consists of single parents with minor age children, 27 percent of whom report being not too happy.

No single study should be taken to show conclusively what causes happiness, but I have reported several studies with congruent conclusions. Taken together, the evidence about changes in happiness and satisfaction over the life cycle strongly suggests that happiness is the result of pursuit of other goals. But there is no reason to believe that people pursue those other goals as subgoals to the higher goal of happiness. Happiness is usually a temporary condition, like other emotions, but goals and the meaning that derives from them can be enduring.

A meaningful life isn't just one where happiness is achieved through accomplishment of goals, but one where there are worthwhile goals to pursue. Many of the goals that people value most—for example, raising children and working at challenging tasks—are not always sources of happiness. The social psychologist Daniel Gilbert argues against the popular belief that having children makes people happy. He cites studies showing that marital satisfaction decreases dramatically after the birth of the first child and increases only when the last child leaves home. New babies can be great sources of positive emotions such as joy and pride, but they also cause worry, sleep deprivation, and unpleasant experiences such as diapering. Work can be a great source of satisfaction, but also of frustration and anxiety arising from deadlines, impossible goals, and difficult interpersonal relations. Nevertheless, such challenging tasks as raising children and pursuing difficult work goals provide meaning to people's lives, despite the daily problems that they bring and their frequent interferences with happiness. Similarly, play goals such as doing your best in a sport may not always produce happiness, but are still valuable in providing motivation and direction to your life.

Hence a meaningful life is not just one in which all your goals are satisfied, but one that provides reasons for doing things. Because meaning requires pursuing goals that are not yet satisfied, it cannot be identified simply with the satisfaction of goals as measured by happiness or well-being. A meaningful life is one where you still have something to do, even if doing it may not make you happy that day, week, or year. In chapter 6, I discussed slacker serenity, the happiness that supposedly comes from abandoning challenging goals and simply accepting what you have. But who has a more meaningful life, the parent struggling to raise children and work a difficult job, or the hermit living an isolated, inactive life? As John Stuart Mill said, "It is better to be a human being dissatisfied than a pig satisfied; better to be Socrates dissatisfied than a fool satisfied." An updated version might be: better a single parent dissatisfied than a wealthy Republican satisfied. Another source of temporary happiness can be drugs such as cocaine and heroin that manipulate the brain's pleasure machinery, but few people would attach meaning to drug use, even if it did not have nasty long-term effects.

In sum, happiness can fleetingly derive from drug use, wealth accumulation, and slacker serenity, whereas pursuit of deeper goals such as raising children and highly challenging work can diminish happiness. You can have happiness without much meaning, and meaning without much happiness; so happiness is not the meaning of life. Happiness is having your goals satisfied, but meaning additionally involves having worthwhile goals that may or may not be satisfied. Hence we cannot simply conclude that the meaning of life is happiness; we need to look in more detail at the nature of goals and how they contribute to meaning. Chapter 8 will argue that deeper goals are ones that satisfy vital human needs.

Goals and Meaning

In chapter 6 I described goals as emotionally valued neural representations of imagined states of the world and self. Imagining things you hope to accomplish can generate positive emotions as you contemplate yourself satisfying such goals as earning a university degree or completing a big project. But imagining also produces anxiety as you contemplate the possibility of failure. Hence merely having goals does not produce happiness, but it does provide you with motivation to perform actions that can contribute to success and help you avoid failure. The goals you aim for do not have to be ones that you are guaranteed to accomplish, as most goals can be accomplished to varying degrees. It would be pointless, however, to maintain a goal that you know you cannot achieve. Hence goal abandonment is an important part of rationality, in addition to goal adoption. How can people acquire goals that make for a meaningful life?

In chapter 4, I claimed that we should think of the meaning of concepts and other representations as multidimensional, involving multiple ways in which they can relate to the world and to other mental states. Similarly, the meaning of life should not be understood as a binary state, something you either have or lack. The opposition of meaningful versus meaningless is far too crude. It is only somewhat better to envision a continuum extending from having a little to having a lot of meaning. This view is still one-dimensional, suggesting that the more goals you have, the better, neglecting the important differences among goals. Later in this chapter I will defend the view that the meaning of life has three key dimensions: love, work, and play. At different stages in their lives, people have varying degrees of goal aspiration and accomplishment with respect to each of these dimensions.

It is hard to say how much of the meaning of life consists of having goals to satisfy and how much depends on having them already satisfied. Whose life is more meaningful, the young person whose major goals have yet to be satisfied, or the very old one who has already accomplished most of what he or she was capable of doing? This question is misleading, because even the young will have accomplished some steps along their way—for example, by finishing some stages of education and making some social progress by developing friendships. Even the very old retain some minor, local goals such as spending time with friends and family, unless they have succumbed to dementia so severe that it hardly seems better than the persistent vegetative state of Terri Schiavo. Hence meaning flows both from goals that need to be satisfied and from goals that are satisfied to an appreciable degree. A crucial philosophical issue yet to be addressed is how meaning depends on having genuinely worthwhile goals that are not just whims.

In sum, your life is meaningful to the extent that

1. you have goals, which are emotionally valued mental representations of situations, consisting of patterns of neural activity;
2. some of your goals have been accomplished to some degree;
3. you have other goals not yet accomplished that you have reasonable prospects of accomplishing;
4. your goals are coherent with each other; and
5. your goals are objectively valuable.

Note that 1–5 should not be construed as necessary or sufficient conditions of having a meaningful life, which would presume the binary view of meaning that I have already rejected. Rather, these conditions are all matters of degree that together determine the varying extent to which a life is meaningful. The assessment of meaning is not with respect to a fixed set of goals, because you may have quite different sets of goals at different stages of your life, through the processes of acquiring, abandoning, and revaluing of goals described in chapter 6. Conditions 2 and 3 concerning goal accomplishment summarize what I have already discussed, that you need to have some goals already satisfied to some degree and others that provide you with something to aim for.

Condition 4 about goal coherence is introduced to handle cases where life is difficult because a person has multiple goals that are not mutually satisfiable. Suppose you want to be both a professional basketball player and a medical doctor. Both pursuits take enormous amounts of time and dedication, so it is very hard to accomplish both of them. There are thus two ways in which the "reasonable prospects" clause of condition 3 can fail: because the nature of the world, including your own abilities, makes it unlikely that you can accomplish the goal—for example, if you are very short and awkward yet want to play basketball; or because your goals are mutually exclusive in the sense that the efforts required for you to accomplish one would make it very hard to accomplish the other. Such incompatibility requires goal abandonment, as described in chapter 6.

Condition 5 about objectively valuable goals is the most philosophically loaded one, because it assumes a distinction between what you value and what is really worth valuing. I include it here to allow for cases where people have goals that matter a great deal to them and provide some motivation and satisfaction, but which others would judge to be pointless. For example, consider someone whose only pursuit consists of playing violent video games and aiming to get higher and higher scores. Such a person may score well in the realm of play but, as a result, fail utterly in the realms of love and work. I won't attempt yet to address the question of what makes a goal objectively valuable, which will require the discussion of human needs and ethical issues in chapters 8 and 9.

Putting the normative aside for now, I want to examine three realms of life that have been the sources of most human goals and accomplishments: love, work, and play. For each of these, I will try to identify how they generate life goals that are represented in human brains. Romantic love and music provide two rich domains in which interesting work has already been done using brain scanning to identify some of the relevant neural processes, and I will speculate about how the brain is likely to be involved in other aspects of love, work, and play. We will then see how these three realms can be important sources of human goals and accomplishments.

Love

Surveys of personal well-being always find that personal relationships are a major source of satisfaction in people's lives. To sustain well-being, people need supportive, positive relationships and social belonging. Only a few misanthropes have denied that loving relationships are a major part of what gives life meaning. Most people value romantic interactions, family ties, and friendship. The 99 percent of people who are not psychopathic are also capable of caring for people beyond their immediate circle, showing compassion for the suffering of others. Understanding of the brain processes that underlie these kinds of social values is just beginning.

The neural mechanisms for romantic love have been investigated by a team that includes the anthropologist Helen Fisher, psychologist Arthur Aron, and neuroscientist Lucy Brown. They cite anthropological evidence that intense romantic love is a cross-culturally and historically universal phenomenon. It is associated with specific physiological, psychological, and behavioral changes, including euphoria, intense focused attention, obsessive thinking, emotional dependency, and increased energy. Fisher and her colleagues used brain scans (fMRI) to investigate the neural systems involved in romantic love. The researchers selected participants who reported having recently fallen in love, and scanned their brains while they looked at a picture of their new romantic interest. Brain activity in this situation was contrasted with activity when the participant looked at a similar but emotionally neutral picture of a familiar acquaintance.

When people looked at pictures of their new romantic partners, their brains showed increased activity in regions that mediate reward via the dopamine system described in chapter 5, particularly the ventral tegmental area and the nucleus accumbens. These are the same areas activated by reward-producing drugs such as cocaine that also lead to exhilaration, sleeplessness, and loss of appetite. Cortical areas associated with emotion were also involved, including the insula, the anterior cingulate, and the amygdala, all of which are included in the EMOCON model of chapter 5. That viewing a romantic partner stimulates brain areas associated with reward and pleasure explains why it feels so good to fall in love. An earlier study of romantic love by Andreas Bartels and Semir Zeki also found increased activation in the insula and the cingulate, but did not detect increased activation in the dopamine system. The differences in the two studies may reflect the fact that the earlier study looked at people in a later stage of romantic love where the intensity of pleasure had diminished.

But love is not just a feeling, as it also provides a spur to actions that serve to bring one closer to another. Fisher and her colleagues also found that people looking at romantic pictures had high activation in a brain region called the caudate nucleus, part of the basal ganglia, which includes the nucleus accumbens. The caudate contributes to the representation of goals, expectation of reward, and integration of sensory inputs to prepare for action. Romantic love can be viewed as a goal-oriented state that leads to specific emotions such as euphoria and anxiety rather than as a specific emotion. Its neurophysiology seems to differ from that of mere sexual attraction and also from that of long-term attachment.

Dopamine is also a key factor in explaining the mating behavior of prairie voles, which are small mouselike animals. When voles mate, both males and females show dramatic dopamine increases, but there are also other chemical changes. Unlike most mammals, including the very similar mountain voles, prairie voles typically retain the same partner for life. The reason for the difference is the activity of the brain chemicals oxytocin and vasopressin, which increase during mating in females and males, respectively. This activity is controlled by a single gene found in prairie voles but not in mountain voles: if the gene is spliced into mountain voles, then they also tend to form a pair bond rather than mating promiscuously. Such chemicals probably also contribute to the romantic attachments that people form. Moreover, oxytocin is heavily involved in inducing maternal behavior in both rats and sheep. In addition, vasopressin and oxytocin contribute to a range of other fear- and anxiety-related behaviors.

Oxytocin increases trust between strangers. In one experiment, two participants interacted in a financial game involving decisions about whether to transfer money. Intranasal administration of oxytocin increased the rate at which one participant trusted the other by 17 percent! People given oxytocin seem to be better able to overcome aversion to being betrayed. You can even find a shady advertisement on the Web offering to sell you Oxytocin Trust Spray, pitched for salespeople and singles, although no one knows whether oxytocin is actually effective for such purposes.

Trust is an important part of friendship, a less intense relationship than romantic love and marriage, but also of great importance to people's satisfaction with their lives. There is a strong correlation between social isolation and diminished well-being. The brain processes involved in interpersonal bonding have much overlap with those identified for romantic and familial attachments. Spending time with friends is highly pleasurable, involving dopamine brain circuitry. With good friends, you feel a real bond and know that you can trust them to look out for your interests, so it is plausible that oxytocin is involved as well.

I have been focusing on the emotionally positive sides of love and friendship that come with their acquisition and maintenance, but most people are also familiar with the negative sides that emerge with their actual or threatened loss. When you are rejected by a lover, divorced by a spouse, widowed, or even just troubled by a falling-out with a good friend, the social pain can be immense. According to the social psychologists Geoff MacDonald and Mark Leary, it is more than metaphorical to describe your feelings as being hurt. Reactions to physical harm and social rejection are mediated by a similar physiological system: social pain really is pain. A brain-scanning study of social exclusion found that social distress is associated with activity in the anterior cingulate cortex, which is known to be an important site for processing physical pain signals. (It is also part of the EMOCON model in chapter 5.) Another brain area involved in both social and physical pain is the periaqueductal gray in the midbrain, which plays a role in both detecting bodily injury and regulating attachment behavior. There thus seems to be a physiological explanation as to why social and physical pain have many shared linguistic and behavioral correlates. Many languages use a term like "hurt" to describe how people feel when they are rejected. The behavior and feelings of anxiety and fear are strongly tied to both physical and social pain, which are also linked to sadness and depression.

In addition, there are chemical similarities between social and physical pain, as both are affected by opioids such as morphine. For example, low doses of morphine reduce the separation distress cries of isolated rat pups. I described the role of oxytocin in bonding behavior, but it also functions to regulate physical pain in rats. For humans, social threats can lead to decreases in pain sensitivity, just as injury does; and rejection leads to increased blood pressure and levels of the stress hormone cortisol. Hence evidence is mounting that social and physical pain have similar mechanisms that can be understood in terms of brain regions such as the anterior cingulate and chemical processes that occur in them. Minds are brains whether they're feeling good or bad.

According to the Christian Bible, you should love your neighbor as yourself. For most of us, it is not psychologically possible to care as deeply about neighbors, acquaintances, and strangers as we do about ourselves and our immediate family members. Intellectually, I can agree that any two people anywhere in the world are as morally important as my two sons, but my personal brain history is such that strangers can never be as emotionally important to me as my children. Nevertheless, people often respond to the misfortunes of strangers with compassion, as we see in many acts of charity such as donations to organizations dedicated to reducing poverty or disease. For example, when a huge earthquake in 2004 caused a tsunami that devastated parts of Indonesia and other countries, people and organizations pledged billions of dollars to help with recovery.

Chapter 9 will discuss mirror neurons, which seem to be part of the brain mechanisms that underlie compassion and empathy: when you see someone in pain, you have activity in the same brain areas that are active when you yourself experience pain. There appear to be interesting changes in the brains of Tibetan Buddhist monks with extensive practice in compassionate meditation. They had spent thousands of hours in a state of "loving-kindness," a kind of life without attachment that promotes an unrestricted readiness and availability to help living beings. Compared to people without such training, the monks showed brain wave differences detected by electroencephalography that measures electrical activity along the scalp: they could self-induce high-amplitude waves and synchrony during meditation. Studies are now under way using brain scans to identify the regions most affected by meditation.

A full account of the brain mechanisms underlying love should be able to accommodate all of its manifestations, from romance to friendship to compassion. Evidence does not yet suffice to guide construction of a comprehensive theory, but enough is known to suggest what some of the neural mechanisms might be. Pleasure-related brain areas such as the nucleus accumbens and circuitry based on neurochemicals such as dopamine and oxytocin are highly relevant. It therefore becomes possible to tie love to the neural emotional processes described in chapter 5. But how does love affect decisions through processes of goal application and goal change?

The philosopher Harry Frankfurt makes the daring suggestion that love is a source of final ends, which are goals that we value for their own sake and not just because they serve other goals:

> How is it that things may come to have for us a terminal value that is independent of their usefulness for pursuing further goals? In what acceptable way can our need for final ends be met?
>
> It is love, I believe, that meets this need. It is in coming to love certain things—however this may be caused—that we become bound to final ends by more than an adventitious impulse or a deliberate willful choice. Love is the originating source of terminal value.

I don't know what kinds of psychological or neurological evidence could be used to assess this claim, but it fits with common experiences of enduring romantic love and love for one's children and parents. Initial romantic love—infatuation—may be driven by sexual desire and other personal goals, but with mature love another person comes to matter inherently, as do children, parents, and close friends. I argued earlier in this chapter that happiness is not our sole goal, since people often pursue love-induced activities that may not contribute much to happiness, such as caring for a disabled child, spouse, or parent. It would be interesting to supplement the kinds of brain scanning experiments that Fisher and her colleagues performed on people newly infatuated with experiments on people who are experiencing more enduring forms of love. According to a preliminary report, there are people who have experienced intense love for twenty years and still show activation in the brain's ventral tegmental area, which is part of the dopamine-based reward system. Even while experiencing grief over the death of a spouse, some people continue to show activation in reward pathways involving the nucleus accumbens.

Douglas Hofstadter insightfully describes the bond created between two people who are together for a long time. In a good relationship, a set of common interests and styles builds up over time, especially when spouses share the common goal of bringing up children. He poignantly describes how he and his late wife shared the same hopes and dreams, encoded as very similar neural patterns realized in two different brains. Such patterns integrate cognitions and emotions, as chapter 5 described, but the details of the encoding remain to be understood.

I would also like to know the neural basis for the difference found by a friend of mine in an informal experiment he conducted with a group of fathers. He asked them whether they would be willing to take a bullet for their wives. After a bit of deliberation, the men reported that they probably would. Then my friend asked them if they would take a bullet for their children, and the answer was immediate: Duh, of course. For these men, love was clearly a source of terminal value. Brain imaging has identified highly specific brain activity (in the medial orbitofrontal cortex) that occurs in response to infant faces but not to adult faces, which may be the neural origin of the strong attachment that most parents feel toward their children.

I find Frankfurt's conjecture about love as a source of value intuitively plausible, but we need evidence to legitimately infer that love is part of the meaning of life. I have sought such evidence from a combination of psychological and sociological studies of connections between personal relationships and reported well-being, and especially from neural studies that inform us how romantic love and affiliation become powerful sources of meaning in people's lives. I do not mean to suggest, however, that we can hope to explain everything about love using just neural and molecular mechanisms. As I argued in chapter 5, understanding human emotions should operate on multiple levels, including attention to psychological mechanisms involving mental representations and social mechanisms involving interactions such as communication. If we want to explain why two people have fallen in love, we will find it useful to take into account such social factors as how they met and how they interacted, as well as such psychological factors as what they thought about each other. These factors should complement descriptions of neural and biochemical changes that are part of falling in love.

Work

Work is another major realm of life that needs to be understood in terms of social and psychological processes as well as neurological ones. You may think of work as something to avoid, but research indicates that many people obtain satisfaction from their jobs, even mundane ones. Some people even prefer work activities to nonwork ones such as leisure and home life. Paid work can provide many benefits, including money, enjoyable activities, social contact, and goals that are engaging and challenging. Rewarding jobs tend to have such characteristics as opportunity for personal control, opportunity for using skills, variety of tasks, being respected, high status, interpersonal contact, and good pay.

One of the purposes of working is to obtain the money one needs to live, but working is not just about income. High income does correlate with happiness and well-being as I mentioned above, but the relation between them is complex. People rank happiness and satisfaction as more important than money. In the last fifty years, American income adjusted for inflation has climbed steadily, with no change in life satisfaction. Wealthy nations tend to be happier than poorer ones, but the differences are small once a basic level of income is achieved. The richest Americans have a high level of life satisfaction, but theirs is not a great deal higher than that of people with middle incomes, and no higher than that of the Pennsylvania Amish, who lead very simple lives. Hence there seems to be no reason to adopt money as a major goal in itself, so work is not just a reason to make money. One complicating factor may be that happiness does not depend on absolute amount of wealth, but rather on how you are doing compared to others. People who are unemployed are significantly unhappier than those who are employed or retired. Some of the reasons for this may be social and financial, but I think there are other cognitive-emotional reasons why work can contribute to happiness.

The brain-based theory of emotions and goals in chapters 5 and 6 helps to explain why work can sometimes be highly satisfying. Goal setting affects both job satisfaction and job performance. Goals serve to direct attention, mobilize effort, increase persistence, and motivate strategy development. Goal setting is most effective when the goals people accept are specific, challenging, within their ability, and accompanied by feedback, rewards, and social support. Under these conditions, goals can possess the positive emotional values represented in the brain through association with areas such as the dopamine system, so that their accomplishment and, to a lesser extent, their anticipation can be rewarded by pleasurable experiences.

Consider how work satisfaction operates in the group with which I am most familiar: academics and scientists. Figure 7.1 displays the role of emotions in scientific problem solving. Scientists generate questions to answer, including empirical questions such as what would happen in a particular experiment and theoretical questions concerning the causes of what is observed. The inspirations for such questions are often tied to emotional reactions like curiosity, surprise, and wonder, as well as to the need to avoid boredom. Attempting to answer questions can generate positive emotions such as hope and happiness when it appears that progress is being made, and negative emotions such as frustration and disappointment when things are not going well. Similarly, an elegant experimental or theoretical result can generate strong feelings of joy and even a sense of beauty, but a failed attempt inevitably brings negative feelings. Fortunately, if you are reasonably good at your job, regular successes should produce a pleasant balance of positive over negative emotions.

Many jobs besides academic ones generate problems that can be solved at least some of the time. A carpenter, for example, can face interesting challenges in figuring out how to construct a piece of furniture or repair a wall, with satisfaction that results from solving the problem. Unfortunately, the

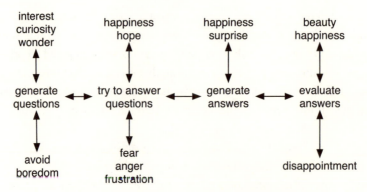

7.1 Role of emotions in scientific problem solving.

most menial jobs, such as working at a fast-food restaurant or on a strictly regimented assembly line, do not offer the possibilities of problem-solving satisfaction, and people suffer boredom and distress.

When problem solving is proceeding optimally, you hardly need to be conscious of it. The psychologist Mihaly Csikszentmihalyi has described the mental state of flow, in which a person becomes fully immersed in an activity that is challenging but closely matched to one's abilities. I sometimes experience this state when I am writing, especially on my best days when an article or chapter almost seems to write itself. Flow can also be a characteristic of other kinds of work activities, and even play activities such as sports. Even without flow, job performance can contribute to job satisfaction and hence to life satisfaction by virtue of success and achievement, effectiveness at specific tasks, progress in accomplishing goals, and the positive moods that come generally with satisfaction of work-generated goals.

Other factors that can contribute to employees' thriving at work include their enjoying a social climate of trust and respect, decision-making discretion, and broad information sharing. People may approach their work as a job (for money), a career (for advancement), or a calling (for intrinsic fulfillment). Some occupations are not only unfulfilling but actually demeaning. A laudable social goal is to make it possible for more people to pursue callings rather than demeaning jobs.

In sum, work can be a major source of meaning in people's lives not only for external reasons such as providing income and social contacts, but especially for internal reasons tied to the neural nature of problem solving.

Jobs that set challenging but reachable goals provide people with motivating tasks that can be inherently enjoyable, because the adoption and accomplishment of goals is a major part of the emotional system in our brains. For most people, finishing challenging tasks is much more satisfying than slacker serenity.

Play

Following an idea misattributed to Freud, I used to think that the meaning of life is love and work. But a friend who had a passion for mountain hiking convinced me that I was missing something important: the many ways that people find to entertain themselves. Play includes more than children's games, and dictionaries describe it more generally as engaging in activity for enjoyment and recreation rather than for a serious or practical purpose. Listening to music and reading novels are clearly play in this sense.

For most people, play supplements love and work as a source of meaning. At the beginning and end of life, work is not expected to be of primary importance. As I have already mentioned, retired people seem to be as happy as those working, and no one expects young children to be doing very much in the way of work. For toddlers, before school and work assume importance, the meaning of life is largely play, although their attachments to parents are also significant.

Even for adults, there are many kinds of activities outside work and personal relationships that people enjoy. According to a 2004 poll of American adults asked to name their favorite leisure-time activities, popular answers included reading (35 percent), watching TV (21 percent), spending time with family and friends (20 percent), movies (16 percent), fishing (8 percent), computer-related activities (7 percent), exercise (6 percent), gardening (6 percent), and walking (6 percent). Other sources of entertainment include good food, recreational drugs such as alcohol, music, drama, sports, and hobbies. In 2005, the average Canadian adult spent 5.5 hours per day on leisure activities.

The neuropsychologist Jaak Panksepp has done extensive research on how the arousal of play circuits within the brain can generate joy. He argues that the brain contains distinct neural systems devoted to the generation of rough-and-tumble play, in organisms from rats to humans. Like human children, rats like to roughhouse with each other, in ways that are intimately linked to somatosensory information processing within the midbrain, the thalamus, and the cortex. Synaptic chemicals that are effective in arousing play include acetylcholine, glutamate, and opioids. Panksepp thinks that play in young animals, including humans, has many important functions, among them the facilitation of learning, physical skills, and social assimilation. The fun of rough-and-tumble play can continue into adulthood, through pursuit of interactive sports such as soccer, basketball, and hockey.

Why is play fun? Rat studies have not identified any particular brain area that seems to be essential for play, which involves neural populations in many brain areas, as does the emotional processing described in chapter 5. Play can be inhibited by environmental manipulations that evoke negative emotional states such as fear, anger, and separation, as well as by bodily disturbances such as hunger and illness. Play produces widespread release of opioids in the nervous system and can be modulated by opioids: low doses of morphine can increase play in rats, and opiate antagonists can reduce it. Activation of serotonin and noradrenaline systems reduces play, and so does blockade of dopamine systems. A full account of the neurophysiology of play remains to be developed, but there is already enough evidence to suggest that play is fun because of its neurochemical effects. The studies to date mostly concern rats, but the relevant neural circuitry and biochemistry are very similar in humans. I described in chapter 5 the evidence that people enjoy recreational drugs such as alcohol because of their effects on various neurochemical pathways, including ones involving dopamine and endogenous opioids.

Little research seems to have been done on the neurochemical reasons why people enjoy playing sports, but the emotional side of the thrill of victory and the agony of defeat is obvious. Much like challenging work, sports clearly involve setting goals and striving to accomplish them. Hence the pleasure associated with winning a game or having a good personal performance likely emanates from the same neural process of goal satisfaction that can make work satisfying. In addition, exercise can stimulate the production of endorphins, natural opioids in the brain that reduce pain and produce feelings of well-being.

Watching sports is an even more popular pastime than participating in them, and there has been extensive research on why people enjoy this kind of entertainment. Emotional motivations for watching sports include the enjoyment that comes from cheering on a favorite team, the increases in arousal and excitement experienced during viewing, the increase in self-esteem associated with a victory by a home team, and escape from the stresses of daily life. People also have cognitive motivations such as learning about players and teams, and social motivations such as companionship and group affiliation. When a group of people identify with a team and each other, the success of the team becomes a goal; unfortunately, these fans have no direct effect on its accomplishment.

There are many kinds of play besides sports. One of the main sources of entertainment is music, whose biological basis is now being extensively researched by psychologists and neuroscientists. In his stimulating book *This Is Your Brain on Music*, Daniel Levitin describes how our musical experiences arise from neural processes of perception and emotion. For example, the ability of people to reproduce the tempo of a song accurately is probably due to activity in the cerebellum, which contains a system of timekeepers for our daily lives. Listening to music and attending to its structure activates a region of the left frontal cortex called the pars orbitalis, which is also involved in language comprehension. But attending to music also involves activation in an analogous area in the right hemisphere not used for language. Perception of music and memory for music have common neural mechanisms that explain how songs can get stuck in our heads, producing so-called earworms that are hard to stop.

Intense musical emotions—thrills and chills—are associated with brain regions involved in reward, motivation, and arousal: the ventral striatum, the amygdala, the midbrain, and regions of the frontal cortex. Levitin used fMRI brain scans to examine whether the nucleus accumbens, which is part of the ventral striatum involved in pleasure and addiction, contributed to musical enjoyment. Here is what he found:

> Listening to music causes a cascade of brain regions to become activated in a particular order: first, auditory cortex for initial processing of the components of the sound. Then the frontal regions, such as BA44 and BA47, that we had previously identified as being involved in processing musical structure and expectation. Finally, a network of regions—the mesolimbic system—involved in arousal, pleasure, and the

transmission of opioids and the production of dopamine, culminating in activation in the nucleus accumbens. And the cerebellum and basal ganglia were active throughout, presumably supporting the processing of rhythm and meter.

The rewarding aspects of music seem therefore to be mediated by dopamine activity in the nucleus accumbens, just like positive aspects of food and drugs. Levitin provides vivid examples of how music has shaped the world through six kinds of songs: friendship, joy, comfort, knowledge, religion, and love.

Other researchers have investigated how music perception affects emotion, the autonomic nervous system, the hormonal and immune systems, and motor representations. Mechanisms underlying musical emotions include cognitive appraisal, brain stem reflexes, emotional contagion, visual imagery, episodic memory, and musical expectancy.

Another of my favorite forms of entertainment is reading, from novels and short stories to poetry and nonfiction. I particularly enjoy reading biographies of people who interest me, such as scientists, writers, and politicians. As I mentioned in chapter 4, much research has been done on the brain processes required for reading. According to Maryanne Wolf, an expert on dyslexia, fluent reading requires recognizing patterns such as letters and words, planning strategies such as interpreting inferential and metaphorical background, and feeling the emotional significance of what is read. The brain's efforts to identify letters and words requires a large amount of processing in visual areas of both hemispheres of the cortex, which becomes much more efficient with practice. Emotional regions of the brain are also important to prioritize and give value to whatever we read. Thus reading, like music, has an emotional component as well as perceptual and cognitive ones.

Like music and rough-and-tumble play, reading requires integrated activity in many brain regions: sensory motor areas, visual areas, auditory and language areas, the temporal lobe, and the cerebellum. Wolf describes research concerning brain deficits that can make it difficult for some children to learn to read, as well as psychological strategies for overcoming these deficits. I am not aware of any studies of how the brain appreciates poetry, drama, and the visual arts, but I expect that the underlying processes of perception, cognition, and emotion are similar.

Another highly enjoyable kind of play is humor, a universal human activity that people frequently experience through laughter. Humor generates the positive emotion of mirth, which arises from a combination of cognitive processes such as the detection of incongruity, and emotional processes such as the perception of physiological changes. Like other emotional experiences, humor depends on the interaction of multiple mechanisms operating at four different levels, from social to molecular. Laughter and play both emerge in infants around the age of four to six months facilitated by similar social contexts. Humor, like music and reading, can facilitate love and work as well as personal amusement and social enjoyment. Here is my favorite joke about psychology, which I include merely to amuse you. Have you heard why psychologists have stopped using rats in their experiments and instead are using lawyers? First, there are now more lawyers than rats. Second, the researchers found that they were getting attached to the rats. And third, there are some things that rats just won't do. Actually, psychologists are going to have to stop using lawyers, because the experimental results don't transfer to humans.

In sum, there is sociological and psychological evidence that play of many different forms is important to people, and neurological evidence concerning how some varieties, such as music, are important. What is missing still is an argument to the normative conclusion that play *ought* to be important to people. Such normative issues will have to wait for the next chapter. I do not claim that all kinds of play are equally meaningful, so please don't attribute to me the view that watching television reruns or getting blind drunk at football games is what makes life worth living. Not all varieties of love and work are equally meaningful either, and some kinds, such as abusive relationships and tedious jobs, are detrimental to human happiness. I will argue in chapter 8 that love, work, and play are objectively valuable when they help to satisfy vital human needs. Biology and psychology provide the crucial link between subjective and objective meaning.

Conclusion

If you want to reduce my book to a slogan, it could be this: The meaning of life is love, work, and play. A more nuanced summary would be better: People's lives have meaning to the extent that love, work, and play provide coherent and valuable goals that they can strive for and at least partially accomplish, yielding brain-based emotional consciousness of satisfaction and happiness.

I have tried to develop a naturalistic theory of the meaning of life, as constituted largely by love, work, and play. Each of these provides rewarding goals, which are brain representations of possible states of affairs imbued with emotional significance through a mixture of neural activities. Observations of the pursuits and happiness of most people provide good reason to reject nihilism, the view that life is meaningless or absurd. There is more to meaning than happiness, which is the result of satisfaction of more basic goals whose pursuit and accomplishment enable human lives to flourish. The meaning of life is multidimensional, requiring the combination and integration of various kinds of goals, the most of important of which concern love, work, and play. Support for the importance of these realms comes from psychological and sociological evidence about their contributions to human well-being, and also from emerging neurological understanding of how they operate in our brains.

Successful pursuit of such goals undercuts Woody Allen's gloomy remark that life is full of misery, loneliness, and suffering—and it's all over much too soon. One philosopher has even advocated the dismal view that universally it is better never to have been born, on the grounds that coming into existence is always a serious harm. Although all lives involve some pain, pain is not unconditionally bad, as there are many cases—surgery, for instance—where it is part of a process that is good overall. Love, work, and even play can all make us vulnerable to pain, but their pursuit and recurring benefits ensure that life is better than nonexistence for most people. Other goals, such as beauty, power, and social harmony, are part of the human condition; but these seem to me subordinate to play, work, and love, respectively.

The neurological basis for romantic love is becoming particularly well understood, but we must extrapolate to other aspects of love, such as parenting, friendship, and general compassion. Work can also be a source of well-being, through satisfaction of goals that include money, social approval, and intrinsic problem solving efficacy. Play might seem too trivial to be a component of the meaning of life, but it is something that frequently occupies adults as well as children, and neuroscience is starting to provide insights into how people enjoy such activities as music.

The major gap in this chapter concerns the normative status of claims about the meaning of life, but these will have to wait for more discussion of ethical issues in the next two chapters. I hope, however, to have provided some reasons for rejecting several inadequate approaches to a meaningful life, including religion, nihilism, and slacker serenity. The realms of love, work, and play can provide ample answers to the question of why life is worth living, but only if we have some grounds for thinking that they furnish not merely goals that people do pursue, but also goals that people *ought* to pursue. The next chapter argues that love, work, and play are normatively appropriate goals because of their contributions to vital human needs.

Chapter Eight

needs and hopes

Wants versus Needs

In the 1960s, the Rolling Stones sang: "You can't always get what you want / But if you try sometimes you might find / You get what you need." Most people want success at love, work, and play, but do they really need it? Our merely wanting something does not show that it deserves to be wanted. People often have frivolous desires acquired from social contagion or advertising—for example, wanting the latest gadget or fashionable clothes. To provide a solid answer to the question of why life is worth living, we need to establish that some goals really are valuable, not just that many people value them. Hence the question of the meaning of life needs to move from the descriptive realms of psychology, neuroscience, and sociology into the normative realm of philosophy.

This chapter argues that needs provide the crucial connection between subjective values and objective ones. Love, work, and play are not arbitrary wants, but are closely tied with vital human needs for relatedness, competence, and autonomy. Vital needs are properties and relationships that people require to live as human beings. Because love, work, and play help to satisfy vital needs, they can constitute the meaning of life normatively as well as descriptively.

Another important normative problem is how to deal with conflicts between important goals such as love, work, and play. People often experience stress and anxiety when they are overwhelmed by such conflicts, as when career goals seem incompatible with family goals. I will discuss strategies for achieving balance in the pursuit of conflicting goals, and will evaluate advice about how to increase the happiness and overall meaningfulness of people's lives. Such strategies show how love, work, and play can provide sources of hope about the value of life.

Vital Needs

According to the philosopher David Wiggins, people need something if they will be harmed by going without it. He rejects the cynical statement that a need is just something you want but aren't prepared to pay for. Needs are much more fundamental than wants or interests: you may want a Hawaiian vacation, but you would be hard-pressed to argue that not getting it would harm you. People have varying interests, which are factors that affect their well-being. But only some of these are *vital* interests, concerning what is required to sustain their functioning as the very kind of being they are. For example, you may have an interest in music, connected with your well-being in that it makes you happy to listen to it. But being deprived of music would not remove your ability to live a life of value. More positively, the satisfaction of needs enables you to live a good human life.

Wiggins does not present evidence to establish which needs really are vital for human functioning. Some biological needs are obvious: you will die if you do not get water for a few days or food for a few weeks. Others are more subtle—for example, when people get sick and function poorly if they have access only to contaminated water or food lacking in nutrients, or if they are unable to sleep, excrete, or exercise. The causal evidence that food, water, and sleep are vital human needs is both negative and positive: when these needs are not satisfied, people are harmed; but when they are satisfied, people thrive. We know that depriving people of water makes them suffer and soon die, whereas providing thirsty people with water makes them happier and capable of living their lives.

For people living in poverty, the vital needs for food, water, and shelter are daily concerns whose pursuit leaves little time and energy for reflection on why life is worth living. In contrast, for those of us whose basic biological needs are taken care of, the key issue of the meaning of life becomes how different kinds of pursuits contribute to human *psychological* needs. If we could identify the deep psychological needs of people, we could evaluate the extent to which the pursuit of love, work, and play contributes to the satisfaction of those needs. What are they?

Psychologists Edward Deci and Richard Ryan have proposed a powerful theory of human motivation postulating three fundamental psychological needs that they call competence, autonomy, and relatedness. Competence is people's need to feel effective in their activities by engaging in challenges and experiencing mastery in the physical and social worlds. The need for competence leads people to seek challenges appropriate for their capacities. Autonomy is people's need to feel that their activities are self-chosen and self-endorsed, enabling them to organize and regulate their own behavior as an expression of their own interests and values. Relatedness is the need to feel a sense of closeness with others through attachments and feelings of security, belongingness, and intimacy. It requires feeling connected to others whom we care for and who care for us. Deci, Ryan, and their collaborators have accumulated a wealth of psychological evidence that these three needs are indeed of great importance to people. Success in satisfying them is associated with well-being, whereas social contexts and individual differences that forestall them are associated with poorer motivation and performance.

Ideally, psychologists should supply evidence that depriving people of competence, autonomy, and relatedness causes them harm, and that providing these three factors enables people to live psychologically satisfying lives. The most convincing evidence would show causation as well as correlation, but for both practical and ethical reasons it is difficult to conduct experiments to determine the causal effects of the three factors. The strongest case for a causal link has been made for relatedness.

Roy Baumeister and Mark Leary comprehensively review evidence that people have a need to belong, and that desire for interpersonal attachment is a fundamental human motivation. The formation of social bonds is characteristic of all human societies, and basic patterns of thought reflect a fundamental concern with social relationships—for example, in the universal use of kinship concepts. The formation of social bonds is generally associated with positive emotions, as in the experience of falling in love. In contrast, threats to social attachments and dissolution of social bonds are a primary source of negative emotions such as jealousy and loneliness. In many cases, the association between social deprivation and negative emotions is clearly causal, as when the death of a spouse, child, parent, or close friend produces intense grief and in some cases ongoing depression. Many studies show that the deprivation of belongingness causes decrements in physical and mental health. Divorced people are at risk for many bad outcomes, including illness, homicide, criminality, and accidental injury or death.

The evidence that autonomy and competence are vital needs is less comprehensive. According to Ryan and Deci, the issue of whether people stand behind a behavior out of their interests and values, or do it for reasons external to the self, is significant in every culture. People whose motivation is self-authored and -endorsed have more interest, excitement, and confidence, resulting in enhanced performance, persistence, and creativity. Autonomy and competence are strongly associated with life events that people identify as most satisfying, and negatively associated with life events that people identify as least satisfying. Distress caused by a controlling boss or spouse shows the importance of autonomy, and sadness caused by failure at work or school shows the importance of competence. Children are more likely to be well-adjusted if their parents support their autonomy rather than controlling them autocratically.

I am not sure that the evidence is now sufficient to support the claim of Deci and Ryan that the needs for relatedness, autonomy, and competence are innate, because not enough is known yet about their evolutionary history and genetic basis. But innateness is not required to establish that these three psychological needs are indeed vital: people thrive in their presence and suffer in their absence. Without competence, autonomy, and relatedness, it is very difficult to function as a human being. Moreover, there is growing evidence presented below concerning the neural mechanisms underlying these needs.

How Love, Work, and Play Satisfy Needs

Activities in the realms of love, work, and play can contribute enormously to satisfaction of the vital psychological needs of competence, autonomy, and relatedness. Work is highly relevant to competence when it is challenging yet doable, so that people can perceive that they are effective. The failure to satisfy the need for competence is a partial explanation of why menial jobs are so unpleasant. Play can also contribute to a sense of competence when it involves challenging activities such as sports, music, and hobbies. Satisfying the need for competence requires a degree of challenge, making it clear why some pastimes, such as watching mindless television, need not be counted as generating much value. Love, which I construed broadly to include friendship and compassion as well as romantic involvement, is clearly the major way to satisfy the need for relatedness. Play of more frivolous sorts not tied to competence might also be justified as a distraction sometimes needed from the stresses associated with the more inherently valuable pursuits of love and work.

Thus work, play, and love are clearly consonant with the needs for competence and relatedness, but what about the proposed need for autonomy? There is some evidence from the sources cited in chapter 7 that work is more satisfying when it is self-chosen and self-regulated, suggesting that the most enjoyable kinds of work help to satisfy the need for autonomy. The problem with tedious jobs is not just that they do not permit feelings of effectiveness needed for competence, but also that they are controlled by others and so do not permit people to choose for themselves and regulate their own behavior. Autonomy also seems important for loving relationships, according to evidence that people tend to be more satisfied with love-based matches than with arranged marriages. I do not know of similar findings for play, but games and entertainment are plausibly more satisfying when they are self-chosen. People don't like being told what they have to do for fun.

If Deci and Ryan are right that competence, relatedness, and autonomy are vital psychological needs, and if there is sufficient evidence that love, work, and play contribute substantially to the satisfaction of these needs, then we have the beginning of an explanation of how activities in these three realms contribute so much to human well-being. The goals that love, work, and play can accomplish are not arbitrary ones acquired through the vagaries of culture and human experience, but ones based in the nature of human minds. To make this story more complete, it would be desirable to find more evidence concerning the neural basis for the needs of competence, relatedness, and autonomy, providing a mechanistic explanation of why being deprived of them causes harm. Of these, the neural basis of relatedness is best understood, thanks to investigation of the mechanisms of interpersonal bonding described in chapter 7. We saw in chapter 5 that loss of relatedness causes psychological harm that is neurologically akin to physical pain.

The need for competence is rooted in neural mechanisms for goal accomplishment, wired into the brain as part of the neurochemical basis for goal representation and reward. According to neuropsychologist Kelly Lambert, the nucleus accumbens and other brain structures implement a system of effort-based rewards that enabled our ancestors to survive by sustaining the high level of activity needed for the acquisition of resources such as food, water, and shelter. Not surprisingly, greater effort can lead to greater reward in the form of pleasure resulting from increased activity of dopamine-transmitting neurons in the nucleus accumbens and the orbitofrontal cortex. It would be valuable to have a more detailed neural explanation as to why challenging goals such as those that motivate the best kinds of work and play are potentially more rewarding than ones whose satisfaction requires little effort. Why does finishing a major project feel better than accomplishing a menial task? The answer is probably related in part to degrees of social approval, but a detailed neural explanation in terms of effort-based rewards should also be developed. Enough is already known, however, to make it clear why slacker serenity is not appealing to most people: little psychological reward comes from pursuing minimal goals that can be accomplished with scant effort.

The need for autonomy is probably tied to brain mechanisms for voluntary control that are located in the frontal cortex and the cingulate. In their second year, the development of frontal control mechanisms allows children to demonstrate voluntary control of actions and to begin to delay gratification by valuing larger, later rewards over immediate, smaller ones. Improved control enables them to have more effective attention and self-regulation. Without the expectation of and desire for autonomy, children would remain content with having their needs met by caregivers. Adolescence brings another major period of development of the frontal cortex, associated with even greater desires for autonomy. Even more than toddlers, teenagers take higher satisfaction from actions they can perform for themselves. It thus seems that interactions between the executive control regions of the brain, the frontal cortex, and the emotional systems yield greater effort-based rewards for goals that are satisfied through the agent's own actions. Psychologists have found that people are happier, healthier, and more hardworking when they are following goals that are authentic: rooted in their own deeply held interests and core values. Further research is needed to describe detailed mechanisms that underlie enhanced satisfaction with the results of self-regulated actions.

At first glance, it might seem that my endorsement of autonomy as a vital need contradicts the rejection of free will in the previous chapter. The brain-based view of decision making is indeed incompatible with a metaphysical notion of autonomy based on the totally free actions of a nonmaterial soul. But the psychological notion of autonomy as people acting in accord with their own interests and values fits perfectly with my neural theory of decision making, because interests and values are represented in brains by activities of neurons. You act autonomously whenever your decisions are based on your own goals, even if the neural process of inference to the best plan is incompatible with the kind of free will that dualism promises but fails to deliver.

Finding a neural basis for the desires for competence, relatedness, and autonomy is important because it shows that they are deep biological needs as well as psychological ones. It is obvious how people are harmed by lack of satisfaction of their basic biological needs such as food, water, and shelter. Hence activities such as eating, drinking, and building houses are understandable and justifiable as crucial for satisfying fundamental human needs. Similarly, love, work, and play are understandable and justifiable as crucial for satisfying vital psychological needs arising from the nature of our brains. That is why they are central parts of the meaning of life, normatively as well as descriptively.

By now, you may be wondering why I don't just say that competence, relatedness, and autonomy are the meaning of life, if these needs explain why people pursue love, work, and play. The reason is that there is much more direct experimental evidence, presented in chapter 7, for love, work, and play as really mattering to people than for the three abstract needs proposed by Deci and Ryan. Eventually, I hope we will have more detailed and brain-based theories about psychological needs that provide more thoroughly mechanistic explanations of why people pursue love, work, and play. For now, however, we must be content with more approximate and conjectural explanations as to why these matter so much to us, hanging on to the more theoretically cautious conclusion that the meaning of life is love, work, and play.

Let me try to clarify the relation between goals and needs. Chapter 6 described goals as emotionally valued neural representations of imagined states of the world and the self. The needs of the self are constituents of states of the world and the self without which the self is harmed. Vital needs are constituents so central to people that they cannot function as human beings without them. Hence the most important goals people have are ones aimed at bringing about states of the world and the self that can satisfy their vital needs. Love, work, and play are goals whose pursuit contributes centrally to the meaning of life because their achievement satisfies vital needs for relatedness, competence, and autonomy.

My view in this chapter is compatible with a significant development in economics and political philosophy: the capabilities approach of Amartya Sen and Martha Nussbaum. They emphasize the importance of people's having the freedom to do the things they have reason to value, such as living a long and healthy life, being able to have social attachments, and having control over their physical and social environments. On my view, people have reason to value those things that contribute to their vital needs, including psychological needs for relatedness, competence, and autonomy.

Peter Railton's idea of an objective interest can also be tied to vital needs. He imagines giving individuals unqualified cognitive and imaginative powers, and full factual information about their physical and psychological constitution and circumstances. We could then ask these idealized individuals what they would want their original selves to want, and the answers would indicate their objective interests as contrasted with their subjective wants. Railton argues that what is morally best depends on the objective interests of all potentially affected. My contention is that psychological and neurological knowledge about vital needs already provides a major part of what we need to know about the generation of such objective interests, which include relatedness, competence, and autonomy.

Compare my justification of love, work, and play as normative sources of meaning with the justification of scientific methods of experiment and reasoning provided in chapter 2. In general, we can use descriptive information to help generate normative conclusions whenever we can identify the appropriate goals. If the appropriate goals of science are truth, explanation, and prediction; and if the history of science reveals that experiments and inference to the best explanation are the best practices for achieving these goals; then these practices are normatively justified as what scientists ought to do. Similarly, if psychology can tell us that the vital needs of human beings include relatedness, competence, and autonomy; and if neuropsychology and sociology can reveal that love, work, and play are the best practices for satisfying these needs; then these practices are normatively justified as sources of objective meaning in people's lives. I will return to the general question of how to be naturalistically normative in chapter 10.

Balance, Coherence, and Change

People are often told that they need to have a good work-life balance, especially if they have been focusing on only a single set of goals—for example, ones connected with pursuing a career. I was narrow in this way in my twenties, when getting a Ph.D. and developing an academic career seemed far more important to me than personal relationships or having fun. By my thirties, however, when I got married and had my first child, I had a much more balanced life, still taking work seriously but valuing my family at least as much.

Unfortunately, trying to achieve a balance among love, work, and play can introduce an emotionally distressing degree of incoherence into people's lives. I mentioned in chapter 6 how we can attain emotional coherence, not just from having particular goals satisfied, but from possessing a set of goals that fit well with each other. The opposite side of this is having a set of goals that are mutually incompatible, as when someone wants a career that requires a one-hundred-hour workweek along with a rich family life and lots of fun surfing and skiing. The major constraints that make it impossible to pursue all these goals are the limited supplies of time, energy, and money. Hence the key to avoiding incoherence is to allocate these supplies so as to ensure that love, work, and play each get enough time, energy, and money to make possible an acceptable degree of life satisfaction. Ideally, every day should have some elements of love, work, and play in them, although balance can be accomplished over larger timescales such as weeks, months, or perhaps even years. Remember to be moderate about everything, including moderation.

Balance of this sort counteracts despair that accomplishing all life goals together is impossible. But in the best of cases, emotional coherence can amount to more than this, if you can manage to find ways to reconcile goals that might otherwise seem to be incompatible with each other. There are various ways of combining love, work, and play, such as finding a job that involves activities you really enjoy, so that work is often like a hobby; integrating work travel and play travel; working in the same field as your spouse, so that you share work as well as romantic interests; taking vacations with your family, combining love and play. These strategies are not possible for all people—I have benefited enormously from the flexibility of an academic life that most people do not have—but they show ways in which life can be not only balanced but coherent.

It might appear that the psychological needs for autonomy and relatedness are incompatible with each other, with one emphasizing personal freedom and the other requiring ties to other people. But autonomy in the sense of Deci and Ryan does not require full independence or detachment from others. Interdependence is compatible with autonomy when attachments are self-initiated as ways of satisfying a person's need for relatedness.

Physiological needs change over time, as people develop from childhood to adulthood to old age, and so do psychological needs. According to Daniel Levinson, the human life cycle evolves through a sequence of four overlapping eras: childhood and adolescence (age 0–22 years), early adulthood (17–45), middle adulthood (40–65), and late adulthood (60+). In childhood one's need for relatedness is satisfied by close family and increasingly by friends, and the potency of needs for autonomy and competence increases into adolescence and adulthood. The transition to early adulthood involves forming new goals about work and love. Late adulthood is commonly a time of reduced need for performance in work and greater opportunities for play. According to Levinson, women go through the same sequence of eras as men, at roughly the same ages.

I have not addressed the question of whether men and women differ in their needs for relatedness, competence, and autonomy, because I don't know of any relevant evidence. My inclination is to say that these needs are equally fundamental for both males and females, so that love, work, and play constitute the meaning of life for all humans. Undoubtedly, however, there is considerable variation across cultures, with some societies insisting that work is more central to men and love is more central to women. I conjecture that need satisfaction and happiness are greatest in societies that have a more egalitarian, gender-neutral view of the importance of love and work. Studies of life satisfaction and well-being do appear to show some correlation with equal sex roles, but it is hard to draw causal conclusions when there are other correlated factors such as economic development.

Hope versus Despair

When Barack Obama ran for U.S. president in 2008, he frequently placed hope at the center of his campaign, but what is hope? From my perspective, hope is the positive feeling that one or more of your goals can be accomplished. Hope can be specific to one goal, as when you hope that you will win the lottery, or it can be more general, a feeling that at least some good things will happen to you. Thus hope can be either an emotion, a specific feeling about some desirable state of affairs, or a mood, a more diffuse positive feeling that good things will happen.

Hope as an emotion fits naturally with the model of emotional consciousness in chapter 5 that integrates cognitive appraisal and physiological perception. Appraisal requires neural representations of future situations and current goals, with evaluation that the goals have some probability of being satisfied. Positive feeling arises from a complex neural representation that combines this appraisal with perception of physiological states. Because there is always uncertainty about the future, hope is usually a mixed emotional state that includes some anxiety about whether the future will bring goal satisfaction rather than disappointment. In the EMOCON model, mixed emotions can occur because of simultaneously occurring appraisals and physiological states.

Despair is the total absence of hope, a feeling that none of your goals can be satisfied. It is different from the belief that life is meaningless, which assumes that there are no goals worth pursuing at all. With despair, you still believe that there are worthwhile goals, such as those that are part of love, work, and play, but you are compelled by life circumstances and/or brain chemistry to conclude that goal accomplishment is tragically beyond your reach.

One way of avoiding despair is to adopt some of the goal revision tactics described in chapter 6, replacing unreachable goals with ones that can be at least partially accomplished. If your only goals are to marry a movie star, create a company that will make you a billionaire, and sail a large yacht around the world, then the chances of satisfaction in love, work, and play are slim. More modest goals, such as having a few good friends, making enough money to live on, and having a bit of fun occasionally, should be satisfiable and sufficient to ward off the depths of despair. Even people who are very old and infirm, confined to nursing homes, can take some pleasure in social contacts, reminiscences of accomplishments, and modest activities. A meaningful life is a hopeful one, not because hope *is* part of the meaning of life, but because it is a summary feeling that there are at least some goals worth valuing and whose pursuit and occasional satisfaction constitute a meaningful life. Specific hopes concern emotionally positive expectations that particular goals relevant to love, work, and play can likely be achieved.

Hope is easier to maintain for people whose past experience has included a high degree of satisfaction of needs for relatedness, autonomy, and competence. If you have a good history of social support and effective actions under your own control, then you have greater reason to expect that at least some of your goals will be satisfied by future events. Previous successes in love, work, and play provide the resilience we need to cope with the inevitable surprises that life throws at us. The general cycle to be desired is to adapt to adversity by remaining hopeful that the future will work out, and engage in the kind of autonomous, competent, and socially supported actions that ensure the future does in fact bring satisfaction of major goals. From this perspective, hope can be viewed not as some vague kind of spirituality, but rather as evidence-based expectations about the future. Hopelessness is unjustified as long as there are some prospects in one's life for satisfaction of some important goals.

My claim that the meaning of life is love, work, and play omits some elements that many people would naturally want to include. We saw in discussing life satisfaction that quality of health is a major factor, but health is less a primary goal than a means to accomplishing other goals. Bad health is a major impediment to pursuing other ends, as well as often being intrinsically unpleasant. But good health is not something you enjoy in itself, since we naturally take it for granted on a day-to-day basis. Adopting practices such as a good diet and a vigorous exercise program fosters good health, thereby making the pursuit of other goals possible. But for most of one's life, health does not need to be a primary pursuit in itself, unlike love, work, and play.

My major omission in this chapter concerns a realm of life that many people report as being very important to them: religion and spirituality. For religious people, theology provides major sources of hope, both in their current lives and in a projected afterlife. People genuinely believe that God will provide, that things work out for the best, that everything happens for a reason, that God loves them and cares for them, and that even if this life is a vale of tears, it does not matter all that much, because an eternal afterlife will be wonderful. These ideas are amazingly appealing, and it is not at all surprising that people eagerly integrate them into their lives. I mentioned in chapter 7 that regular churchgoers report being happier than less religious people.

If my approach were purely descriptive, I would have to include religion and spirituality in the meaning of life, for most people. From a normative perspective, however, it is not reasonable to include religion as a legitimate part of meaning, because of the lack of evidence for a caring God or a redeeming afterlife. Like immortality and free will, divine love and eternal bliss would be nice, but you just have to learn to live without them. Fortunately, love, work, and play are real and realizable, putting a substantially meaningful life within reach of most people. The reassurance provided by religion and spirituality that everything will work out is illusory, but most people have the intellectual and material resources to achieve meaningful lives through the moderately successful pursuit of love, work, and play. Perhaps one of the main reasons why religious people are happier is that attending services and identifying oneself as a member of a religious community contributes to belongingness. If so, spirituality is not a vital need but rather a stand-in for relatedness, which can be satisfied through secular communities.

In the self-help section of your local bookstore or public library, you can find many attempts to give people advice about increasing the happiness and overall quality of their lives. These books are mostly faith based, like *The Purpose Driven Life,* or simply made up to appeal to the gullible, like *The Secret.* A striking exception is *The How of Happiness,* by social psychologist Sonja Lyubomirsky, which is based on a wealth of recent research on the sources of positive emotions. She recommends a dozen concrete activities that have been shown experimentally to contribute to happiness:

1. Expressing gratitude
2. Cultivating optimism
3. Avoiding overthinking and social comparison
4. Practicing acts of kindness
5. Nurturing social relationships
6. Developing strategies for coping
7. Learning to forgive
8. Increasing flow experiences where one is absorbed in an activity
9. Savoring life's joys
10. Committing to your goals
11. Practicing religion and spirituality
12. Taking care of your body through physical activity

Except for number 11, these all fit very well with the emphasis in this chapter on how people can develop happiness and meaning in their lives through the pursuit of goals concerning love, work, and play.

Lyubomirsky's engaging book shows that self-help can be evidence based and can steer people intelligently to improve their lives without blind faith or wishful thinking. Less obvious is *why* these activities increase happiness, although many clearly contribute to satisfaction of vital needs. For example, expressing gratitude, practicing acts of kindness, and nurturing social relationships can contribute to satisfaction of the need for relatedness, and increasing flow experiences and committing to your goals can contribute to the need for competence. The effects of other activities can naturally be understood on the basis of the integrated account of emotions presented in chapter 5. Developing strategies for coping and savoring life's joys make for positive cognitive appraisals, while meditation and physical activity contribute to positive emotions through bodily changes.

I've written at length about the meaning of life, but what about the meaning of death? Without religious illusions to rely on, death has none of the appeal associated with eternal reward, nor any of the terror inspired by the possibility of eternal punishment. From a naturalistic perspective, it's all over when it's over. Such finality should not be a cause for despair, because at death you cease to have goals along with all other mental representations. The good news is that you cease to have unsatisfied goals, and unhappiness is as impossible as happiness. Hence death should be no cause for despair, even if it is not something to look forward to. Nonreligious people are actually less likely than religious ones to request aggressive measures such as mechanical ventilation and respiration to prolong their lives, which shows that faith is not required for a person to face death bravely.

Regardless of belief in an afterlife, you can still expect that some of your life's accomplishments, such as the help you gave to people you cared about and the labors you have performed, will have some continuing influence after you have ceased to be. If your pursuit of love and work have found some success, then you can reasonably hope that your life will have some enduring value even after it ends. Religions such as Christianity have provided a conceptual and emotional framework for dealing with death, but a better way to manage fear of nonexistence is simply to strive to ensure that by the time you die, you will have largely accomplished your goals and abandoned the unreasonable ones. Consider John Stuart Mill's last words to his stepdaughter: "You know I have done my work." Mill's biography shows he was largely done with love and play as well.

Conclusion

I have tried to show how needs can provide a link between what people value and what they ought to value, elevating the empirical claim of the previous chapter that people find meaning in love, work, and play to the normative claim that these realms are justified sources of meaning. People have deep biological and psychological needs that generate goals whose pursuit and accomplishment are inherently meaningful. Psychological evidence supports the existence of fundamental human needs for relatedness, competence, and autonomy. The successful pursuit of love, work, and play is the best available means for satisfying these needs, so they both are and ought to be the realms that offer valuable and meaningful lives. Understanding the neural basis of psychological needs such as relatedness, competence, and autonomy enables us to see how psychological needs *are* biological needs.

I have not tried to write a self-help book, but this chapter does have implications for what to do if you feel that your life is futile and lacking in meaning. Set yourself reasonable goals concerning love, work, and play; and expend time, energy, and money in pursuit of them. Review the methods of goal acquisition and revision proposed in chapter 6, and avoid the ways of making bad decisions described there. Aim for balance among the three main realms of life, and strive for coherence, wherever possible, by combining and integrating the pursuit of love, work, and play. Practice happiness-enhancing activities such as those suggested by Lyubomirsky. If you are seriously depressed or considering suicide, you urgently need to consult a clinical psychologist or psychiatrist who can provide evidence-based help through a combination of cognitive therapy and medication.

Why life is worth living is only one of the normative questions that philosophy seeks to answer. I now want to consider more generally what makes actions right or wrong, beginning with an examination of the neuropsychological basis for moral judgments.

Chapter Nine

ethical brains

Ethical Decisions

Suppose you work for your country's main security agency and you have apprehended a man who you strongly suspect is involved in a terrorist conspiracy. You have some reason to believe that other members of his group are planning a major attack that will cost many lives, but the man refuses to identify them despite extensive interrogation. Your moral dilemma is whether you should torture the terrorist in order to extract from him information that might prevent a major disaster.

Now you have to make a decision that is not just about satisfying your personal goals. Rather, you have to deal with a conflict between competing ethical principles: the strict rule that torture is always wrong, and the more flexible rule that you should pursue the greatest good for the greatest number of people. You now have to face the last major philosophical question identified in chapter 1: what makes actions right or wrong?

Some philosophers such as Nietzsche have rejected the whole idea of moral objectivity. Maybe there are no absolute standards of right and wrong, so that morality is relative to particular individuals, situations, or cultures. Perhaps we should say that torture is wrong if your society thinks so, but OK otherwise. Or even more subjectively, perhaps torture is wrong for you if you don't like it, but fine for me if I do. Many religious thinkers have thought that these kinds of moral relativism would unavoidably result from the rejection of theology. Without God, anything is permissible.

In contrast, my aim is to develop a theory of objective morality that fits well with a general naturalistic, evidence-based approach and with particular findings about how brains think. Many philosophers would view this as a hopeless task, because of Hume's famous injunction that you cannot derive an *ought* from an *is*. I do not claim to have produced such a derivation, as Hume was undoubtedly right that there are no sound deductive arguments that can take you from empirical facts about the world to the acceptance of particular or general moral judgments.

Rather, I will move toward a moral theory that is highly coherent with what is known about how brains make moral decisions, and with other psychological and social facts. This moral theory should be a central part of a general account of wisdom and why life is worth living. As in chapter 8, the crucial bridge between *is* and *ought* is provided by human needs that point to a general theory of what makes actions right and wrong. I will discuss brain mechanisms such as mirror neurons that enable and encourage people to care about others as well as themselves.

Conscience and Moral Intuitions

When I was a child, I was told by my religious teachers that God had given me a conscience to use so that I could tell whether something I was doing was right or wrong. But even without any remaining religious beliefs, I still have a conscience, providing a gut reaction about the rightness or wrongness of my own actions or those of others. For example, when I wanted an iPhone and thought about putting it on my research grant, I got a bad feeling that this would be a misuse of government funds. More seriously, the arbitrary retention and torture of people who are vaguely suspected of being terrorists strikes me as wrong, not just in an abstract, purely cognitive way, but as part of a visceral, emotional reaction. The 99 percent of people who are not psychopaths also react emotionally to moral issues, although different people respond differently to different situations. The accounts of emotions and emotional decisions offered in chapters 5 and 6 should help us to understand the neuropsychological origins of moral judgments. Such understanding is not sufficient by itself to establish a moral theory, but can provide some of the empirical theory and evidence with which we should expect a moral theory to cohere.

Contemporary ethical theory has largely abandoned the idea of conscience but makes much of the similar idea of moral intuition. People have moral intuitions that some things are right and others wrong. On the theological view, these feelings might be God talking to you via your conscience. If you believe that such intuitions derive instead from convictions based on a priori truths, then you should still be inclined to take them very seriously. On the other hand, the skeptical, relativist view would respond that moral intuitions are just arbitrary expressions of your past experiences, with no import at all for what is objectively right or wrong. Many philosophers have adopted a view that we can develop our ethical theories using an ongoing process of adjusting our theories and intuitions with respect to each other, aiming to achieve a good balance that John Rawls called *reflective equilibrium*. However, a closer look at the neuropsychology of moral intuitions will show the implausibility of reflective equilibrium views as well as theological, a priori, and relativist ones.

Moral intuitions are instances of emotional consciousness as described in chapter 5. They are obviously conscious, as people are always aware of their feelings that something is right or wrong. There can be unconscious emotions, as when someone is behaving in a highly angry way while refusing to recognize the feeling of anger, but I have never heard of an unconscious moral intuition. Indeed, the terms "conscious" and "conscience" have the same Latin root.

But are moral intuitions always emotional? Many of them clearly are, as we witness in the intensity of debates about such issues as abortion, but perhaps some people are capable of making completely dispassionate moral judgments. I do not want to make the strong claim that emotions are *essential* to moral judgments, because essences are necessary properties and I have already rejected, in chapter 2, any idea of necessary truths. Nevertheless, introspection and observation of other people support the claim that moral intuitions are generally emotional reactions. Hence it is reasonable to conclude that moral intuitions are one kind of emotional consciousness.

Then the argument that emotional consciousness is a brain process of the sort sketched in the EMOCON model has a major consequence. Moral intuitions are brain processes that combine cognitive appraisals with bodily perceptions through neural mechanisms of parallel constraint satisfaction. Intuitions do not have to be mysterious, impenetrable, black boxes. They are just brain processes like all the many other kinds of judgments that people make. The often visceral, gut-reaction character of moral intuitions is explained by the bodily perception aspect of emotional consciousness. It really is your gut that is telling you what to do, along with your heart, lungs, and other parts of your body whose states are reported to brain areas such as the insula and the amygdala.

Your gut and other bodily reactions are not all there is to emotional consciousness, which also requires cognitive appraisal of your situation. For moral judgments, the situation you are appraising is not just your individual, personal one but usually involves other people also. Because we have no direct access to all the neural processes involved in bodily perception, cognitive appraisal, and their interaction, moral intuitions seem ineffable. But neuroscience is beginning to explain their origins.

The hypothesis that moral intuitions arise from the neuropsychological mechanisms of emotional consciousness explains several important aspects of ethical thinking. First, it shows how conscience can be both emotional and cognitive, combining a physical gut reaction with a judgment about something in the world. When people react with revulsion to descriptions of torture, there is often both a physiological response akin to disgust and a cognitive representation of the acts such as visualization of people being tortured. The bodily perception component of the EMOCON model of emotional consciousness explains why moral intuitions usually involve a visceral reaction. But the model also shows how such intuitions have substantial cognitive content as well, both in respect to the acts that they represent and in respect to appraisal concerning goals. Purely somatic or purely cognitive theories of emotion would not be able to capture the dual aspect of ethical thinking.

Second, understanding moral intuitions as neural processes of emotional consciousness can start to explain why there is both much agreement and much disagreement about what is right and wrong. Agreement is explained in part by the fact that almost all people share the same neurological structures described in the EMOCON model, including areas such as the amygdala and the insula needed for bodily perceptions and structures such as the prefrontal cortex and the dopamine system needed for cognitive appraisal. Hence there is evidence that the underlying mechanisms for moral intuitions are nearly universal. Moreover, people often share cognitive appraisals of the ethical significance of situations because they have similar goals. Most people care about the survival and well-being of themselves and others, so their cognitive appraisals of many practices can be similar. For example, most people approve of helping those who are suffering because they have emotional goals that help to make them act in compassionate ways. Hence the existence of substantial amounts of moral agreement can be explained by the similarities of people with respect to physiology and social goals.

But there is also considerable disagreement that needs to be explained. Some people, for example, have no qualms about torturing suspected terrorists. Psychopaths are people completely lacking in conscience and constitute approximately 1 percent of the population. They display characteristics such as superficial charm, grandiose sense of self-worth, impulsivity, and irresponsibility. The most famous examples are serial killers such as Jeffrey Dahmer, who killed and ate many people, but more intelligent psychopaths can thrive by exploiting people in less dramatic ways—for example, through financial scams.

Why some people lack the normal capability for moral intuition is just beginning to be understood at the neural level. One prominent theory is that psychopaths have amygdala damage that interferes with the kind of emotional learning one needs to acquire moral reactions to other people's experience of harm. If this account of psychopaths is correct, then the starkest kind of moral disagreement—not caring ethically about anybody or anything—has a neural explanation. This explanation fits well with my model of emotional consciousness, which includes the amygdala as an important component. Differences in moral judgments can also result from damage to other brain areas, such as the ventromedial prefrontal cortex.

Less extreme differences in moral intuitions can arise in people with intact brains because of differences in goals arising from socialization. Cognitive appraisal is affected by the existence and priority of goals, beliefs about how to accomplish goals, and other beliefs about people and the world. Chapter 6 described how goals come to be adopted and adjusted through people's life experience. People vary substantially in their cultural environments, particularly their religious upbringings; this variation leads to very different goals that can then dramatically affect their cognitive appraisals. In the torture case, people who think that by far the most important goal is national security may be cavalier about how potential terrorists are treated. But if your parents and religious teachers taught you to care deeply about the well-being of all people, then torture will violate your emotionally important goals. Different upbringings can also produce different factual beliefs—for example, concerning whether life begins at conception—leading to different judgments about the morality of abortion.

We thus have evidence that moral intuitions are instances of emotional consciousness as characterized by the EMOCON model, which shows why conscience can combine emotion and cognition and lead to both considerable moral agreement and considerable moral disagreement. I will try later to connect this view of moral intuition to general moral theories about the nature of right and wrong. First I want to use recent work in neuroscience to address a crucial question for moral reasoning: why might you be concerned with the goals and well-being of other people besides yourself? It turns out that you have special kinds of neural populations that make concern for others very natural.

Mirror Neurons

The discovery of mirror neurons has been hailed as one of the major recent breakthroughs in neuroscience, with possible implications for the explanation of many important cognitive functions, including action understanding, imitation, language, and empathy. Mirror neurons were first identified in the 1990s by Giacomo Rizzolatti and his colleagues at the University of Parma. They found that the monkey prefrontal cortex contains a particular class of neurons that discharge both when the monkey does a particular action and when it observes another individual doing a particular action. Similar classes of neurons have been found in humans, capable of mirroring not only physical actions but also pain and disgust.

When a monkey grasps an object, there are neurons in area F5 of its premotor cortex that fire. Much more surprising is the serendipitous discovery by Rizzolatti and his colleagues that the same region contains neurons that fire both when the monkey grasps an object and when it observes another monkey or a human grasping an object. There are mirror neurons in F5 for grasping both with hands and with mouths, and another area, the superior temporal sulcus, contains mirror neurons for walking, turning the head, bending the torso, and moving the arms. The observations represented by mirror neurons are visual-motor, integrating the visual and motor experiences of monkeys.

Rizzolatti argues that the mirror neuron system is the basis for both action understanding and imitation. Not only does a monkey's mirror neuron system give it a direct understanding of what another monkey is doing when it moves; it also facilitates imitating those motions that might be useful for its own goals, such as finding food. Mirror neurons can work with auditory-motor representations, as well: there are neurons in the monkey premotor cortex that discharge when the animal performs a specific action and when it hears the related sound.

The evidence for mirror neurons in monkeys comes from direct recording of single neurons, but evidence for analogous systems in humans is largely indirect, from brain scanning. Many studies show that the observation of actions done by others activates in humans a complex network formed by visual and motor areas. Evidence that a mirror system exists in humans comes from many kinds of brain experiments, including imaging and transcranial magnetic stimulation, which uses magnetic pulses to affect neural activation in the cortex. Hence observing the physical actions of others prepares people not only to understand what they are doing but also to imitate them.

In humans, mirror neurons may be relevant for how people understand emotions as well as actions. A mirror-neuron system involving visceral-motor centers may enable people to understand each other's emotions, just as one involving visual-motor centers enables people to understand each other's actions. Investigators have used fMRI brain scans to compare how people react to disgusting smells with how they react to video clips of people reacting to disgusting smells. They found that the brain's anterior insula, which is known to collect information from various visceral centers, is activated both during the emotion of disgust evoked by unpleasant odors and during the observation of facial expressions of disgust. Additional overlap was found in the anterior cingulate cortex. Hence it appears that these two cortical areas, the insula and the anterior cingulate, enable people to grasp other people's emotions of disgust. Both these areas are part of the EMOCON model.

Similarly, neuroimaging found that perception of facial expressions of pain engages cortical areas also engaged by the firsthand experience of pain, including the anterior cingulate and the insula, the same areas that had been shown to mirror disgust. Another study found that the insular cortex and the anterior cingulate cortex were activated both by the experience of pain and by the observation of a loved one in pain. Further support for the mirroring of pain is found in the studies that used transcranial magnetic stimulation to detect evidence for the presence of empathic appreciation of the sensory qualities of the pain of others.

Empathy

Empathy, where you imagine yourself in someone's situation and get some indication of their emotional state, is important in enabling us to understand other people and to make moral decisions about them. Allison Barnes and I developed an account of empathy as a kind of analogical mapping relying largely on verbal representations of someone's situation. Mirror neurons make possible a more direct kind of empathy employing visual-motor representations.

Barnes and I analyzed empathy on the basis of the cognitive theory of emotions, according to which emotions are primarily indications of the extent to which personal goals are or are not being achieved. From this perspective, empathy consists of reasoning that someone in a situation similar to one that you have dealt with is probably feeling an emotion similar to what you experienced in your situation. For example, if you want to understand a friend who seems sad because of a disappointment, you can remember a situation, such as a job rejection, where you were sad because your career goals were not accomplished. Empathy is thus analogical mapping between someone else's situation and your own.

In contrast, Tania Singer and her colleagues advocate a perception-action model of empathy, in which observation or imagination of another person in a particular emotional state automatically activates a representation of that state in the observer. Singer and her colleagues used functional magnetic resonance imaging (fMRI) to measure brain activity in volunteers who observed others receiving painful stimulation to their hands. As expected, mere observation of another's pain produced increased activation in the pain network of the observer, including the insula and the anterior cingulate. People who scored higher on standard empathy scales had higher activity in these brain areas. It thus appears that more empathic people have more active mirror neuron systems for appreciating the pain of others.

In Singer's study, the people who received painful stimulation had previously engaged in a game where some had behaved fairly and others unfairly.

Men, and to a lesser extent women, showed much less pain-related brain activation when observing those sufferers who had acted unfairly. Moreover, men but not women showed greater activation in the reward-related area of the nucleus accumbens when observing unfair people being punished. Thus men more than women took pleasure in the pain of wrongdoers.

The studies of Singer and her colleagues suggest a need to expand the largely verbal account of empathic analogical mapping provided by Barnes and me. The analogy starts with my own experience of what I felt as the result of stimulation:

> visual/tactile representation of my stimulation →
>   sensory/affective representation of my pain.

Then, when I see you stimulated similarly, the analogical result is:

> visual representation of your stimulation →
>   sensory/affective representation of my AND your pain.

This mental operation is still a sort of analogical inference, in that it involves grasping a relational similarity between two situations, but it is much more direct than the verbal sort performed by computer programs for reasoning with analogy. The arrows indicate a sequence of sensory-motor neural representations, not a verbal description. Thus my feeling your pain can sometimes be a direct reaction based on observation, not an intellectual exercise I perform in seeing systematic mappings between two people's situations and goals. The intellectual, verbal kind of empathy may still occur, but it probably depends on the visual/motor/sensory/affective neural pathways generating the emotional response that is the hallmark of empathy. I may feel your pain as the result of thinking about your situation and seeing parallels with my own experiences, but observing you in pain much more immediately gives me a sense of your pain.

Empathy as verbal analogy fits well with the cognitive aspects of the EMOCON model, whereas empathy as physical experiences fits better with the physiological aspects. We saw that a full theory of emotion should incorporate both cognitive and physiological processes, and so should an account of the full range of empathy. Mirror neuron areas help us to understand the emotions of other people because they fire when we see others expressing their emotions.

My mirror-neuron account makes it clear how even the physically direct kind of empathy differs from emotional contagion, which involves picking up an emotion from someone else without any inference. According to Hatfield, Cacioppo, and Rapson's theory of emotional contagion, one person "catches" another's emotions as follows:

1. In conversation, people tend automatically and continuously to mimic and synchronize their movements with the facial expressions, voices, postures, movements, and instrumental behavior of others.
2. Subjective emotional experiences are affected, moment to moment, by the activation and/or feedback from such mimicry.
3. Given propositions 1 and 2, people tend to "catch" others' emotions, moment to moment.

In contrast, empathy via mirror neurons requires neither mimicry nor behavioral synchronization, but only the perception of another's situation, which activates a kind of perceptual/motor schema that generates an analogous feeling.

In sum, empathy can be based on the kind of verbal analogical mapping discussed by Barnes and me; but it can more fundamentally involve direct perceptual detection of the relation between someone's situation and your own via your mirror neurons. Either way, the phrase "I feel your pain" is not just a touchy-feely cliché but rather an expression of genuine appreciation of the experiences of others. Moreover, feeling the pain of others can contribute enormously to caring about them and being motivated to act ethically in general. Empathy is a major factor in the moral development of children.

Moral Motivation

Why be moral? This question is fundamental for ethics, because even if people can figure out what are the right things to do, we can still ask why they would in fact do those things. The problem of moral motivation—what makes people do what is right—has two classes of answers, rationalist and sentimentalist. The traditional philosophical responses to the problem have been rationalist: we should be moral because it would be irrational to do otherwise. The rationality of morality might derive from a priori truths about what is right, or from arguments that it is rational for people to agree with others to be moral. The philosopher Sean Nichols argues that a major problem for rationalism is that psychopaths, with no impediments in abstract reasoning, nevertheless see nothing wrong in harming other people.

Nichols argues convincingly that what is wrong with psychopaths is not their reasoning but their emotions. I mentioned earlier in this chapter the theory that psychopathy, whose symptoms include antisocial behavior, lack of guilt, and poverty of emotions, is the result of impairments to emotional learning that derive from disrupted functioning of the amygdala.

According to Nichols, an adequate account of ethical thinking must explain how emotion plays a role in linking moral judgment to motivation, while also allowing a place for reason in moral judgment. His explanation of ethical norms is cultural and historical: "Norms are more likely to be preserved in the culture if the norms resonate with our affective systems by prohibiting actions that are likely to elicit negative affect." Norms that prohibit harm to others are virtually ubiquitous across cultures because of this "affective resonance." The adoption of norms enables us to reason about what is right and wrong, but these norms have an emotional underpinning that intrinsically provides a connection between morality and action: people are moral because of their emotional commitment to normative rules.

What is missing from Nichols's otherwise plausible account is an explanation of *why* people have such a basic emotional reaction to harm to others. There is no mystery concerning why you do not want harm to yourself, because experiences such as pain and fear are intrinsically negative. Appreciating harm to others might be achieved by abstract analogical reasoning, but there is no guarantee that such reasoning will be motivating: I may understand that you experience pain and fear, but why should I care? What makes emotional moral learning work?

As my discussion of empathy indicated, mirror neurons provide the plausible missing link between personal experience and the experience of others. People not only observe the pain and disgust of others; they experience their own versions of that pain and disgust, as shown by the mirroring activity in cortical regions such as the insula and the anterior cingulate. Normal children do not need to be taught moral rules as abstract theological principles ("Thou shalt not kill!") or rational ones ("Act only in ways that could become universal"). Normal children do not need to reason about why harm is bad for other people; they can actually feel that harm is bad. Thus mirror neurons provide motivation not to harm others by virtue of direct understanding of what it is for another to be harmed.

It would be elegant if there were evidence that psychopaths have deficiencies in the functioning of their mirror neurons, but the relevant experiments have not yet been done. It is possible that psychopaths' deficits in emotional learning that involve disrupted functioning of the amygdala are partly due to mirror neuron malfunctioning. Children who are incapable, for genetic or environmental reasons, of feeling the pain of others will not be able to become motivated to follow rules that direct them not to harm other people. Blair and his colleagues discuss moral socialization in terms of aversive conditioning, as when caregivers punish children for their wrongdoings. They claim that the sadness, fearfulness, and distress of a victim act as a stimulus to instrumental learning not to produce harm. The involvement of mirror neurons shows why instrumental learning can be especially effective when people can fully appreciate what is negative about their behavior.

I have argued that mirror neural mechanisms contribute to solution of the philosophical problem of moral motivation by showing how biologically normal people naturally have at least some understanding of and concern about harm to other people. Feeling the pain of others is not the whole story of moral motivation, for there are many cognitive and social additions in the form of rules and expectations that can be built on top of neural mirroring. The motivating reason to be moral is not just that morality is rational, but rather that feeling the pain of others is biologically part of being human. For ethics, the capacity to care about others is at least as important as the ability to reason about them.

Caring has a neural basis, in that mirror neurons enable brains to get a kind of direct comprehension of the pain and emotions of others. Mirror neurons are neither necessary nor sufficient for ethical evaluations, but they help enormously to enable children and even adults to appreciate the experiences of others. Hence they provide a causal basis for empathy and moral motivation, encouraging us to feel and care about the pain of others and to act so as to alleviate it. The capacity for such caring is built into our neural circuitry, but needs to be fostered by moral education that can lead us to care more about people beyond our immediate circles of acquaintance.

Mirror neurons and emotional contagion get us started on moral appreciation of the interests of others, but much socialization is required to improve it. We need moral education to reinforce resistance to the psychopathic suggestion that self-interest is the highest good.

Hence empathy enhanced by mirror neurons is an important part of moral thinking, but far from the whole story. When you try to judge whether torturing terrorists can ever be ethical, you can be influenced by the empathy that you may feel for the victims of both torture and terror, but you need much more guidance to resolve moral dilemmas involving the pain and suffering of more than one person. I don't think that evidence about the brain is by itself sufficient to direct us to any one ethical theory that we ought to adopt, but I will try to show that such evidence puts some constraints on the evaluation of ethical theories.

Ethical Theory

An ethical theory is an attempt to answer generally the question of what makes actions right or wrong. For most people today, the answer to this question is religious. If you are Christian or Muslim, for example, you probably believe that the rightness and wrongness of actions is determined by the commandments of God as laid down in the Bible or Koran. But making morality dependent on religion has all the problems that chapter 2 identified about faith. First, which religion should you look to for moral guidance? Islam, Hinduism, Judaism, and the many variants of Christianity offer different moral prescriptions, and you ought to have some reason rather than the accident of your birth for following a particular moral code. Second, even if you buy into a particular religion, how do you know that the divine prescriptions of that religion are moral? For example, in the Old Testament, God tells Abraham to sacrifice his son Isaac, an extraordinarily cruel request that causes Abraham much anguish. Third, even if you were right in adopting a particular religion, there are often uncertainties about what to do in particular situations because of the difficulties of applying fairly coarse rules. A commandment accepted by many religions is that you should not murder, but that does not seem to help settle the dilemma of whether to torture a terrorist.

Accordingly, philosophers since Socrates have looked for nontheologi-cal answers to the question of what makes actions right or wrong. One of the most influential approaches is to try to find moral principles that can be justified as true a priori, as was done by the eighteenth-century Ger-man philosopher Immanuel Kant. Unfortunately, attempts to find necessary truths in ethics have been no more successful than the attempts to find necessary truths about reality that I criticized in chapter 2. If there were any a priori, necessary truths about right and wrong, you would think that many centuries of philosophical reflection would have identified some. The Kantian view is that there are general principles, establishing rights and duties that determine right and wrong. For example, one could argue that torture is wrong because it violates a fundamental human right, so that everyone has a duty not to torture. But debates continue to rage both about the acceptability of general moral principles and about their application to particular cases.

We need a moral theory that fits better with the empirical findings de-scribed earlier, including the following:

1. people have vital biological and psychological needs without whose satisfaction they are harmed;
2. moral intuitions are the result of neural processes that combine cognitive appraisal and bodily perception; and
3. mirror neurons are a major source of empathic appreciation of harm done to others, motivating people to care about others.

I will now show how these findings fit much better with consequentialist ethics than with theological, Kantian, and relativist approaches.

Consequentialism is the philosophical view that whether an act is right or wrong depends only on the effects it has on all people concerned. There are many philosophical varieties of consequentialism, not all of them fully consistent with what I have said about the brain. The classic version of consequentialism was hedonistic utilitarianism, defended by Jeremy Ben-tham and John Stuart Mill. They said that an action is right if it produces the greatest good for the greatest number of people, where good is equated with pleasure and the avoidance of pain. At first glance, it might seem that my account of emotional consciousness could fit with hedonism, the view that good is pleasure, and with the idea that good can be measured by a single metric, utility. After all, my theory of emotions attributed to every emotional experience a positive or negative valence, which sounds a lot like utility. One might even try to associate pleasure and pain with particular brain areas because of the high correlations between activity in the nucleus accumbens and pleasurable experiences, and the correlations of negative emotions with brain areas such as the amygdala and the insula. However, the EMOCON model fits better with a version of consequentialism in which there are other goods besides pleasure and the avoidance of pain.

Most notably, the discussion of the neural representation of goals in chapter 6 did *not* attempt to reduce goals to the single one of obtaining pleasure and avoiding pain. People operate with a multiplicity of goals, many of the most important of them concerned with love, work, and play. There is nothing in the brain suggesting that all goals can be reduced to a "common currency." I argued that happiness is not in itself a source of meaning, and that there are pursuits such as raising children that are valuable independent of how well they generate happiness. I have frequently mentioned the dopamine system as providing a mechanism for positive evaluation, but this system is only part of how the brain estimates the value of different situations. The nucleus accumbens is important, but so are the orbitofrontal cortex, the anterior cingulate, and other brain areas. In addition to dopamine, other neurotransmitters such as serotonin undoubtedly contribute to neural processes of goal evaluation. Hence instead of trying to reduce the good to a single goal, pleasure, we can allow that many goals can be relevant to assessing the good. This view is called *pluralistic* consequentialism, because it allows a variety of goals whose accomplishment can constitute good consequences. The argument in chapter 7 that people aim for multiple goals and not just happiness suggests that pluralistic consequentialism is more plausible than hedonistic utilitarianism.

Adopting a pluralistic version of consequentialism provides ways around some of the most damaging objections that have been made to utilitarianism. One standard objection is that consequentialism can be used to justify horribly unfair actions. For example, it might seem that torture could easily be justified whenever the pain and suffering produced in one individual could be expected to be less than the pain and suffering of other people. If a terrorist is probably involved in a conspiracy that would kill dozens of people, then torturing him would save many lives at the cost of at most one.

It would therefore seem that consequentialism could justify the violation of human rights in many instances, showing the need for a Kantian theory of rights as an alternative or at least as a supplement to consequentialism. Some acts seem to be wrong even if they do produce the overall greatest good for the greatest number of people. An extreme example would be the immorality of torturing an innocent on television just because it would provide enjoyable entertainment for millions of sadistic watchers.

The best way to deal with this objection is not to abandon consequentialism but to modify it to include the adoption of some general principles or rules. Many religious traditions, going back to the ancient Greeks, have some variant of the golden rule, that you should treat others as you yourself want to be treated. This rule could be viewed as an abstract intellectual exercise, like John Rawls's proposal that when we try to establish moral principles, we should place ourselves behind a "veil of ignorance" that takes us away from our own personal situation and requires us to think of people in general. But I think that the effectiveness of the golden rule depends instead on its role in reminding us to care about other people in roughly the same way we care about ourselves. If you are asked how you would feel if you were treated in a cruel way that you are considering for someone else, then you will be spurred to imagine yourself in the situation of the other. Such imagination may then trigger empathy via mirror neurons, in which you feel some approximation to what the other people would feel as the result of mean treatment. Thus the golden rule is a tool for empathy and caring, not for intellectual exercises such as the veil of ignorance or Kant's categorical imperative, which tells you to act in ways that you can will to be universal. The natural psychological progression is from mirror neuron activity to empathy to emotional and intellectual appreciation of the needs of others.

But what aspects of others should we care about? The hedonistic utilitarian view says that we should be concerned only with happiness construed as pleasure and the avoidance of pain, which makes no distinction between wants and needs. A broader view says that ethical decisions should take into account human rights based on people's vital interests.

The philosopher Brian Orend uses Wiggins's conception of needs to develop a rich and plausible account of human rights. According to Orend, there are five items that are vital interests, required for minimal functioning as a person:

1. personal security providing reliable protection from violence;
2. material subsistence, with secure access to resources such as food and shelter required for biological needs;
3. elemental equality, being regarded as initially equal in status to other agents;
4. personal freedom from interference with life choices; and
5. recognition as a worthy member of the human community.

Lacking any of these five items damages one's ability to live a minimally good life. Orend arrives at the core principle that people have rights not to have grievous harm inflicted on them in connection with their vital needs.

The items that Orend identifies are all consonant with the golden rule. You know that you do not want to be physically threatened, starved, discriminated against, coerced, or rejected as a human being. Hence empathy should motivate you to treat others in ways that do not threaten *their* vital interests. Human rights on this view are not products of pure reason; rather, they derive from empirically based reflection on what is required to be a minimally functioning human being. Recognizing that people have human rights provides constraints on some of the less appealing implications of consequentialism, militating against diminishing the happiness of one person just to increase the happiness of a bunch of others.

Unfortunately, recognition of human rights does not provide an easy answer concerning what to do in cases where it may be necessary to violate one person's rights in order to prevent the violation of the rights of others. Hedonistic utilitarianism has a way out of this problem, telling us to calculate what produces the greatest happiness for the greatest number of people. Such calculations are very difficult to make, but even more complicated is the assessment of the extent to which different actions would violate the diverse needs of different people.

Orend's vital interests include not only personal security and material subsistence, but also more social ones involving equality, freedom, and recognition. Equality and freedom are closely tied to the psychological needs of competence and autonomy discussed in chapter 8, and recognition is one aspect of the need for relatedness. Hence there is a good fit between what Orend sees as the basis for human rights and what Deci and Ryan see as fundamental psychological needs of all people.

Another major problem with consequentialism is that it seems to demand too much of people. It expects us to consider the consequences for all people equally, which means that we should consider strangers as on a par with ourselves and with people we are close to, like family members. But very few people are capable of counting the happiness of themselves and people they love as no more important than that of people they will never meet. For this problem, we need a more detailed account of how the need for relatedness explains why close relationships are much more important than more casual friendships and associations. If people have a deeper need for relatedness based on close family relationships than for relatedness based on more casual acquaintances, then they naturally feel greater concern for how consequences affect their loved ones than for how they affect people in general. Thanks to mirror neurons and the cognitive and bodily aspects of emotional intuition, people are capable of caring about other people in general. But we cannot expect them to put aside a special concern for the well-being of their loved ones.

Hence ideas about vital needs can be used to overcome the most serious objections to consequentialism as an ethical theory by making it pluralistic, compatible with rights, and sensitive to social ties. In contrast, the problems of theological and a priori approaches to ethics are insurmountable. We can assess actions as right or wrong according to how well they satisfy human needs, especially vital needs such as material subsistence, but also social and psychological needs such as relatedness and autonomy. Actions that violate needs cause harm to people, whom we can care about not only for intellectual reasons but also because our mirror neurons give us a direct empathic sense of what happens when people suffer. Moral intuitions, like emotional consciousness in general, involve both cognitive appraisal and bodily perception. Although they cannot be taken as indicators of a priori truths or used as any sort of direct evidence of moral reality, they can nevertheless be highly informative in particular situations about what ought to be done. Their informativeness depends on the extent to which the cognitive appraisals and bodily perceptions that generate them are based on broad experience of the positive and negative consequences of previous actions. Thus needs-based consequentialism is the most plausible ethical theory currently available, and opens the possibility that judgments about right and wrong might be objective.

Moral Objectivity

Because of the difficulty of establishing general moral principles to which everyone will agree, it is sometimes tempting to abandon the idea of moral objectivity. The philosopher Jesse Prinz defends moral relativism, the view that moral judgments are just reflections of cultural values that vary from one society to another. He describes the large divergence of moral views across individuals and cultures on issues such as monogamy, homosexuality, and cannibalism, practiced by many peoples. He thinks that there is nothing more to the rightness or wrongness of an action than emotional attitudes of approval or disapproval.

Most of the traditional routes to moral objectivity do not work. I have already criticized the religious route based on faith and the a priori route based on pure reason. Another possibility is that all humans are born with innate ethical principles that constitute a moral universal grammar. There are several problems with this suggestion. First, there is little evidence that there are any ethical principles that are culturally universal. It is not hard to identify cultures whose practices include murder, cannibalism, infanticide, and incest, so any attempt to root our favorite ethical principles in universal properties of mind seems implausible. Second, if particular ethical principles are innate, it should be possible to identify specific brain areas for moral reasoning where the principles are stored and processed, akin to the dedicated areas in the brain for vision. But the emotional consciousness model and the rapidly increasing studies involving brain scans of moral reasoning suggest that many interacting brain areas are involved in moral reasoning, not some localized module.

Third, even if there are principles that are culturally universal and biologically based, they might not be ethically acceptable. For example, suppose people had an innate xenophobic principle derived from our evolutionary history that prescribed the inferior treatment of members of groups other than our own. This principle would be innate but wrong, just as I argued in chapter 2 that innate beliefs about the world such as Euclidean geometry can be wrong. Like scientific knowledge, moral judgments should be assumed to be fallible and subject to reevaluation based on accumulating evidence. Hence I see no reason to believe that there is a moral universal grammar that might provide some basis for moral objectivity.

Many contemporary philosophers look to the method of reflective equilibrium as providing a route to objectivity. This method consists of reflectively adjusting our moral intuitions and moral principles until equilibrium is reached in the form of a rich set of intuitions and principles that fit well with each other. There are two major problems with reflective equilibrium as a source of moral objectivity.

The first problem is the highly subjective nature of moral intuitions as revealed by the emotional consciousness account given above. We have little idea why we have the particular emotional reactions that we do to different situations, because the brain processes described in the EMOCON model are not accessible to consciousness. Your initial moral intuitions may be based on rich and valuable personal experiences of what benefits people's lives, but they may also be based on the unsubstantiated moral prejudices of teachers and caregivers. Many contemporary ethicists like to treat moral intuitions as evidence, akin to experimental data that are to be explained by theories. But the method described in chapter of 2 of evaluating theories on the basis of data relied on the general robustness of the results of observation and experience. Moral intuitions have no similar robustness and therefore should not be treated as data. There is thus no reason why they should be allowed as input to the process of reflective equilibrium, even if the consideration of principles can be expected to lead to the revision of intuitions.

Second, the method of reflective equilibrium is flawed because it is often much too easy to reach equilibrium without achieving anything like objectivity. Rawls got the equilibrium idea by analogy with what he thought goes on in logic, where logical principles are supposedly developed that fit with evolving intuitions about what kinds of inference are legitimate. On this view, logical principles such as modus ponens (if p then q; p, therefore q) and statistical inference are not true a priori but instead are arrived at through a process of mutual adjustment with logical intuitions. The problem, however, is that people can settle into equilibrium states with a good fit of intuitions and principles that nevertheless are not very logical. Many people subscribe to the gambler's fallacy—for example, if a tossed coin has turned up heads many times in a row, then tails is due to turn up. In ethics, it has been historically easy for people to become highly content with principles such as that what the Bible says about right and wrong is true.

Hence reflective equilibrium provides at best a weak method of pursuing moral objectivity, not any kind of defense of it.

We saw in chapter 4 that evidence based on observation and experiment provides a way of making the coherence of theory and data more than a purely internal matter. We need a similar way to break out of the circle of intuitions and principles that the method of reflective equilibrium generates. Vital needs provide the most attractive direction, because the question of what we need to function minimally and maximally as human beings is at least partly empirical. Biology tells us that people cannot live without food and water. For a broader account of successful functioning as a human being, we need to look to other empirical sources such as psychology, anthropology, and sociology.

If there are objective vital needs that provide the basis for human rights across cultures, then we have grounds for rejecting Prinz's leap from descriptive relativism (morals vary across cultures) to normative relativism (morals are subjective). Consider, for example, cannibalism, formerly common in many cultures. It is easy to see that killing people in order to eat them violates the vital needs of the victims, although eating people dead of natural causes would be a different matter. Equally obviously, homosexuality does not violate any human rights in Orend's sense, and discrimination against it is a threat to elementary equality and personal freedom, as well as to the psychological need for autonomy. A more difficult case is polygamy, in hypothetical cases where breaking the usual Western one-to-one correspondence between husbands and wives does not damage the vital interests of women who are voluntarily involved. In practice, however, polygamy has usually been accompanied by violations of the rights of women with respect to equality, freedom, and recognition, and sometimes even personal security.

In sum, moral objectivity becomes possible if we look, not to theology or a priori reasoning, but to evidence drawn from biology and psychology. Needs-based consequentialism fits well with the brain-based emotional consciousness account of moral intuition and with the cultural diversity of moral behavior. The difficulty of arriving at indisputable moral principles is the result not of moral relativity, but rather of the huge complexity of determining the range and importance of human psychological needs and calculating the consequences of the available range of actions. Moral judgments are very difficult decisions, but we can still strive to use all we know about the nature of the world and human minds to make them the best we can.

Responsibility

But does it make any sense to talk of striving if moral judgments are just brain processes based on neurochemical mechanisms? What happens to the idea of moral responsibility if minds are brains and free will is an illusion? Suppose you apprehend a sadistic torturer who inflicted massive pain and damage on victims on the vaguest suspicion that they might have some useful information. On the traditional view of mind as soul, the torturer can be held responsible and punished for the sinful act of torture. But if the decision to torture was just a physical process of neurons firing in response to sensory stimuli such as instructions from the torturer's supervisor, then it might seem illegitimate to blame someone for an act that could not be controlled. The response to any evil act might be "It's not my fault—my brain made me do it." The Brain Revolution would have the extreme consequence that the idea of moral responsibility would have to be abandoned along with immortality and free will, a cost that many people would find unacceptable.

The distinguished neuroscientist Michael Gazzaniga accepts the view that decisions and actions are determined by brain processes, but argues that we can hold on to the idea of responsibility as a property of persons, not brains. He maintains that responsibility is a human construct that exists only in the social world, not a property of brains. Proponents of religious concepts of morality would reply that this is much too weak a notion of responsibility to be morally interesting, hardly better than abandoning the concept altogether.

The behaviorist psychologist B. F. Skinner wrote a book called *Beyond Freedom and Dignity* that did completely reject the traditional notion of moral responsibility. If what you do is just the result of past reinforcement learning that yields predictable patterns of responses to stimuli, then the notion of responsibility does seem to be pointless. There would be no more reason to hold someone responsible for torturing than there would be for holding a rat responsible for chewing on its cage. But we saw in chapter 6 that human decision making is far more complex than such stimulus-response pairings could allow. A decision is the result of an inference to the best plan achieved through the emotional evaluation of actions with respect to multiple goals. Then holding someone responsible for acting immorally does have a point: we want to try to ensure that future decisions, by the person blamed as well as by other people, are made on the basis of goals that include the interests and needs of all those concerned. For people contemplating committing torture, we want their decisions and moral judgments to take into account the pain and suffering of their potential victims. Holding people responsible for their actions is legitimately intended to have the socially beneficial result of making them behave better, by encouraging them to take into account social goals that include caring for other people, not harming them, and avoiding disapproval. It is morally legitimate to hold people morally responsible for their actions because doing so has good social consequences. Punishing people is justified to the extent that it prevents them or others from acting badly. Putting criminals in jail unfortunately limits their satisfaction of needs for autonomy and relatedness, but should serve to keep them from harming others.

Hence the Brain Revolution does not require abandoning the idea of moral responsibility, but it does change it substantially. On the traditional, dualist view, a person is a mind that is a soul, and actions are the result of free choices not fully determined by physical causes. People who make bad choices of their own free will can be held responsible for them and *deserve* to be punished. But on the view I have been defending, actions are the result of decisions that are physical brain processes, so the point of responsibility and punishment cannot be the sinful nature of what a person has done. Rather, holding people responsible for their actions and punishing them are justified if they have the good social consequences of reducing harm to people in the future. As Gazzaniga suggests, we should think of a person as a social being, understood in terms of relationships to other persons, not just as a brain or body. If persons are conceived as social and the point of holding them responsible is social improvement, then the idea of moral responsibility survives.

The neuropsychologists Joshua Greene and Jonathan Cohen reach similar conclusions about the relevance of neuroscience to legal issues about punishment. They argue that neuroscience shows that free will is an illusion, and requires abandonment of the traditional justification of legal punishment as retribution for wrong acts. If people are not souls freely choosing their immoral acts, we cannot say that they really deserve to be punished as the result of absolutely free will. However, neuroscience does not undermine the alternative consequentialist justification of punishment as needed for social good, both to serve as a deterrent against harmful acts and to remove criminals from society so that they cannot commit additional offenses. I argued above that consequentialism is consistent with a needs-based view of human rights that would circumvent the standard objection that consequences can be used to justify arbitrary and unjust punishments.

At first glance, it might seem that my rejection of free will is incompatible with the need for autonomy. How can people feel that their activities are self-chosen if their decisions are just neural activity? The answer requires replacing the traditional concept of the self, an immortal soul free of physical constraints, with a concept informed by neuroscience. Then the self can be viewed as a complex neural system encompassing representational structures and processing capacities that differentiate between (a) actions that are generated by internal decision making based on intrinsic interests and (b) actions that are externally coerced or motivated. Moreover, in keeping with the multilevel systems view defended in chapter 5, the self can also be understood as a social and psychological system. Love, work, and play are usually parts of social systems, not just neural ones. Hence the need for autonomy is fully compatible with the rejection of free will and the adoption of social responsibility. A fully responsible self should be able to make autonomous inferences to the best moral plan that take into account both personal goals and the interests of other people.

Conclusion

The revolution that recognizes minds as brains requires us to abandon familiar and valued concepts such as immortality and free will. But ethical ideas about right, wrong, and moral responsibility can survive in altered forms. We can even maintain the old idea of conscience, as long as it is understood as a brain process rather than as a communication from God to soul. Judgments about right and wrong are instances of emotional consciousness, produced by interactions among multiple brain areas that combine cognitive appraisal with bodily perception. Such moral intuitions might appear to us as direct perceptions of right and wrong, but they are actually very complex brain processes arising from past experiences, both personal and educational. Moral intuitions by themselves are not evidence that something is right or wrong, and must be evaluated as to whether they reflect objective moral concerns or merely previous biased experience or coercive and arbitrary inculcation by bogus moral authorities. The idea of sin as a free act against a divine being must be abandoned as based on false assumptions about souls and gods. But social emotions such as guilt and shame and the consonant idea of moral responsibility can still be appropriate, if they contribute to the vital needs of all those concerned. Consideration of vital psychological needs such as competence, relatedness, and autonomy provides an explanation and justification for the proposition that the meaning of life is love, work, and play.

According to neural naturalism, moral objectivity does not rest on theological prescriptions, a priori truths, moral universal grammar, or reflective equilibrium. The basis for morality is that people have objective vital needs without which they would be harmed in their ability to function as human beings. Actions have consequences that affect the needs of people; an action is right to the extent that it furthers those needs, and wrong to the extent that it damages them. Moral judgments are inherently emotional in that we feel approval toward what we take to be right and disapproval toward what we take to be wrong. Like emotional experience in general, moral judgments have an element of cognitive appraisal that should include assessment of the consequences of an action for the needs of the people involved. The assessment is not just a cold calculation of costs and benefits, but should include an element of caring about those who are affected. Such caring enlists the physiological aspects of emotions and the functioning of mirror neurons.

Neuroscience is just beginning to use brain scans and other technologies to acquire evidence concerning how brains make ethical judgments: the relevant research dates back only to 2000. A fuller account of ethical brains will have to take into account such fascinating findings as these:

- Patients with damage to the prefrontal cortex can become flagrantly immoral.
- Brain scans of people given moral dilemmas to solve reveal different kinds of neural activity that correspond to different moral

intuitions depending on whether they engage in personal or impersonal judgments.

- People can be induced to trust others by nasal sprays of the hormone oxytocin, which affects the brain to increase feelings of affiliation.

This chapter has not attempted to give a full theory of moral psychology, but has pointed to some of the key factors such as mirror neurons and emotional consciousness that are relevant to an understanding of the nature of ethical judgments in the brain.

This understanding does not leap across the fact/value barrier by any deductive inference, but rather assembles many kinds of psychological, neurological, and anthropological evidence that cohere or fail to cohere with philosophical theories about right and wrong. You cannot derive an *ought* from an *is*, but you can appreciate that some proposed *ought*s fit much better than do others with what we know about minds, brains, and cultures. Consequentialism about vital needs is coherent with biological and psychological knowledge, and therefore provides a better approach to normative ethics than do alternatives such as theological and Kantian ethics. Indeed, moral objectivity is possible because there are psychological, neurological, and social facts about what humans need to function and thrive. For moral progress, we need to appreciate the needs of other people intellectually and also to care about them emotionally. Our brains' ability to discern right from wrong is consonant with their ability to know reality, feel emotions, make decisions, and pursue meaningful lives. In the concluding chapter, I will summarize how these abilities fit together, and will suggest answers to other questions, such as what kind of government people need, and why there is something and not nothing.

making sense of it all

Connections Made

In one of my favorite jokes, a man goes into a movie theater and is surprised to see a woman enter with a dog. When the movie starts, the dog watches it, laughing at the funny parts, crying at the sad parts, and bouncing up and down at the exciting ending. When the movie finishes, the man chases after the woman and says: "Excuse me, I was amazed that your dog actually seemed to be enjoying the movie." The woman responds: "I was surprised too—he hated the book." Like most jokes, this one is funny because it sets up one coherent set of expectations and then violates them in another coherent direction. Jokes make sense in surprising ways.

Scientific and philosophical explanations are not generally funny, but they also achieve coherence in surprising ways. I have tried to pursue an integrated approach to what I take to be the four most important philosophical problems: What is reality? How do we know it? Why is life worth living? What is right and wrong? Coherence comes in part from a commonality of method, relying on evidence drawn from observations and scientific experiments rather than from religious faith, a priori arguments, or thought experiments. I have tried to keep in mind the Jewish proverb "For example is not proof." Anecdotes are at best a weak form of evidence, and the made-up thought experiments favored by many philosophers are not evidence at all.

I have used more systematic forms of evidence to argue for two main claims about reality, that minds are physical systems constituted by brains interacting with bodies and the world, and that the world exists independently of anyone's mind. We know reality not just by collecting the results of observation and experiment, but also by forming theories that we can evaluate to see whether they are part of the best explanation of the full range of available evidence. Scientific theories such as Newtonian mechanics, electromagnetism, and the germ theory of disease have been hugely successful in enabling humans to interact with the world, providing strong indication that the method of evidence-based inference is far more effective than methods based on faith or intuition.

Similarly, scientifically collected evidence can aid us in developing the kinds of normative theories we need to answer questions about ethics and the meaning of life. There is no simple leap possible from "this is how things are" to "this is how things should be," but evidence is nevertheless highly relevant to questions of value. Such relevance is most easily seen in instrumental reasoning, where something is assigned value because it is a way of achieving something else already identified as valuable. For example, if we value truth, and scientific method is a good road to truth, then scientific method can also be valued. The main problem is how we manage rationally to assign value to our top-level goals, such as truth and explanation. I have ruled out any transcendent, a priori arguments for such goals, so it might seem that one must be either arbitrary or circular in defending them.

I have tried to show that coherence of goals with each other and with various kinds of evidence provides a middle way between arbitrariness and circularity. Just as scientific theories and experiments are justified because of their fit with each other, similarly we can look for general descriptive and normative accounts that are justified because of their mutual coherence. The specter of circularity is avoided through the relative objectivity of evidence collected through the senses, which we know to be generally reliable because of past experience and growing scientific understanding of the underlying physical mechanisms by which vision, touch, hearing, and smell interact with the physical world. Sciences such as biology and psychology enable us to identify the needs of human beings, which are the factors that enable us to operate as persons in our complex physical and social worlds. Truth and explanation are such factors, because we cannot operate as human beings without some reliable understanding of how the world works around us. Other objective needs include material subsistence, autonomy, and social relatedness.

The easily recognized importance of such factors enables us to reject nihilism about the meaning of life as well as the minimalist pursuit of slacker serenity. I have tried to show how it is possible to be naturalistically normative about knowledge (chapters 2 and 4), the meaning of life (chapters 7 and 8), and questions of right and wrong (chapter 9). Figure 10.1 provides

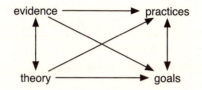

10.1 How descriptive information can be
relevant to normative conclusions.
Arrows indicate inferential relevance.

a schematic summary of the use of scientific evidence and theories to inform
deliberation about the justification of practices through their contributions
to appropriate goals. We can use evidence to help us select theories and to
identify practices and goals, at the same time that evidence is influenced by
theories, and practices and goals are influencing each other.

The kind of parallel process presented in figure 10.1 can be hard to
grasp, so here is a more linear depiction of how descriptive evidence can
help to establish prescriptive norms. I will call this sequence the *normative
procedure*.

1. Identify a domain of practices, such as scientific inference (chapter 2) or ethical reasoning (chapter 9).
2. Identify candidate norms for these practices, such as inference to
   the best explanation (chapter 2) or consequentialism (chapter 9).
3. Identify the appropriate goals of the practices in the given domain,
   such as truth (chapter 4) and vital needs (chapter 8).
4. Evaluate the extent to which different practices accomplish the relevant goals.
5. Adopt as domain norms those practices that best accomplish the
   relevant goals.

Step 3 is the trickiest, because it requires complex consideration of relevant goals, taking into account evidence, theory, and practices, as shown
in figure 10.1. To establish goals for inference about what to believe and do,
we can ask such questions as the following. What do people aim for? Why
do they have those aims? Are the aims coherent with other goals? Step 4

is also difficult, because it requires evidence about what practices causally produce goal satisfaction, not just correlations between practices and goals. Nevertheless, these steps provide a way of using descriptive evidence to address normative questions, as I will illustrate later in this chapter with respect to the nature of government.

I certainly don't pretend in this short book to have made sense of everything, but I have tried to identify some connections among plausible answers to the most serious philosophical problems. Questions about how to pursue knowledge and how to pursue morality require answers that are both descriptive and normative. We want to know both how we do form beliefs and how we ought to form beliefs, just as we want to know both how people behave and how they ought to behave. In both epistemology and ethics, however, the descriptive and normative questions can be tied together by considerations of past experience and coherence of different kinds of practice with different kinds of goals, such as the most fundamental needs and interests. Such links between descriptive and normative conclusions fit well with the naturalistic view of reality that minds are a complex, brain-based part of an entirely physical universe.

The same combination of empirical, theoretical, and normative considerations has served to generate answers to the question of why life is worth living. Goals concerning love, work, and play are connected to vital needs of human beings that can be identified through empirical investigation. This research is often part of the social sciences, using empirical techniques established in psychology, economics, and sociology. But insights are increasingly streaming from the investigation of the biological mechanisms operating in human brains. We know more and more about how activities are marked as rewarding through interactions of brain areas involved in cognition and emotion, such as the prefrontal cortex, the amygdala, and the nucleus accumbens. These investigations enable us not only to use the social sciences to identify *that* love, work, and play matter to people, but also to use neuroscience to learn *how* they matter to people through brain functioning. We thus get an understanding of how the goals related to these realms of life are tied to the deep objective interests of human beings.

I have, however, steered clear of many strong claims that have been made in recent years about the direct relevance of evolutionary biology. I have no doubt that the human brain evolved by natural selection, but available evidence does not particularly well support claims commonly made by proponents of evolutionary psychology that the brain is a collection of special-purpose innate modules such as ones for language and social behavior. Given the current lack of evidence about just how brains evolved, it is at least as plausible that the major effect of natural selection has been to allow the development of powerful methods of individual and social learning. The brain clearly has a built-in architecture of areas such as the dopamine-based reward system, but it functions more in the direction of flexible learning strategies than in the direction of fixed modules. The Brain Revolution does not condemn us to using patterns of thinking fixed in the Stone Age by biological wiring.

Rather, cultural developments such as literacy, mathematics, argument, and scientific experiments have opened rich possibilities for developing human societies in ways that can immensely enrich the lives of people. I argued in chapter 5 for a multilevel approach to explaining the mind that is neither reductionist nor antireductionist. We should draw on all the insights about mental processes that the Brain Revolution is providing, while acknowledging the continuing relevance of psychological and social explanations to understanding how things are and how they can be improved.

Wisdom Gained

Many readers will unavoidably be disturbed by my evidence-based arguments for the conclusions that minds are brains, that reality is independent of our thinking of it, and that the meaning of life and morality is to be sought in human biology and psychology rather than in some transcendent realm. Historically, people have found it hard enough to undergo the cognitive change required to reorganize our conceptual systems to think that humans are just another kind of animal and that the earth is just another planet among billions of solar systems and galaxies. Even more psychologically difficult is the emotional conceptual change that requires abandoning feelings about the cosmic centrality of human existence, along with naturally valued ideas about immortality, free will, and a caring God. The cognitive conceptual change is justified by the overwhelming evidence for scientific theories such as the theory of evolution by natural selection and the big bang theory of the universe. These theories also put heavy pressure in the direction of emotional conceptual change, because they challenge the assumptions needed for religion-based views about souls.

But the emotional conceptual changes accompanying the replacement of faith by evidence do not have to be entirely negative, nor need they generate an existential crisis of deep despair. Hope is to be sought not in eternal deliverance or divine oversight, but in the much more mundane and realistically achievable pursuit of goals connected with love, work, and play. Secular lives do not have to be empty or immoral, but can have the same primary pursuits as those of religious people, who also have families, jobs, and entertainment. Moreover, people can avoid the tedium of church services and the terrifying threat of eternal punishment. The fact that the universe doesn't care about you should not be horribly distressing as long as there are people who do. If you can develop confidence that moderately successful pursuit of love, work, and play will satisfy your vital needs for relatedness, competence, and autonomy, then you shouldn't need the religious belief that God is looking out for you or the spiritual belief that everything happens for a reason. Recognizing that minds are brains is unavoidably a conceptual revolution, but it does not have to be a complete emotional revolution, because the values that drive most of people's activities in everyday life can be retained.

In chapter 1, I characterized wisdom as knowledge about what matters, why it matters, and how to achieve it. I hope you agree that evidence-based answers to questions about the nature of reality, knowledge, morality, and meaning constitute important kinds of knowledge that matter. In particular, I have tried to show that the realms that do and should matter most in people's everyday lives are love, work, and play, rather than happiness or the pursuit of wealth. I have not gone into detail about how to accomplish goals associated with love, work, and play, but for such practical advice you would do better to consult psychologists rather than philosophers.

Many important philosophical, neuropsychological, and social questions remain. Although I will not attempt to answer any of them in depth, I want to sketch the kinds of answers to some key questions that can be developed within the neural naturalistic framework that I have defended. What kind of government should countries have? How can creative change be produced?

What is mathematical knowledge? Why is there something and not nothing? My answers to these questions will be very preliminary but will serve to indicate some of the future tasks for neural naturalism.

What Kind of Government Should Countries Have?

The central question in political philosophy concerns what kind of state is most legitimate. This is not the descriptive question of what forms of government different countries have used, but rather the normative question of what form of government ought to be used. We can attempt to answer the question using the normative procedure outlined earlier in this chapter.

The first step is to identify a domain of practices. Around ten thousand years ago, humans began to settle in larger groups than the hunter-gatherer clans that were the original social organizations. The development of farming in river valleys in Mesopotamia and Egypt allowed for greater concentration of populations, which required centralization of power for economic and military purposes. Governments formed and over the following millennia took on different organizational structures, which constitute the domain of political practices that is our current concern.

The second step is to identify candidate norms for these practices, which consist of actual and hypothetical forms of government. Early governments were monarchies, but subsequent centuries have brought new forms such as liberal democracy, state socialism, fascism, and hypothetical forms of anarchism in which the state is ideally abolished in favor of either mutual cooperation (left-wing anarchism) or free market forces (libertarianism). Looking around the world today, we can identify different forms of government that can serve as candidate norms concerning how the state should be run, including the following:

- Liberal democracy, with representative government and individual freedom, e.g., the United States
- Communism, with state ownership and one-party control, e.g., Cuba
- Religious nationalism, e.g., Iran
- Absolutism, with no constitutional government, e.g., Saudi Arabia

Within these forms, there are important variants, such as the social democracies like Sweden that place more emphasis on economic equality than countries such as the United States that emphasize economic freedom.

The third step in my normative procedure is to identify goals of political practices, which requires asking what the state is for. Some conservatives prefer the minimalist answer that the state is legitimately concerned only with keeping people from harming each other, whereas religious fundamentalists see the state as ideally dedicated to pursuing divine commands. Should the state be primarily concerned with people's freedom, or with issues of fairness and social justice, or with some other goals? My preferred answer to this question follows directly from the needs-based ethics developed in chapters 8 and 9: the appropriate goals of the state are to help meet people's vital needs. These include basic physiological needs such as safety, food, shelter, and health care, and also the fundamental psychological needs of autonomy, relatedness, and competence.

We should not expect the state to provide complete equality with respect to wealth or happiness, as long it works to promote equality with respect to the satisfaction of vital needs. Once again, the concept of need straddles the descriptive and the normative: needs can be identified through evidence about what people require to avoid harm and to thrive; needs then generate obligations that people and the state work toward satisfying those needs. Empathy and caring are a crucial part of this generation, as the structure of our brains gives most of us the human capacity to appreciate the needs of others.

Now we can proceed to the fourth, more directly evidence-based step of evaluating the extent to which various forms of government accomplish the goals of satisfying vital human needs. Here we have a wealth of data to consult, such as the United Nations Human Development Index, which calculates average values for 177 countries based on how well they succeed in providing their citizens with a long and healthy life, education, and a decent standard of living. In 2008, the top ten countries on the Human Development Index were Iceland, Norway, Canada, Australia, Ireland, the Netherlands, Sweden, Japan, Luxembourg, and Switzerland.

Another way to try to assess human needs satisfaction in different countries is to look at surveys of subjective well-being that have been made since 1981. The countries with highest subjective well-being include Mexico,

Denmark, Columbia, Ireland, Iceland, Switzerland, the Netherlands, Canada, and Austria. Looking at the countries on both lists, we might reasonably conjecture that the currently available form of government most conducive to satisfaction of human needs consists of a liberal democracy operating in a capitalist economic system with substantial state support for education, health care, and other egalitarian social requirements.

Obviously, we would need much more evidence and argument to advance to the fifth step in the normative procedure of concluding that liberal-capitalist-social democracy should be adopted as the norm for governing states. Difficult issues about the relative importance of particular needs such as autonomy and relatedness must be discussed, along with whatever evidence is available for assessing how the world's countries succeed in meeting those needs. We should also not rule out the possibility that some form of government not currently practiced might actually be better for meeting vital human needs than those now in operation. Perhaps future social experiments will find creative new ways of governing states that will be more effective than those now observed.

How Can Creative Change Be Produced?

Where do new ideas come from, and how can creative solutions be found for the serious problems that the world now faces? Pressing global problems include economic crises, poverty, unemployment, climate change, overpopulation, and looming energy shortages. Dealing with these problems will require major social innovations emanating from creative decisions that arise through psychological, neural, and molecular processes in human brains. Here I will sketch some research just beginning on the emergence of new concepts through interconnected patterns of brain activation.

At its simplest, creativity can be understood as a process of novel conceptual combination, in which existing concepts are joined for the first time to produce something new. My home town of Waterloo, Ontario, is the headquarters for Research in Motion, the company that makes the popular Blackberry wireless handheld device. In the mid-1990s, this company was a tiny manufacturer of wireless pagers, when its founder, Mike Lazaridis, got the idea of developing ways of using pagers for electronic mail. The concept of wireless communications was already widespread, and email had been around for decades, but the conceptual combination *wireless email* was new and creative, as shown by the subsequent huge success of the Blackberry and the development of Research in Motion into a multibillion-dollar company.

If chapters 3 and 4 are on the right track, then concepts such as *wireless* and *email* are patterns of neural activation. My collaborators and I are working on a neurocomputational model of how a new pattern of activation can emerge in a neural population integrating the patterns of activation in two neural populations that encode two previous concepts. We are trying to identify neural mechanisms by which new concepts can be formed out of the neural activations that constitute existing concepts. These mechanisms should suffice for explaining how creative concepts such as *wireless email* can emerge, and also how other forms of novelty can arise. We hope to build a unified neural account that applies to how scientific hypotheses such as Darwin's theory of evolution can arise (chapter 4), as well as to how creative new goals can be generated (chapter 6). Explaining creativity in areas as diverse as conceptual combination, hypothesis formation, and goal generation would be another piece of evidence that minds really are brains, as chapter 3 argued.

Of course, generating new ideas in brains is not the only process needed for developing solutions to social problems. As chapter 5 argued, we need to think of people in terms of multilevel systems that include social, psychological, and molecular mechanisms as well as neural ones. Here are some conjectures about how best to attempt to change complex systems such as human minds and societies:

1. To change a multilevel system, intervene at all accessible levels.
2. At a particular level, intervene by understanding the relevant mechanisms in sufficient detail to identify the manipulations of parts, interactions, and feedback loops that are most likely to produce the desired changes.
3. Pay attention to the interactions between mechanisms at various levels.
4. Coordinate interventions so that they are complementary rather than incompatible.

For a concrete example of change in multilevel systems, consider the most effective treatment for cases of serious depression. The available evidence suggests that the best way to improve the mood of depressed people is a combination of cognitive therapy and antidepressant medication. This combination intervenes at all four relevant levels: social, psychological, neural, and molecular. A cognitive therapist assists patients at the psychological level by helping them to identify and overcome negative beliefs, goals, and emotions. The therapist often also assists the patient in improving personal and work relationships, so cognitive therapy intervenes at the social level as well. Antidepressants such as Prozac and Wellbutrin affect levels of neurotransmitters including serotonin and dopamine, so they operate at the molecular level, but they also change the firing rates of neurons, as well as the generation of new neurons in the hippocampus. Hence it seems that the combination of cognitive theory and antidepressant medication is beneficial owing to their synergistic intervention at all four relevant levels of mechanisms. More effective interventions will become possible through greater knowledge about the social, psychological, neural, and molecular mechanisms underlying depression, including their interconnections described in conjectures 2–4.

Many more examples of changes in complex systems are needed to evaluate the plausibility of my conjectures about system change. We desperately need to develop further evidence-based theories about how to change psychological, political, and social systems in ways that can address the daunting list of problems that humans now face. The account of multilevel explanations that I defended in chapter 5 should pave the way for multilevel interventions that avoid simplistic models of causality.

Figure 10.2 displays four commonly advocated views of such relations. The most familiar is (A), the classical reductionist view that changes at lower levels cause changes at higher levels. On this view, causality runs upward, and so should explanation: social changes are explained as the result of psychological changes, which are the result of neural changes, all the way down to subatomic changes. In the social sciences, some writers go far in the other direction, suggesting that the social level is the key source of causality, as in (B). On this view, causality and explanation run only downward, from the social to the psychological, and everything is a social construction; the neural and molecular levels are largely ignored.

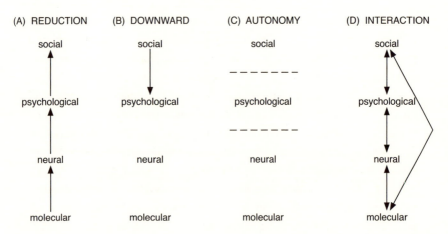

10.2 Four views of the relations between levels of explanation in cognitive science. Arrows
      indicate causality. © Cognitive Science Society.

A more moderate, less imperialistic form of antireductionism is the autonomy view, (C) in figure 10.2, where the dotted lines indicate that explanations at each level can proceed independently. This view is popular
among sociologists, economists, and anthropologists who want to maintain
their independence from psychology without making strong claims of social constructivism. Similarly, some psychologists and philosophers of mind
have wanted to defend psychology from the rapidly increasing incursion of
neuroscience. The autonomy view is dwindling in plausibility, as cognitive,
social, clinical, and developmental psychology are being increasingly tied
to neural processes. Similarly, at the social level, economics is coming to be
influenced by behavioral and neural approaches.

My own preferred view is the highly interactive one (D), in which there
are causal interactions and hence explanatory relations among all levels.
This view is not reductionist, because it rejects the one-way causal connections shown in (A), nor is it antireductionist, because it recognizes that
molecular processes are part of the explanation of neural events, neural processes are part of the explanation of psychological events, and psychological
processes are part of the explanation of social events. I hope that increased
knowledge about interconnected multilevel mechanisms will be useful for

explaining human thinking, and, further, for creating new ways to approach difficult social problems. Then philosophy and neuroscience will serve not only to interpret the world, but also to help change it.

What Is Mathematical Knowledge?

Interpreting the world remains a large objective, and one important unanswered question concerns the nature of mathematical knowledge. Why is it true that $3 + 4 = 7$? In chapters 2 and 4, I briefly mentioned how mathematical knowledge has spurred numerous philosophers and mathematicians to reject naturalism. For Plato and many successors, there must be an a priori basis for truths of arithmetic, geometry (such as the Pythagorean theorem), and many other branches of mathematics. They think that it is necessarily true (in all possible worlds) that $3 + 4 = 7$, in a way that natural science cannot explain.

Puzzles about how people manage to grasp mathematical truths have long been a source of the view that ideas are supernatural. A full-blown plausible naturalistic alternative requires learning much more about the nature of mathematical concepts as they develop in human brains. Already there is some understanding of concepts of number in animals and infants, but the neural underpinnings of mathematical knowledge are just beginning to be investigated.

As a first pass, we can say that mathematical concepts from *three* to *right triangle* to *infinite number* are all patterns of brain activation of the sort discussed in chapter 4. This does not assume that such concepts are derived directly from experience, because we have seen that new concepts can be formed by conceptual combination that go far beyond perception. Moreover, some basic concepts like *object* may be innate. Activation of concepts like *number* and *addition* may begin with specific examples when children observe collections of objects and are taught to count and add, but conceptual combination can quickly generate abstract combinations such as *number divisible only by itself and 1*. The kinds of neural mechanisms I mentioned in discussing creativity should suffice equally well for producing representations of mathematical abstractions.

But there is a crucial difference between theoretical entities such as *sound wave* and mathematical entities such as *infinite number*. Even though we cannot observe sound waves, we are justified in believing that they exist by inference to the best explanation. We cannot hear or see sound waves, but we can observe their causal effects whenever we hear sounds. In contrast, purely mathematical entities like numbers do not have any direct causal effects, so how can we be justified in thinking they exist?

I was once tempted to say that numbers exist because numbers are concepts, and concepts are patterns of neural activation that exist in real brains. The problem with this view is that there would seem to be far more numbers than patterns of brain activation. Assuming that neurons can fire or not fire about 100 times per second, and that there are 100 billion neurons, then we can calculate that there are at least $(2^{100})^{100,000,000,000}$ possible patterns of activation in the human brain. This is an extraordinarily large number, far greater than the number of kinds of things there are in the universe, which is usually estimated to contain only about 10^{80} elementary particles. But the number of integers $(1, 2, \ldots)$ is infinite, because we can always produce a greater integer just by adding 1. (A similar proof shows that there are an infinite number of reality TV shows, because an even worse one is always coming along.)

Intensifying the problem, the nineteenth-century mathematician Georg Cantor showed that there are more real numbers (e.g., pi, $3.14159 \ldots$) than there are integers, and indeed that there are an infinite number of sets of infinite numbers of different sizes, an infinity of infinities. Clearly the brain cannot hold an infinite number of patterns. So numbers cannot all be brain concepts, any more than they can be theoretical entities inferred by inference to the best explanation.

I think the most plausible way out of this impasse is to conclude that numbers and other mathematical objects are just fictions: they don't exist in the real world, any more than Harry Potter, Hamlet, and angels do. Then purely mathematical claims are fictional too, although they can be plausible or implausible within the context of the fictional worlds they describe. Fictionally, Harry Potter is a boy wizard rather than a dog, and angels have wings rather than jet engines. Similarly, within the context of the axioms of number theory, numbers can be infinitely large or small; and within the context of set theory, there is an infinity of infinite sets. But numbers, sets, and wizards do not exist in the real world.

The major problem with understanding mathematical objects as fictions resides in comprehending how mathematics can be so useful in describing and explaining the world. It seems that there are straightforward arithmetical truths such as 2 + 2 = 4, and many branches of mathematics, such as algebra and calculus, that are invaluable in scientific fields ranging from physics to theoretical neuroscience. How can mathematical models of brain functioning tell us anything about thinking if math is fictional?

The most plausible answer is that many mathematical claims can be understood as being about the real world rather than about some abstract domain of objects. I think that the following claim is true: Putting 2 objects together with 2 other objects makes a total of 4 objects. This is a claim about objects, not about numbers, so it can be true of the real world. Similarly, algebra and calculus are neither true nor false, but they are used to express evaluable claims about physical systems, claims that can be judged to be true or false on the basis of experimental evidence and inference to the best explanation. Mathematical statements are not true a priori, nor are they generalizations about the world; but we can combine mathematical concepts with concepts about things and processes to make claims about the world. Abstract mathematical statements such as those in set theory and number theory are fictional assertions rather than necessary truths.

Yet these fictions do sometimes turn out to be very useful for describing the real world. Imaginary numbers and group theory, for example, were ideas developed in pure mathematics that turned out to be important for theories in physics. I think that pure mathematics sometimes turns out to be scientifically useful for the same reason that good fiction can tell us much about human psychology and social relations. Harry Potter and wizards do not exist, but J. K. Rowling's characters are based on her familiarity with and understanding of human social relations. My favorite authors (such as Shakespeare, Tolstoy, and Carol Shields) produce intensely interesting fictional characters and events because they know so much about human nature derived from their own experience. Similarly, the abstractions that mathematicians produce are often not pure creations; rather, mathematicians develop them by imaginatively combining concepts that originated in reflections on aspects of the real world. The writer Julian Barnes said that the novel tells beautiful, shapely lies which enclose hard, exact truths. Mathematics tells beautiful, exact lies that sometimes approximate to messy truths.

To make this view of mathematics plausible, we need to know much more about the nature of mathematical concepts. A wealth of experimental evidence is accumulating concerning the nature of numerical thinking in human adults and infants, as well as in other animals. In accord with the view of concepts defended in chapter 4, mathematical concepts are patterns of neural activation that encode many different kinds of representation— visual and spatial as well as verbal and formal. But the development of mathematics will not be well understood until we have a better account, to be provided by theoretical neuroscience, of the mechanisms by which neural populations in multiple brain areas can generate new, more abstract mathematical concepts.

Why Is There Something and Not Nothing?

Surely there is one major question that I haven't been able to answer, one central issue that a naturalistic approach cannot possibly address. Why does anything exist at all? Much astrophysical evidence supports the theory that the universe emerged from a very hot, dense state around fourteen billion years ago, in a big bang that instituted time and space. But where did the big bang come from? Few educated people now buy the biblical picture that the world was created just six thousand years ago, but there is still some appeal to the idea that God made the big bang and thereby created the universe. Problems with this view are easily spotted, such as how a nonmaterial being managed to create matter and energy, but there is something more satisfying about the idea of a creator than about the idea of our universe just popping into existence through some kind of inexplicable quantum fluctuation. Theology still seems more explanatory than does magic.

Recently, however, an alternative to both theology and magic has been proposed by two distinguished physicists, Paul Steinhardt and Neil Turok. They have developed a new theory of a cyclic universe, according to which our universe came into existence because of the repeatable collision between two strange objects called *branes*. The cyclic model is based on the leading approach to fundamental physics, string theory, according to which matter is composed of vibrating stringlike objects operating in more dimensions than the one temporal and three spatial ones familiar from our everyday experience. A brane (short for "membrane") is a multidimensional surface that can move, stretch, curve, and collide with similar constituents. According to Steinhardt and Turok, our universe began with a violent transition from a low-energy density state to a very high-energy density state consisting of the hot plasma that constituted the big bang. The energy produced will eventually decay, leading back over a trillion years or so to the state in which a brane collision could produce another big bang, with repetitions at regular intervals throughout cosmic history, past and future. In each cycle, there is a big bang followed by stages dominated successively by radiation, matter, and energy, leading to contraction and eventually another big bang.

Steinhardt and Turok present evidence that the cyclic theory matches all the current astronomical observations with the same accuracy as the modified big bang theory, and show how it potentially can explain and unify some aspects of the universe beyond the range of the big bang theory. No one yet knows whether the cyclic universe theory will become an accepted part of astrophysics, in part because it has been difficult to perform experiments to provide evidence that would support the acceptance of string theory, which the cyclic theory presupposes. Nevertheless, I mention the cyclic model here because it shows the possibility of an evidence-based answer to the question of why there is something and not nothing. According to the model, there has always been something, namely, branes, which are the historical causes of the existence of an infinite number of universes, including ours. The main explanation of the existence of familiar things such as the sun, the planets, and members of our own species is the big bang history of our universe, which originated through the brane mechanism that Steinhardt and Turok propose. Perhaps the cyclic universe is not emotionally satisfying, because it stands far from providing any kind of reassurance about the meaning of the universe and our place in it. But it is potentially cognitively satisfying because it provides a nonmysterious mechanism by which our universe could have come to be. If I someday write a second edition of this book, I hope it will have a chapter section called "Branes and the Meaning of Life."

Steinhardt and Turok reject the popular *anthropic principle,* according to which the complexity of the universe is connected with our ability to exist in it as observers, as if the universe were somehow fine-tuned to produce humans. They grant that the physical laws and conditions that govern the universe must be compatible with the fact that life exists, but this fact tells us nothing about the origins of those laws and conditions. Some physicists suggest that our planet lies in an unusual universe out of a multiverse of possibilities, finely tuned as a prerequisite for life to evolve. In contrast, the cyclic model sees our universe as arising from physical mechanisms, not abstract ideas such as the multiverse and fine tuning to support life.

I see the anthropic principle as yet another attempt to stage a Ptolemaic counterrevolution, aiming to put human minds back at the center of reality. This attempt is no more successful than its many predecessors, including Kant's theory of knowledge, Husserl's phenomenology, Buddhist mysticism, New Age wishful spirituality, postmodernism, the Wittgensteinian defense of everyday concepts, and consciousness-based interpretations of quantum mechanics. Rejecting idealism and the lure of dualism, we need to comprehend the insights of physics, biology, and neuroscience that our minds are just another physical process in a vast universe. The cyclic theory shows how this universe might have come into existence through a physical mechanism, without generating spurious reassurance about the centrality of human thinking to reality. Only in the past few hundred thousand years, out of the many billions of years that the universe has existed, have human minds been around to interpret reality. We have no way of ever knowing whether other kinds of minds evolved in previous cycles of expansion before our universe was formed, or whether new kinds will evolve in future cycles trillions of years from now.

The Future of Wisdom

I wonder how long the human species will survive. Perhaps disasters such as epidemics, drastic climate change, or nuclear war will prevent *Homo sapiens* from enjoying the few million years that most vertebrate species last. More optimistically, given our intelligence and adaptive powers, we may be able to hang on for the five billion years or so before the sun starts to die from lack of hydrogen. If scientific knowledge continues to expand at the increasingly rapid rate of the past few centuries, humans may even have the capability to move on to other solar systems.

Much more immediately, we can look forward to a far richer understanding of how the brain produces the mental processes that I have discussed in this book. Within the next decade or two, I hope to see major neuroscientific advances concerning the kinds of thinking people do to know reality, feel emotions, make decisions, act morally, and lead meaningful lives. I expect to see continuing rapid progress concerning the neural mechanisms responsible for basic cognitive processes such as perception, memory, learning, and inference. I hope to see a deeper understanding of how scientific thinking works, especially the most creative processes in which new hypotheses and concepts are generated. New neurocomputational models should shed light on the nature of people's understanding of causality.

In addition, much more remains to be learned about the neural basis of human emotions, including their integration with cognitive processes and their generation of conscious experience. I have been able only to sketch some of the neural mechanisms underlying emotional consciousness, and much more detailed accounts are needed of particular emotions such as fear and anger. I expect that these accounts will include both cognitive appraisals and bodily perceptions, but will provide more specific details about how the brain generates particular kinds of emotional experiences. One of my major plans for future research is to develop a neural model of emotional change that will apply both to individual psychology and to social improvement. A new collaborative project is attempting to identify the emotional deep structure of national conflicts.

Innovative mechanistic theories of cognition and emotion should pave the way for much richer accounts of human decision making, including ethical evaluations. Much more needs to be said about how goals are represented in human brains and how we use them to choose among possible actions for both instrumental and ethical reasons. I hope that a fully developed neural theory of goal-based decision making will provide the basis for a more psychologically realistic theory of economic behavior. In particular, a richer theory of goal revision should provide the basis for an explanation of the major emotional changes that take place in human enterprises ranging from psychotherapy to social innovation. Ideally, it would also suggest more creative forms of conflict resolution that would provide insights into disputes between individuals and between groups.

Finally, much fuller neural theories of cognition, emotion, decision making, and consciousness should point the way to a better understanding of the kinds of wisdom that we all depend on when we face difficult life decisions. Psychology and philosophy need more investigation of how realms of life such as love, work, and play help to satisfy people's basic needs. I look forward to detailed theories about the neural mechanisms that underlie such phenomena as romantic attachment, friendship, job satisfaction, and entertainment. The academic disciplines most in need of these developments are literary and cultural theory, which have tended to rely on philosophical and psychological ideas borrowed from evidence-poor research traditions. Fortunately, cognitive approaches to literature and neural approaches to aesthetics are starting to emerge.

The legal scholar Anthony Kronman chides universities for having given up the attempt to understand the meaning of life, and argues for the importance of the humanities in this endeavor. I certainly agree that much can be learned about the meaning of life from the appreciation of great works of literature and art, as well as from consideration of classical philosophical and historical issues. But I have tried to show that neuropsychology is also valuable for investigating what makes life worth living, and I hope to see much richer connections in the future between the humanities and the social sciences. My intent has not been to use science as a replacement for philosophy, which remains important for pursuing very general descriptive and normative questions. But I have tried to show how we can evaluate answers to those questions using evidence from neuroscience and other areas of science. I said in chapter 1 that philosophy originates in anxiety as well as in wonder, and both motivations are better served by naturalism than by faith or pure reason.

Problems about reality, knowledge, morality, and meaning are all connected, not by transcendental truths, but by the history and nature of human beings in a physical universe. The resulting naturalistic system of evidence-based philosophy is, I hope, highly coherent both with the available scientific information and with reasonable aspirations for human life. I have displayed a strong fit between coherentism as a theory of knowledge and constructive realism as a theory of what exists. Both support the multidimensional theory of the meaning of life based on love, work, and play, as well as the consequentialist theory of morality tied to objective human needs.

Like science, evidence-based philosophy is never a finished project, and I hope to see metaphysics, epistemology, and ethics evolve further in step with scientific developments. Unlike the quick fixes offered by faith and a priori reasoning, naturalism requires patience and tolerance as scientific theories and evidence fallibly develop. Faith-based thinking should increasingly be understood as a cultural tradition stemming from motivated inferences that can be defused by recognition of how love, work, and play can suffice to meet human needs. Julian Barnes wrote: "I don't believe in God, but I miss him." Appreciation of how love, work, and play provide life's meaning should quell such yearning.

When I was an undergraduate, professors often smoked in class. One day, my logic teacher threw a match into the wastepaper basket, setting the paper in it on fire. When he tried to extinguish the fire by stomping it out, his large foot got caught in the basket, as students looked on with a combination of horror and hilarity. Similarly, philosophers sometimes start intellectual fires that they have trouble escaping, but that is not because the most important problems they pursue arise from minor errors in language or logic. Rather, philosophical problems arise whenever there are challenging questions about action and belief. Such questions are inescapable at the frontiers of science and technology, as well as in the dilemmas of people's personal lives.

The physicist Richard Feynman is supposed to have said that scientists need philosophers like birds need ornithology, but philosophical issues abound in cutting-edge science, such as current attempts to develop a theory of quantum gravity. Let me reformulate what Santayana said about history: Those who ignore philosophy are condemned to repeat it. To amplify, let me adapt what Keynes said about economic theory: Those who disparage philosophy are usually slaves of some defunct philosopher. Philosophical issues about knowledge, reality, meaning, and morality cannot be ignored by anyone who wishes to think deeply about what to believe and what to do.

It has become unfashionable to propose systems of philosophy, but I have tried to show that scientific evidence provides grounds for an integrated set of answers to the most fundamental and important philosophical questions. Despondent obsession with problems of doubt, death, and power can give way to more positive reflections on how humans frequently manage to achieve knowledge, morality, and lives that meet vital needs through the pursuit of love, work, and play. The Brain Revolution will continue to generate insights into how we think, feel, and make decisions, including ones about the morality of actions and good directions for a meaningful life.

Notes

Chapter 1
We All Need Wisdom

1   Albert Camus began his book *The Myth of Sisyphus*: Camus 2000a, p. 11. For a fictional presentation of absurdity, see his novel *L'Etranger,* translated into English as *The Outsider*. See chapter 7 for further discussion of Camus.

1   Such a struggle is not rare among young adults: an American survey of university students: Jamison 2000, p. 36. More than half of American students reported having at least one episode of suicidal thinking: http://www.apa.org/releases/suicideC08.html.

1   Baltimore Catechism: http://www.gutenberg.org/files/14552/14552.txt.

2   Martin Seligman remarked that the three great realms of life are love, work, and play: http://www.apa.org/monitor/aug98/pc.html. He does not, however, assert that the meaning of life is love, work, and play, and primarily discusses happiness, e.g., in Seligman 2003.

4   The ancient Greek philosopher Epicurus: http://www.epicurus.net/en/menoeceus.html.

5   Philosophers have sought wisdom for thousands of years: For philosophical work on wisdom and the meaning of life, see Klemke and Cahn 2007; Flanagan 2007; and these Web sites: http://plato.stanford.edu/entries/wisdom/; http://plato.stanford.edu/entries/life-meaning/. For psychologists on wisdom and the meaning of life, see Sternberg 2003 and Baumeister 1991. For the relevance of the humanities, see Kronman 2007 and Eagleton 2007. For a broad but shallow survey, see http://en.wikipedia.org/wiki/Meaning_of_life.

5   The approach to philosophy that I favor . . . called *naturalism:* Other philosophers whose work had a substantial naturalistic component include Aristotle, John Locke, David Hume, John Stuart Mill, Charles Peirce, and W.V.O. Quine 1968. Many of the contemporary philosophers of mind discussed in later chapters are also naturalists.

5   Wittgenstein . . . claimed that philosophy "leaves everything as it is": Wittgenstein 1968, paragraph 124. For the therapeutic view of philosophy as conceptual clarification, see Wittgenstein 1971. I criticize this view in chapter 2.

6   I call my approach neural naturalism: The pioneers of neurophilosophy are P. S. Churchland 1986 and P. M. Churchland 2007. For more about the nature of philosophy and its relation to science, see Thagard 2009.

7   Galileo used the newly invented telescope: Drake 1978.

7   Today the interdisciplinary field of cognitive science: Boden 2006; Thagard 2005a.

8   Together, these advances made possible the field of cognitive neuroscience: Ward 2006; Smith and Kosslyn 2007.

12 Plato said that philosophy begins in wonder: Plato, *Theaetetus,* http://classics.mit.edu/Plato/theatu.html.

Chapter 2
Evidence Beats Faith

14 Today, most leading scientists are atheists or agnostics: Larson and Witham 1998.

14 Stephen Jay Gould argued that science and religion: Gould 1999.

14 According to the Web site adherents.com: http://www.adherents.com/Religions_By_Adherents.html.

16 American president George W. Bush and Arab leader Osama bin Laden: Mansfield 2003; Randal 2004.

16 Once children are exposed to particular religions, their doctrines can become highly coherent: see the account of the emotional coherence of religion in Thagard 2006, ch. 14. For further discussion of goals and beliefs, see chapter 6.

16 Religious faith meshes with tendencies in human thinking that are very natural: Gilovich 1991; Kunda 1990, 1999. Even perception can be affected by motivation: Balcetis and Dunning 2006. Motivated inference can contribute to confirmation bias, as one of the effects of wanting to believe something is selective attention to evidence that supports your views. The pioneering research on motivated inference was done by the brilliant social psychologist Ziva Kunda, who died of cancer in 2004. She was only forty-eight, and our sons were twelve and fourteen. My reflections on why life is worth living originated in attempts to deal with my wife's illness.

17 The philosopher Charles Taylor: Taylor 2007, p. 4.

18 I was walking across a bridge one day: This was the winner in a 2005 contest for the funniest religious joke run by http://www.shipoffools.com. I actually thought their third-place joke was funnier: see the first paragraph of chapter 5. It's lucky for me that blasphemy is a victimless crime.

19 An egregious example of New Age motivated inference is the 2006 best-selling book *The Secret:* Byrne 2006.

19 Strikingly, this process can lead to the abandonment of beliefs previously held: See Thagard 1992 on scientific revolutions. For descriptions by many scientists of contemporary cases where they have changed their minds on the basis of evidence, see http://www.edge.org/q2008/q08_index.html. For an analysis of belief revision about climate change, see Thagard and Findlay (forthcoming-a).

20 But it also appears that some of the jurors were motivated to find Simpson not guilty: Bugliosi 1997; Thagard 2003, 2006, ch. 8.

21 Philosophers call this kind of reasoning *inference to the best explanation*: Harman 1973, 1986; Thagard 1988, 1992; Lipton 2004.

22 Choosing the best explanation requires not just counting the pieces of evidence explained, but also evaluating: For my general theory of coherence, including algorithms for computing coherence and the best explanation, see Thagard 1989, 1992, 1999, 2000.

23   Much more seriously, we can consult the history of science for many examples of inference to the best explanation: For documentation of the Darwin case, see Thagard 1989 or 1992. For physics examples, see Thagard 1992; Eliasmith and Thagard 1997; and Nowak and Thagard 1992a, 1992b. On dinosaur extinction, see Thagard 1991. For detailed legal examples, see Thagard 1989, 2003, 2004. For a detailed medical example, see Thagard 1999.

23   First, explanations in science employ detailed mechanisms: For defense of this claim, see Bechtel and Richardson 1993; Bechtel and Abrahamsen 2005; Bechtel 2008; Craver 2007; Machamer, Darden, and Craver 2000; Salmon 1984; Thagard, 1999, 2006.

25   But the use of carefully designed and controlled experiments is relatively recent: See, e.g., Hall 1962.

25   Galileo was one of the pioneers: Drake 1978.

28   The movement for evidence-based medicine: See, e.g., Guyatt et al. 1992.

29   The placebo effect is well known in medicine: Harrington 1997. Television's Dr. House corrected Marx's comment about religion's being the opiate of the people: it's actually a placebo.

30   Although randomized, controlled trials are rightly touted as the highest standard: For a critical philosophical look at evidence-based medicine, see Worrall 2007. Although Worrall rightly criticizes the extreme view that *only* randomized, controlled trials constitute evidence, he does not sufficiently appreciate their contribution to inference to the best competing medical explanations.

30   Incidentally, carefully controlled clinical trials seem to show that taking large doses of vitamin *C* does *not* actually help: http://www.quackwatch.com/01 QuackeryRelatedTopics/DSH/colds.html.

30   But it is very difficult to separate the reliable from the anecdotal or spurious, given that doctors are prone to cognitive and emotional biases just like other people: Groopman 2007.

30   Of course, religious leaders also advocate prayer, but experiments have found that heart patients do not benefit from prayers for their recovery: Benson et al. 2006. Sloan and Bagiella 2002 review many studies and conclude that there is little empirical basis for assertions that religious involvement or activity is associated with beneficial health outcomes.

31   Another worry is that many trials are conducted by pharmaceutical companies: Angell 2004 provides a scathing review of drug company practices.

32   The two most compelling arguments for divine existence: See Thagard 2000, ch. 4, for more detailed discussion. Swinburne 1990 provides an evidence-based defense of the existence of God. Theory evaluation can also be modeled on the basis of Bayesian probability theory, an approach criticized in Thagard 2000, ch. 9.

33   Scientific cosmology has found experimental support for the big bang theory: http://www.big-bang-theory.com/.

33   Where the big bang came from remains speculative, but recent work in string theory: Steinhardt and Turok 2007. See chapter 10 for further discussion.

34   There are even some studies suggesting that religious people are happier: See references to studies about happiness in chapter 7.

34   If faith-based approaches to knowledge are inferior to evidence-based ap-
     proaches, why does religion still dominate: Thagard 2006, ch. 14. For infor-
     mative naturalistic discussions of religion, see Dawkins 2006; Dennett 2006;
     Flanagan 2007; and McCauley and Lawson 2002. Even philosophers and sci-
     entists who recognize the evidential emptiness of religion are inclined to try to
     naturalize spirituality (Flanagan 2007) or reinvent the sacred (Kaufman 2008).
     Kaufman recognizes the natural occurrence of emergent processes but inflates
     emergence into creativity, which is a property of special kinds of processes that
     currently occur, as far as we know, only in human brains and their computa-
     tional analogs. He then inflates creativity into God and calls the whole confu-
     sion sacred. For a more reasonable account of emergence, see Bunge 2003. I
     prefer to dispense with the spiritual and the sacred altogether, and to satisfy the
     need for meaning that inspires them by methods that are secular and evidence
     based; see chapters 7 and 8.

35   The ontological argument of Anselm: http://plato.stanford.edu/entries/ontological
     -arguments/.

37   Hilary Putnam: Not every statement is both true and false: Putnam 1983.

37   Some Hegelians and Marxists claimed that to understand motion: Hegel 1969;
     Engels 1947.

37   A contemporary philosopher has asserted that paradoxical statements . . . are
     best understood as *both* true and false: Priest 2006.

38   The concept of necessity . . . should be dispatched to the dustbin of history,
     along with deity and monarchy: Other philosophical ideas that are tied to ne-
     cessity and can be dispatched with it are essentialism, supervenience, constitu-
     tivism, and possible worlds.

38   Douglas Hofstadter considers the exercise of imagining: Hofstadter 1979, p. 639.

38   Much philosophical writing assumes that thought experiments: http://plato
     .stanford.edu/entries/thought-experiment/. For defense of thought experi-
     ments, see Shepard 2008 and Williamson 2007. Their arguments fail to show
     that thought experiments can be anything more than suggestive.

39   Philosophy can be experimental and theoretical much as science can: On the re-
     cent upswing in experimental philosophy, see Knobe and Nichols 2008; Appiah
     2008; and http://experimentalphilosophy.typepad.com/. My view of philosophy
     as evidence based is much broader than Knobe and Nichols's notion of experi-
     mental philosophy, which mostly uses surveys of people's intuitions rather than
     investigations of cognitive and neural processes. For further discussion of the
     nature and value of philosophy, see Thagard and Beam 2004 and Thagard 2009.

40   The philosopher Karl Popper is often cited as having shown that the crucial
     difference between science and nonscience is falsifiability: Popper 1959. For
     critiques, see Lakatos 1970; Thagard 1988.

Chapter 3
Minds Are Brains

43   Philosophers call the claim that states and processes of the mind are identi-
     cal to states and processes of the brain the *identity theory*: http://plato.stanford

.edu/entries/mind-identity/. For the 1950s versions, see Place 1956; Feigl 1958; and Smart 1959. For powerful contemporary defenses of neural approaches to mind, see P. S. Churchland 1986, 2002, and P. M. Churchland 1995, 2007. The assertion that minds are brains is shorthand for a number of claims that need to made more precise. It can be subdivided into two claims: the local one that each particular mental state and process in an individual is a particular state and process of the individual's brain (token identity), and the more global one that *kinds* of mental states and processes occurring in many individuals are *kinds* of neural states and processes (type identity). You can accept local claims while denying global ones—for example, agreeing that your perception of a bear is a process in your brain, but denying that all perception of bears is an identifiable kind of neural process on the grounds that there is too much variation across humans, other animals, and thinking machines. I endorse the local claim, but can say little about the global one until much more is known about the relevant kinds of mental and neural states.

44   It was not always obvious that brains have much do with thinking: For the history of neuroscience, see Finger 1994. A chronology is at http://faculty.washington .edu/chudler/hist.html.

46   Much is known about the physical basis of how these senses work: See, for example, Banich 2004 and Smith and Kosslyn 2007.

49   The American neuroscientist Eric Kandel: Kandel 2006.

50   According to Hebb: Hebb 1949.

50   The psychiatrist Norman Doidge has written an accessible book: Doidge 2007.

50   John Anderson is a psychologist: Anderson 2007.

51   Vinod Goel has used brain scanning: Goel 2005.

51   Jerome Feldman has proposed a neural theory: Feldman 2006.

51   Maryanne Wolf points out that literacy is a recent development: Wolf 2007.

51   More mundanely, how do neurons carry out basic forms of inference such as deduction, generalization from examples, and analogy: For some relevant work on these problems, see Smith and Kosslyn 2007 and Thagard 2005a.

52   In scientific reasoning, the best way to show causation rather than mere correlation is to introduce an intervention: Woodward 2004.

52   Much is now known about the neural and molecular mechanisms that draw people to recreational drugs: Meyer and Quenzer 2005.

53   How these drugs alleviate depression: Kramer 2005.

55   Many mediums and psychics have been exposed as frauds: http://www.skepdic .com/medium.html.

55   Out-of-body experiences can be induced by laboratory experiments that produce confusion between the senses: Ehrsson 2007; Blanke et al. 2005.

56   The Greek philosopher Epicurus: http://classics.mit.edu/Epicurus/menoec.html.

57   Historically, efforts to validate parapsychology have not been even moderately successful: Diaconis 1978; Kurtz 1985; http://www.csicop.org/si/9603/claims .html.

60   The conceptual schemes that we acquire from our cultures are inherently dualist: Macdonald 2003; Bloom 2004. Evidence is now insufficient to support the claim that dualism is innate. If dualism is innate, it is another example of

how a priori beliefs can be false, as chapter 2 pointed out. Similarly, I don't buy arguments that religion is innate, as it more plausibly results from more basic psychological processes such as emotion and explanation (Thagard 2006, ch. 14). But if religion were innate, it could be yet another case of a priori beliefs undermined by scientific investigation.

61　The most prevalent is the "zombie" argument: Chalmers 1996.

61　There are several things wrong with the zombie argument: P. S. Churchland 2002; Dennett 2005.

61　Some philosophers think that ascription to the brain of psychological properties such as consciousness is incoherent: Bennett et al. 2007. The philosophical idea of a category mistake is a mistake about categories: Thagard 2009.

62　This view is called functionalism: Putnam 1975. For critiques see Bechtel 2008; P. M. Churchland 2007; and Thagard 1986.

62　Computer intelligence has had some remarkable successes: Russell and Norvig 2003.

63　This research suggests that mental processes are both neural *and* computational: Churchland and Sejnowski 1992.

63　Minds are embodied: e.g., Gibbs 2006; Dreyfus 2007; Thompson 2007. I am prepared to endorse the moderate embodiment thesis that cognition is closely tied to sensorimotor processes, as we will see in the discussions of causality in chapter 4 and emotion in chapter 5. But I reject the extreme embodiment thesis that cognition is just embodied action and therefore incompatible with computational-representational approaches to how brains work. Many kinds of thinking, including causal reasoning, emotion, and scientific theorizing, take us well beyond sensorimotor processes. The "extended mind thesis" of Clark 2008 is too vague to be evaluated with respect to evidence.

64　The neuroscientist Joseph LeDoux eloquently writes: LeDoux 2002, p. 31. Bechtel 2008 has a rich discussion of the self from a neuroscience perspective. We need to understand the self as an emergent process combining multilevel mechanisms. Accounts of emergence sometimes verge on the mystical, but for insightful discussions, see Bechtel 2008; Bunge 2003; and Chi 2005. Thagard and Findlay (forthcoming-b) argue that one of the great difficulties people have in understanding human minds as a product of biological evolution is seeing how one emergent process (natural selection) can produce another emergent process (minds). Emergence is a far more useful way of thinking of the relation between mechanistic levels than is the philosophical notion of supervenience.

Chapter 4
How Brains Know Reality

67　Constructive realism: The term is taken from Giere 1999.

68　Some ancient Greek philosophers: http://plato.stanford.edu/entries/skepticism-ancient/.

68   An influential current form of skepticism is found in postmodernist philoso-
      phers and literary theorists: http://plato.stanford.edu/entries/postmodernism/.
      On reality as more than a social construction, see Hacking 1999.

68   The philosopher Immanuel Kant thought that he had accomplished a kind of
      Copernican revolution: Kant 1965. The phrase "Ptolemaic counterrevolution"
      is from Russell 1948. There are many contemporary variants of this Ptolemaic
      attempt to make reality dependent on mind; see chapter 10. Kant said he had
      to deny knowledge to make room for faith; my strategy is the opposite.

69   Jerry Fodor claimed that there is a language of thought: Fodor 1975.

69   Many contemporary philosophers assume that knowing is a propositional at-
      titude: Richard 1990. For critiques of the idea of propositional attitudes, see
      P. M. Churchland 2007 and Thagard 2008. On neuroimaging of belief, disbe-
      lief, and uncertainty, see Harris, Sheth, and Cohen 2008.

72   Some psychologists writing on hallucinations: Behrendt and Young 2005.

74   Our assessment of the truth of what people say to us is a matter of inference to
      the best explanation: Thagard 2005b.

75   Paul Churchland has found: P. M. Churchland 2007, ch. 10.

76   Greg Murphy's *Big Book of Concepts:* Murphy 2002.

77   In the 1970s, some philosophers, psychologists, and computer scientists ad-
      vocated a more relaxed view of concepts as *prototypes*: In philosophy, see Witt-
      genstein 1968 and Putnam 1975. In psychology, see Rosch and Mervis 1975.
      In artificial intelligence, see Minsky 1975.

77   This view points to the large role that concepts play in providing explanations:
      Medin 1989.

78   The psychologist Larry Barsalou reviews evidence: Barsalou et al. 2003.

79   The philosopher and theoretical neuroscientist Chris Eliasmith has been devel-
      oping interesting ideas about how brains can deal with such relations: Eliasmith
      2005a; Eliasmith and Anderson 2003; Eliasmith, Stewart, and Conklin forthcom-
      ing. Eliasmith's technique builds on the holographic reduced representations of
      Plate 2003. For an application to explanatory inference, see Thagard and Litt 2008.

80   Artificial neural populations can have the desired properties required for mod-
      eling exemplars, prototypes, and relations among concepts: For prototypes,
      see Rumelhart and McClelland 1986. For exemplars see Kruschke 1992. For
      relations, see Eliasmith and Thagard 2001.

80   The conceptual atomism of Jerry Fodor: Fodor 1998. My view of concepts is
      also incompatible with the common philosophical assumption that concepts
      are essentially linguistic. I see no reason to deny that infants and nonhuman
      animals have concepts. Philosophical debates about whether there is "non-
      conceptual content" presuppose a narrowly linguistic view of concepts.

80   For example, the concept *chair* construed as a pattern of neural activation has
      meaning: Eliasmith 2005b. For a different view of neurosemantics, see P. M.
      Churchland 2007. Vagueness is not an aberrant property of deficient concepts,
      but an unavoidable and often valuable characteristic of patterns in neural popu-
      lations. On meaning in robots, see Parisien and Thagard 2008. For critique of
      the philosophical doctrine of propositional attitudes, see Thagard 2008.

83   A theory such as Lavoisier's oxygen theory has both explanatory breadth and simplicity, in that it explains a lot with a small set of assumptions: See the discussions of simplicity in Thagard 1988, 1992.

84   These two aspects of highly developed science, involving progressive broadening and deepening of explanations over time: See Thagard 2007a for further discussion. Newtonian mechanics might be taken as an example of a broad theory that turned out to be false, but it was never deepened and in any case remains approximately true for midsize objects. For further defense of realism about science, see Bunge 2006 and Thagard 1992, 1999, 2000. Realism is also needed to explain such common aspects of science as the reliability of many instruments and surprising experimental results.

84   It has become common in some areas of the humanities and social sciences to claim that science is socially constructed: For critical discussion, see Thagard 1999 and Hacking 1999. For advocates, see Latour and Woolgar 1986; Latour 1987.

86   Much philosophical discussion of explanation: see Salmon 1984, 1989; Thagard 1989; Woodward 2004; http://plato.stanford.edu/entries/scientific-explanation/. For a neural account of explanation and causality, see Thagard and Litt 2008.

86   Even at 2½ months, human babies act surprised: Baillergeon, Kotovsky, and Needham 1995.

87   Even very sophisticated ideas about causality, such as Bayesian networks: Pearl 2000.

87   But we still need an account of how brains integrate many competing claims about explanations to make an inference to the best explanation: For a much more detailed and rigorous exposition of my theory of explanatory coherence, including algorithms for computing it, see Thagard 1989, 1992, 2000.

88   Figure 4.2 shows a simple network that has units representing competing hypotheses in the Simpson case: For a more detailed analysis, see Thagard 2006, ch. 8.

89   This method of maximizing explanatory coherence: Thagard 1989, 1992, etc.

90   Our computer simulations show that more biologically realistic neural networks: Thagard and Aubie 2008.

91   A set of representations such as a theory is approximately true: For further discussion, see Thagard 2000, 2007a.

Chapter 5
How Brains Feel Emotions

95   The view that emotions conflict with reason goes back at least to Plato: Plato 1961, p. 499, in the *Phaedrus*.

95   The mind does not just have concepts and beliefs, but also attaches values to them: For evidence from experimental psychology, see Fazio 2001 and Zajonc 1980. On the neuroscience of valuing, see Montague 2006.

96   Recordings of neuron firings in animals and brain-scanning experiments in humans show the amygdala is important for emotions: LeDoux 1996; Phelps 2006. On affective neuroscience, see Panksepp 1998; Davidson et al. 2003; and Rolls 2005.

96   Feelings of pleasure and anticipation of desirable outcomes are associated with a circuit of neurons: Knutson and Greer 2008.

98   Philosophers and psychologists have long debated the nature of the emotions, and their proposed theories fall into two main camps: Cognitive appraisal theorists include Nussbaum 2001; Oatley 1992; and Scherer, Schorr, and Johnstone 2001. Bodily perception theorists include Damasio 1994; James 1884; and Prinz 2004.

99   According to bodily perception theories, your emotion is your brain's response to such physiological changes, as expressed in a famous quote from the American psychologist/philosopher William James: http://psychclassics.yorku.ca/James/emotion.htm.

100 In an attempt to explain emotional consciousness, I developed the EMOCON model shown in figure 5.2: Thagard and Aubie 2008. See also the neuronal workspace model of Changeux 2004; the component process model of Grandjean, Sander, and Scherer 2008; and the neural theory of consciousness of Rolls 2005. Emotional consciousness is an emergent property of neural networks, in that it is a property of a whole system, not of individual neurons; see Bunge 2003. A crucial open research question is how neural representations in different parts of the brain are bound together; see Thagard and Stewart forthcoming.

102 Although bodily perception theories of emotion have become popular in recent years, they fail to account for the full range of emotional phenomena: Barrett 2006; Rolls 2005.

103 People with damage to this area have great difficulty making good decisions: Thagard 2006, ch. 6.

103 Hence the brain can accomplish cognitive appraisal of a situation: For much more neurocomputational detail, see Thagard and Aubie 2008, which describes simulations of parts of the EMOCON. See also Litt, Eliasmith, and Thagard 2008, and Wagar and Thagard 2004.

105 What it is like to feel happy or sad: For philosophical arguments that science cannot address what it is like to be conscious, see Nagel 1979 and Chalmers 1996.

106 The reason that it feels good to be happy is neural: Phan et al. 2004.

106 There is research showing that being *more* hateful involves *more* activity in areas such as the insula, and that anticipation of greater rewards correlates with increased activity in the nucleus accumbens: Zeki and Romaya 2008; Knutson et al. 2001.

106 People's preference for Coke over Pepsi correlates: McClure, Li, et al. 2004; Montague 2006.

108 Mechanistic explanations are starting to emerge for other kinds of consciousness: e.g., Damasio 1999; Koch 2004; Tononi and Koch 2008.

108 Feelings provide succinct information about anticipated benefits and risks: See the "mood as information" account of Schwartz and Clore 2003, and the "risk as feeling" account of Loewenstein et al. 2001.

109 The molecular level is important for understanding how neurons work: Thagard 2006, ch. 7; Lodish et al. 2000.

111 The best approach to explaining mental events requires attention to multiple levels: Bechtel 2008; Craver 2007; McCauley 2007; Thagard 2006.

112 Emotions are widely thought to be bad for you: But for the contrary view that emotions can often contribute positively to rationality, see Damasio 1994; de Sousa 1988; Frank 1988; and Thagard 2006.

112 Such inferences are not usually pure wishful thinking: Kunda 1990.

112 Motivated inference can contribute to bad decisions arising from conflicts of interest: Thagard 2007c.

113 An even more common affective affliction is weakness of will, which occurs when you find yourself doing something that you know is not in your best interests: Stroud and Tappolet 2003; Thagard 2007c.

113 Weakness of will is fostered by the operation of separate neural systems for immediate and delayed rewards: McClure, Laibson, et al. 2004.

113 Many people suffer occasionally or chronically from depression: Kramer 2005.

114 At the other extreme, some people have bouts of mania: Goodwin and Jamison 2007.

115 The simplest but nevertheless valuable rule I have heard is Michael Pollan's suggestion: http://www.nytimes.com/2007/01/28/magazine/28nutritionism.t.html.

115 Far more effective and pleasant motivations come from positive emotions such as the many variants of happiness: Seligman 2003.

Chapter 6
How Brains Decide

119 If you have ever tried to make an important decision about careers or relationships using such quantitative methods: Using quantitative means to make decisions was proposed by Benjamin Franklin. For modern mathematical decision theory, see Luce and Raiffa 1957.

120 Analogously, I propose that decisions are made on the basis of inference to the best plan: Thagard and Millgram 1995; Millgram and Thagard 1996.

122 Described in words, this all sounds rather mysterious, but there are computer algorithms available for assessing just such highly connected kinds of coherence: Thagard 2000; Thagard and Millgram 1995.

122 There is psychological evidence that successful goal pursuit has a positive effect on well-being: Wiese 2007. Given the practical importance of goals and emotions, and the strong interconnections of cognitive and emotional processes in the brain, it is not surprising that people are so susceptible to the bias of motivated inference discussed in chapter 2.

124 Humans differ from other animals in that our representations are not confined to immediate situations: Penn, Holyoak, and Povinelli 2008.

124 A crucial part of the brain's representation of goals is their association with rewards and punishments: Rolls 2005.

124 Brain scans of people making purchasing decisions have found that product preferences correlate with activation of regions associated with anticipating gain: Knutson et al. 2007. Soon et al. 2008 report that the outcome of a decision can be encoded in brain activity seconds before it enters consciousness.

125 Then the complex computation of what combination of actions produces the best overall plan can be accomplished by the parallel firing of all the relevant neurons: For details about how this might work neurocomputationally, see Wagar and Thagard 2004 (also in Thagard 2006, ch. 6); Litt, Eliasmith and Thagard 2008; Thagard and Aubie 2008.

126 Similarly, the brain's evaluation of actions with respect to goals can also lead to reevaluation of the importance of goals: Simon, Krawczyk, and Holyoak 2004.

126 Twentieth-century economists devised a less mentalistic conception of utility: Frey and Stutzer 2002.

126 Traditional expected utility theory often fails to account for human choice behavior: Kahneman and Tversky 2000; Ariely 2008.

127 The artificial intelligence pioneer Marvin Minsky has an intriguing idea: Minsky 2006. For a similar idea and evidence about social contagion of goals, see Wild and Enzle 2002. According to Josephs et al. 1992, the goals that govern people's decisions include avoiding damage to self-esteem. See also the theory of goal setting in Locke and Latham 1990. Another major issue about goal acquisition concerns brain mechanisms enabling people to generate creative goals that are novel to them and to others; see Thagard and Stewart forthcoming.

128 Evidence that people are often altruistic: Batson 1991; Sober and Wilson 1998.

129 William James eloquently remarked: "To give up pretensions": James 1961, p. 53.

129 Clinical psychologists have found that disengagement from unattainable goals has benefits for health and general well-being: Wrosch et al. 2007.

131 There is experimental evidence that when people make decisions, they alter judgments about goals: Simon, Krawczyk, and Holyoak 2004.

131 Neuroscientist Read Montague's *Why Choose This Book* provides a good introduction to the role of the dopamine system in decision making: Montague 2006. For more on the exciting new field of neuroeconomics, see Camerer, Loewenstein, and Prelec 2005. Traditional economic theory makes many unrealistic assumptions about human behavior, which render it unable to explain important changes such as economic booms and busts: Akerlof and Shiller 2009. Neural models of economic decision making can explain why people deviate from neoclassical assumptions about preferences, in accord with the experimental results of behavioral economics; see, for example, Litt, Eliasmith, and Thagard 2008. Whereas economists usually take preferences as given, affective neuroscience can explain why people have the preferences that they do. Even more ambitiously, it should be possible to construct neuropsychological

explanations of both the irrational exuberance that fuels economic booms and bubbles, and the desperate fear that instigates crises and crashes. Both are instances of emotional consciousness as analyzed by Thagard and Aubie 2008.

131 Aristotle said that deliberation is of means, not ends: Kolnai 1978.

131 Here are some ways to really screw up your decisions: For positive advice, see Russo and Schoemaker 1989; Bazerman 1994.

134 If you use analogies in your decision making: Holyoak and Thagard 1995, ch. 6, discuss good and bad analogical decision making.

134 Maureen Dowd's comment: http://www.nytimes.com/2008/06/01/opinion/01 dowd.html.

135 The psychological finding that people are often not very good about emotional forecasting: Gilbert 2006.

135 Your brain can primarily employ the midbrain dopamine system rather than frontal and parietal regions needed for assessing long-term implications of your actions: McClure, Laibson, et al. 2004.

137 Intuitions can be reasonable: See the method of informed intuition advocated in Thagard 2006, ch. 2. Some routine decisions can best be made quickly and intuitively, as described by Dijksterhuis 2004; Gigerenzer 2000; and Gladwell 2005. But I think that important decisions deserve deliberation to ensure that a full canvas of goals and actions has been made. Unfortunately, I don't know of a systematic body of evidence indicating when decision making should be done deliberatively. For psychological research on when emotions help or hurt decision making, see Vohs, Baumeister, and Loewenstein 2007.

137 Psychologists such as Daniel Wegner have compiled substantial evidence against the everyday view of conscious action: Wegner 2003.

137 Many behaviors result not from decisions but from established habits, which are acquired through neural learning mechanisms: Barnes et al. 2005.

138 Philosophers such as Daniel Dennett and Owen Flanagan: Dennett 2003; Flanagan 2002. For an introduction to philosophical controversies about free will, see http://plato.stanford.edu/entries/freewill. For discussions of free will and self-control informed by neuroscience, see Bechtel 2008; P. S. Churchland 2009; Hebb 1980; and Roskies 2006.

141 The psychologist Drew Westen pointed out in 2007 the repeated failures of American political strategists who tried to approach voters through dispassionate, issue-oriented campaigns: Westen 2007, p. 418.

Chapter 7
Why Life Is Worth Living

142 Camus did not kill himself: Todd 1997.

143 Camus' novel *L'Etranger*: Camus 2000b, p. 68.

144 Camus' character Meursault: Camus 2000b, p. 115.

145 The American essayist Roger Rosenblatt: Rosenblatt 2000.

145 Counting against nihilism is the empirical finding that most people are happy: Biswas-Diener, Vittersøe, and Diener 2005.

145 According to Kay Jamison: Jamison 2000, p. 100.

146 An extensive body of research has developed in the past decade using surveys to identify the extent and the sources of human happiness: Deaton 2008; Diener and Seligman 2004; Easterlin 2006; Harris poll—http://www.harrisinteractive .com/harris_poll/index.asp?PID=900.

146 Nathaniel Hawthorne wrote: "Happiness is as a butterfly": This quote is all over the Web, but I have been unable to find the original source.

147 The American economist Richard Easterlin: Easterlin 2006.

147 Widowhood and divorce both produce strong drops in life satisfaction: Lucas et al. 2003.

147 Another study, conducted by the Pew Research Center: http://pewresearch.org/ pubs/301/are-we-happy-yet.

148 Happiness is usually a temporary condition, like other emotions: Lazarus 2003.

148 The social psychologist Daniel Gilbert: Gilbert 2006, pp. 220–222.

149 As John Stuart Mill said, "It is better to be a human being dissatisfied than a pig satisfied": Bentham and Mill 1973, p. 410. The quote is from Mill's essay *Utilitarianism*, ch. 2.

152 Surveys of personal well-being always find that personal relationships are a major source of satisfaction in people's lives: Baumeister and Leary 1995; Diener and Seligman 2004.

152 The neural mechanisms for romantic love have been investigated by a team that includes the anthropologist Helen Fisher: Fisher 2004; Aron et al. 2005; Fisher, Aron, and Brown 2005.

153 An earlier study of romantic love by Andreas Bartels: Bartels and Zeki 2000.

153 Dopamine is also a key factor in explaining the mating behavior of prairie voles: Insel and Young 2001.

154 Oxytocin increases trust between strangers: Kosfeld et al. 2005. On the neural correlates of trust, see Krueger et al. 2007.

154 The brain processes involved in interpersonal bonding: Depue and Morrone-Strupinsky 2005; Panksepp 1998, ch. 14.

154 According to the social psychologists Geoff MacDonald and Mark Leary: Mac-Donald and Leary 2005.

155 A brain-scanning study of social exclusion: Eisenberger, Lieberman, and Williams 2003; Eisenberger and Lieberman 2004.

156 There appear to be interesting changes in the brains of Tibetan Buddhist monks: Lutz et al. 2004.

156 The philosopher Harry Frankfurt makes the daring suggestion: Frankfurt 2004, p. 55.

157 According to a preliminary report, there are people who have experienced intense love for twenty years and still show activation in the brain's ventral tegmental area: http://www.sciencenews.org/view/generic/id/38653/title/Still_ crazy_(in_love)_after_all_these_years.

157 Even while experiencing grief over the death of a spouse, some people continue to show activation in reward pathways involving the nucleus accumbens:
O'Connor et al. 2008.

157 Douglas Hofstadter insightfully describes the bond created between two people
who are together for a long time: Hofstadter 2007, pp. 222–224. I like his suggestion that this bond can create a new, emergent, higher-level entity.

157 Brain imaging has identified highly specific brain activity (in the medial orbitofrontal cortex) that occurs in response to infant faces but not to adult faces:
Kringelbach et al. 2008.

158 Research indicates that many people obtain satisfaction from their jobs: Diener
and Seligman 2004; Spector 1997; Dawis 2004.

158 Rewarding jobs tend to have such characteristics as: Judge et al. 2001.

158 High income does correlate with happiness and well-being as I mentioned
above, but the relation between them is complex: Diener and Seligman 2004;
Deaton 2008.

159 Goal setting affects both job satisfaction and job performance: Judge et al.
2001; Locke et al. 1981.

160 Figure 7.1 displays the role of emotions in scientific problem solving: Adapted
from Thagard 2006, p. 177.

160 Mihaly Csikszentmihalyi has described the mental state of flow: Csikszentmihalyi 1997.

160 Other factors that can contribute to employees' thriving at work: Spreitzer et al.
2005.

161 Following an idea misattributed to Freud: Freud 1962, p. 23, denies that life
has a purpose, but says that people strive after happiness, to which love and
work contribute. According to Haidt 2006 (which contains many interesting
reflections on happiness), Freud may have said in conversation that the meaning of life is love and work.

161 According to a 2004 poll of American adults asked to name their favorite
leisure-time activities: http://www.harrisinteractive.com/harris_poll/index.asp?
PID=526.

161 In 2005, the average Canadian adult spent 5.5 hours per day on leisure activities: http://www4.hrsdc.gc.ca/indicator.jsp?lang=en&indicatorid=52.

161 The neuropsychologist Jaak Panksepp: Panksepp 1998, ch. 15. On the neuroscience of hunor, see Martin 2007.

162 In addition, exercise can stimulate the production of endorphins: Thoren et al.
1990.

163 Emotional motivations for watching sports: Raney 2006; Gordon 2008.

163 Daniel Levitin describes how our musical experiences: Levitin 2006.

163 Listening to music causes a cascade of brain regions to become activated in a
particular order: Levitin 2006, p. 187.

164 Levitin provides vivid examples of how music has shaped the world through
six kinds of songs: Levitin 2008.

164 Other researchers have investigated how music perception affects emotion:
Koelsch and Siebel 2005.

164 Mechanisms underlying musical emotions: Juslin and Västfjäll 2008.

164 According to Maryanne Wolf: Wolf 2007. Zunshine 2006 says that people read fiction because it cognitively engages our theory of mind, but I think that emotional simulation is at least as important. See chapter 8 on mirror neurons and Goldman 2006.

166 One philosopher has even advocated the dismal view that universally it is better never to have been born: Benatar 2006 argues that self-assessments of the quality of life are unreliable.

Chapter 8
Needs and Hopes

169 According to the philosopher David Wiggins, people need something: Wiggins 1987, p. 14. My discussion here draws on Orend 2002, whose application of needs to human rights is discussed in chapter 9. For the relevance of needs to ethics, I am also indebted to a lecture by Patricia Churchland in Waterloo in April 2008. Braybrooke (1987) provides a comprehensive philosophical discussion of needs, including a plausible list of physiological and social needs.

169 Psychologists Edward Deci and Richard Ryan: Deci and Ryan 2000, 2002. See http://www.psych.rochester.edu/SDT/ for many other papers providing evidence for their theory of self-determination. Abraham Maslow's famous hierarchy of basic needs (physiological, safety, love, esteem, and self-actualization) has little evidential support.

170 Roy Baumeister and Mark Leary comprehensively review evidence that people have a need to belong: Baumeister and Leary 1995. I described in chapter 7 how widowhood and divorce both produce strong drops in life satisfaction: Lucas et al. 2003. This kind of longitudinal study shows a causal link between belongingness deprivation and harm.

171 According to Ryan and Deci, the issue of whether people stand behind a behavior out of their interests and values, or do it for reasons external to the self, is significant in every culture: Ryan and Deci 2000. See also Sheldon et al. 2001.

171 Children are more likely to be well-adjusted if their parents support their autonomy rather than controlling them autocratically: Ryan et al. 2006. This paper is a broad and deep discussion of the importance of autonomy. Walton, Devlin, and Rushworth 2004 show differences in brain activation depending on whether people are making their own decisions or being told what to do.

171 I am not sure that the evidence is now sufficient to support the claim of Deci and Ryan that the needs for relatedness, autonomy, and competence are innate: See Richardson 2007 for the dangers of postulating innate mechanisms without the kinds of evidence appropriate for evolutionary explanations. Basic emotions such as happiness and sadness are plausibly innate, as there is much evidence concerning their cultural universality and biological basis. Quartz and Sejnowski 2002 argue that the main evolutionary legacy of the human brain is a strong capacity to learn. Debates about whether various behaviors and

concepts are innate are often based on simplistic models of development; see Stiles 2008. Nevertheless, I strongly suspect that the need for relatedness is innate, and perhaps also the other two. As many authors have pointed out, humans are social animals.

172 Evidence that people tend to be more satisfied with love-based matches than with arranged marriages: Xiahoe and White 1990.

172 Of these, the neural basis of relatedness is best understood, thanks to investigation of the mechanisms of interpersonal bonding: Depue and Morrone-Strupinsky 2005.

172 According to neuropsychologist Kelly Lambert: Lambert 2006.

173 In their second year, the development of frontal control mechanisms allows children: Posner and Rothbart 2007.

173 Adolescence brings another major period of development of the frontal cortex, associated with even greater desires for autonomy: Sylwester 2007.

173 Psychologists have found that people are happier, healthier, and more hard-working: Lyubomirsky 2008, p. 210; Sheldon 2002.

175 The capabilities approach of Amartya Sen and Martha Nussbaum: Sen 1999; Nussbaum 2000.

175 Peter Railton's idea of an objective interest: Railton 2003, p. 11.

177 According to Daniel Levinson, the human life cycle evolves through a sequence of four overlapping eras: Levinson 1978, 1996. His surveys seem to show more difficulties in the lives of women than in those of men, although he acknowledges that "in every person's life there is an admixture of joy and sorrow, success and failure, self-fulfillment and self-defeat" (1996, p. 416).

177 Studies of life satisfaction and well-being do appear to show some correlation with equal sex roles: e.g., Inglehart et al. 2008.

178 Hope is usually a mixed emotional state that includes some anxiety: Lazarus 1999.

180 *The How of Happiness,* by social psychologist Sonja Lyubomirsky: Lyubomirsky 2008. This book is based on *positive psychology*, a major trend in current clinical and social psychology to study scientifically the nature and causes of optimal human functioning. I would like to see a trend of *positive philosophy* (not positivist!) that develops theories of the accomplishment of knowledge, morality, and meaning that counter skepticism, relativism, and nihilism.

181 Nonreligious people are actually less likely than religious ones to request aggressive measures: Phelps et al. 2009.

182 Consider John Stuart Mill's last words to his stepdaughter: "You know I have done my work": Capaldi 2004, p. 356.

Chapter 9
Ethical Brains

183 Some philosophers such as Nietzsche: http://plato.stanford.edu/entries/nietzsche/. See also the discussion below of Prinz 2007.

183 Hume's famous injunction that you cannot derive an *ought* from an *is*: Hume 1888.

185 John Rawls called *reflective equilibrium*: Rawls 1971.

185 I do not want to make the strong claim that emotions are *essential* to moral judgments: contrast Prinz 2004.

186 The hypothesis that moral intuitions arise from the neuropsychological mechanisms of emotional consciousness: For further discussion, see Thagard and Finn forthcoming.

187 Psychopaths are people completely lacking in conscience and constitute approximately 1 percent of the population: Hare 1993. Perhaps psychopaths have needs that differ from those of normal people, but we shouldn't tie ethics to a pathological minority, any more than we should tie epistemology to schizophrenics with a skewed sense of reality.

187 One prominent theory is that psychopaths have amygdala damage: Blair, Mitchell, and Blair 2005. Psychopathic behavior can also result from damage to the ventromedial prefrontal cortex, as in the case of Phineas Gage, and (I conjecture) from reading Ayn Rand.

187 Differences in moral judgments can also result from damage: Koenigs et al. 2007. Other important work on neuroscience and ethics includes Greene et al. 2001; Moll et al. 2005; and Casebeer and Churchland 2003.

188 Mirror neurons were first identified in the 1990s by Giacomo Rizzolatti: Rizzolatti and Craighero 2004. The next few sections are taken from Thagard 2007b. Iacoboni 2008 provides a fascinating review, including the observation that media violence can encourage violent social behavior via mirror neurons. Goldman 2006 relates mirror neurons to philosophical issues about understanding other minds.

190 Allison Barnes and I developed an account of empathy: Barnes and Thagard 1997. See also Thagard 2006, ch. 3, on emotional analogies.

190 Tania Singer and her colleagues advocate a perception-action model of empathy: Singer et al. 2006. See also Preston and de Waal 2002; Decety and Jackson 2004; Jackson et al. 2006; and Singer et al. 2004.

191 Mirror neuron areas help us to understand the emotions of other people because they fire when we see others expressing their emotions: Iacoboni 2008.

192 According to Hatfield, Cacioppo, and Rapson's theory of emotional contagion: Hatfield, Cacioppo, and Rapson 1994, pp. 10–11.

192 Empathy is a major factor in the moral development of children: Hoffman 2000.

193 The philosopher Sean Nichols: Nichols 2004.

193 "Norms are more likely to be preserved in the culture": Nichols 2004, p. 140.

194 Blair and his colleagues discuss moral socialization: Blair, Mitchell, and Blair 2005, p. 128.

194 For ethics, the capacity to care about others: On the ethics of care, see Held 2006 and Slote 2007.

196 German philosopher Immanuel Kant: Kant 1959.

196 Consequentialism is the philosophical view that whether an act is right or wrong depends only on the effects: http://plato.stanford.edu/entries/consequentialism/.

198 Many religious traditions, going back to the ancient Greeks, have some variant of the golden rule: http://www.religioustolerance.org/reciproc.htm.

198 John Rawls's proposal that when we try to establish moral principles, we should place ourselves behind a "veil of ignorance": Rawls 1971.

198 The philosopher Brian Orend: Orend 2002.

200 Thus needs-based consequentialism is the most plausible ethical theory currently available: To defend this fully, I would have to critique alternative ethical theories such as contractarianism, expressivism, and virtue ethics. Some neurophilosophers have seen an affinity between neuroscience and virtue ethics (Casebeer and Churchland 2003; P. M. Churchland 2007). I find virtue ethics—the view that an action is right if it is what a virtuous agent would do in the circumstances—unappealing for both philosophical and psychological reasons. Philosophically, it is less than helpful, because it leaves open what constitutes a virtuous agent, which on my view requires caring about the needs of others. (The advice you get from virtue ethics is rather like the punctuation advice "Don't use commas like a stupid person.") Psychologically, virtue ethics faces the problem of dealing with the large amount of experimental evidence that people's behavior is often a function more of their circumstances than of their character. See http://plato.stanford.edu/entries/moral-psych-emp/.

201 The philosopher Jesse Prinz defends moral relativism: Prinz 2007.

201 Another possibility is that all humans are born with innate ethical principles that constitute a moral universal grammar: Hauser 2006; Mikhail 2007. This view is based on the increasingly dubious approach to linguistics that postulates universal grammars for language. In both language and morals, there is considerable diversity that points to the power of learning mechanisms rather than to innate principles.

202 The problem, however, is that people can settle into equilibrium states with a good fit of intuitions and principles that nevertheless are not very logical: Stich and Nisbett 1980. For other critiques of reflective equilibrium, see Thagard 1988 and Harman and Kulkarni 2007.

204 The distinguished neuroscientist Michael Gazzaniga: Gazzaniga 2005.

204 The behaviorist psychologist B. F. Skinner: Skinner 1972.

205 As Gazzaniga suggests, we should think of a person as a social being: On the relational view of persons, see also Koggel 1998. Bechtel 2008 has a philosophically and scientifically rich discussion of freedom and dignity consistent with an understanding of mental mechanisms.

205 The neuropsychologists Joshua Greene and Jonathan Cohen: Greene and Cohen 2006. Ongoing discussion of the relevance of neuroscience for understanding freedom and responsibility is occurring in the burgeoning field of neuroethics: http://www.neuroethics.upenn.edu/websites.html.

206 Hence the need for autonomy is fully compatible with the rejection of free will and the adoption of social responsibility: For similar views, see Ryan et al. 2006.

208 Consequentialism about vital needs is coherent with biological and psychological knowledge: For a rigorous account of coherence, including ethical coherence, see Thagard 2000.

Chapter 10
Making Sense of It All

211 Adopt as domain norms those practices that best accomplish the relevant goals: For further discussion of the relation between the descriptive and normative, see Thagard 1988, 2000; and Hardy-Valée and Thagard 2008.

212 Available evidence does not particularly well support claims commonly made by proponents of evolutionary psychology that the brain is a collection of special-purpose innate modules such as ones for language and social behavior: See, for example, Richardson 2007.

213 Given the current lack of evidence about just how brains evolved, it is at least as plausible that the major effect of natural selection has been to allow the development of powerful methods of individual and social learning: Quartz and Sejnowski 2002.

215 Early governments were monarchies: Trigger 2003. For further discussion of the question of what kind of state is most coherent with human experience, see Thagard 2000, ch. 5.

216 The human capacity to appreciate the needs of others: Ignatieff 1985.

216 In 2008, the top ten countries on the Human Development Index were: http://hdr.undp.org/en/statistics/.

216 Another way to try to assess human needs satisfaction in different countries is to look at surveys of subjective well-being that have made since 1981: http://thehappinessshow.com/HappiestCountries.htm. See also Inglehart et al. 2008, according to which subjective well-being is increasing in most countries.

217 Pressing global problems include economic crises, poverty, unemployment, climate change, overpopulation, and looming energy shortages: Homer-Dixon 2007.

218 My collaborators and I are working on a neurocomputational model of how a new pattern of activation can emerge: Thagard and Stewart forthcoming. For an excellent cognitive-historical discussion of scientific creativity, see Nersessian 2008.

219 The available evidence suggests that the best way to improve the mood of depressed people is a combination of cognitive therapy and antidepressant medication: Kramer 2005.

219 Figure 10.2 displays four commonly advocated views of such relations: This figure and a few sentences are taken (with permission of the Cognitive Science Society) from Thagard 2009, which contains further discussion. For a video of me talking about changing complex systems, see http://video.google.com/video play?docid=1880605980833989.

221 Already there is some understanding of concepts of number in animals and infants, but the neural underpinnings of mathematical knowledge are just beginning to be investigated: For a comprehensive discussion, with many recent references, see Kadosh and Walsh 2009, who argue that numerical representation is supported by neural populations in the parietal cortex.

222 I think the most plausible way out of this impasse is to conclude that numbers and other mathematical objects are just fictions: Bunge 2006; see also Maddy 2007.

224 The writer Julian Barnes said that the novel tells beautiful, shapely lies which enclose hard, exact truths: Barnes 2008, p. 78.

224 Paul Steinhardt and Neil Turok: Steinhardt and Turok 2007.

228 Fortunately, cognitive approaches to literature and neural approaches to aesthetics are starting to emerge: For an example of neuroaesthetics, see Levitin 2006 on music. Mar and Oatley 2008 illustrate the value of cognitive psychology for understanding fiction literature. For an approach to allegory based on neural processes, see Thagard forthcoming. I would also like to see neurocognitive/emotional theories of film, dance, and painting, all of which constitute part of the meaning of life through their contributions to play, work, and even sometimes love. My hope is that neural naturalism can help to rescue cultural studies from the pit of postmodernism, which combines obsolete psychology (Freud) with outmoded politics (Marx) and obscure philosophy (Heidegger).

228 The legal scholar Anthony Kronman: Kronman 2007. Another writer who appreciates the value of the humanities but neglects neuropsychology is Eagleton 2007.

229 Julian Barnes wrote: "I don't believe in God, but I miss him." Barnes 2008, p. 1.

229 Philosophical problems arise whenever there are challenging questions about action and belief: See Thagard 2009 for more detailed discussion of the relevance of philosophy to science.

Glossary

A priori knowledge — Knowledge that is gained by reason alone, independently of sensory experience.

Amygdala — Brain area located centrally below the cortex, important for emotions such as fear.

Anthropic principle — View that the existence of human observers is relevant to explaining the nature of the universe.

Autonomy — Psychological need to self-organize and regulate one's own behavior and avoid control by others.

Bodily perception — Component of emotion that uses internal sensors to detect bodily states such as heart and breathing patterns.

Brain revolution — The emerging replacement of the belief that minds are souls by the hypothesis that minds are brains.

Brain scanning — The use of imaging techniques such as functional magnetic resonance imaging (fMRI) to investigate the structure and function of the brain.

Cognitive appraisal — Component of emotion that assesses the impact of a situation on a person's goals.

Cognitive neuroscience — Investigation of mental functions linked to neural processes.

Cognitive science — The interdisciplinary study of mind and intelligence, embracing philosophy, psychology, neuroscience, linguistics, anthropology, and artificial intelligence.

Coherentism — The epistemological theory that beliefs are justified by how well they fit with other beliefs and with sensory experience.

Competence — Psychological need to engage optimal challenges and experience physical and social mastery.

Confirmation bias — The tendency of people to search for evidence that supports rather than challenges their beliefs.

Consciousness — Mental state involving attention, awareness, and qualitative experience.

Consequentialism — The ethical theory that whether an act is right or wrong depends on its effects on people. Needs-based, pluralistic consequentialism says that the effects to be considered concern vital human needs.

Constructive realism — The view that reality exists independently of minds, but that our knowledge of reality is constructed by mental processes.

Cortex — Outer layer of the brain, responsible for many higher cognitive functions.

Descriptive — Pertaining to how things are, as opposed to how they ought to be.

Dopamine — Neurotransmitter used in reward pathways in the brain.

Dualism — The view that a person consists of two kinds of substances, a spiritual mind and a physical body.

Electroencephalography — The use of electrodes placed on the scalp to record electrical activity in the brain.

Embodiment—The view that our thinking depends heavily on the ways our bodies enable us to perceive the world and act on it.

EMOCON—Model of how brain areas interact to produce emotional consciousness through the interaction of working memory, cognitive appraisal, and bodily perception.

Emotion—Brain state involving positive or negative appraisal of a situation and perception of physiological changes.

Empathy—The capacity to appreciate the states of mind of others by imagining oneself in their place.

Empiricism—The philosophical view that all knowledge is based on sense experience.

Epistemology—The philosophical study of the nature of knowledge.

Ethics—The philosophical study of the basis of right and wrong.

Evidence—Information gathered by careful observation, especially through scientific experiments.

Evidence-based philosophy—Philosophical investigation tied to the observational, experimental, and theoretical results of science rather than to faith or a priori reasoning.

Explanation—Specification of how a state or process results from an underlying causal mechanism.

Faith—A belief in, trust in, and devotion to gods, leaders, or texts, independent of evidence.

fMRI—Functional magnetic resonance imaging. A brain-scanning technique that uses the flow of blood in the brain to measure activity in brain areas.

Free will—The ability to make choices that are uncaused by physical processes.

Functionalism—The philosophical view that mental states are defined by their functional (input-output) relations to each other, not by any particular kind of physical realization.

Goal—Emotionally valued neural representation of imagined states of the world and self.

Happiness—Emotion characterized by positive experience with intensity ranging from contentment to intense joy.

Hebbian learning—Process in neural networks that strengthens the association between two neurons that are simultaneously active.

Hippocampus—Brain region involved in the acquisition of memories.

Hope—Brain process that produces a positive feeling about future goal satisfaction.

Hypothesis—A conjecture about what factors might explain why something happens.

Idealism—The philosophical view that reality is inherently mental.

Identity theory—The hypothesis that mental states and processes are states and processes of the brain.

Inference to the best explanation—The acceptance of a hypothesis on the grounds that it provides a better explanation of the available evidence than do alternative hypotheses.

Inference to the best plan—Decision making by choosing an action on the grounds that it is part of the best means for accomplishing goals.

Intuition—Apparently immediate conscious judgment arising from unconscious brain processes.

Materialism—The metaphysical view that nothing exists except matter and energy.

Mechanism—A system of connected parts whose interactions produce regular changes.

Metaphysics—The philosophical study of the fundamental nature of what exists.

Mirror neurons—Neurons that fire both when an animal acts and when it perceives the same action in another animal.

Motivated inference—The tendency to use memory and evidence selectively in order to arrive at beliefs that facilitate our goals.

Multimodal representation—Brain structure that may involve different kinds of sensory and emotional as well as verbal information.

Naturalism—The view that we can best address philosophical questions by taking into account scientific evidence and theories rather than supernatural sources.

Need—Condition without which a person would be harmed.

Neural naturalism—The version of naturalism that emphasizes knowledge gained from neuroscience in addition to other sciences.

Neural network—Interconnected group of neurons.

Neuron—nerve cell.

Neuropsychology—The investigation of mental functions linked to neural processes.

Neurotransmitter—Molecule that transmits nerve impulses across a synapse.

Nihilism—The view that life has no meaning at all.

Normative—Pertaining to how things ought to be, as opposed to how they are.

Nucleus accumbens—Brain area located below the cortex, important for pleasure and positive emotions.

Parallel constraint satisfaction—Process, naturally performed by neural networks, in which a problem is solved through the simultaneous discovery of the best assignment of values to interconnected aspects of the problem.

Philosophy—The search for answers to fundamental questions about the nature of reality, knowledge, morality, and the meaning of life.

Positive philosophy—Approach to philosophy, analogous to positive psychology, that emphasizes the achievement of knowledge, morality, and meaning rather than doubt and despair.

Ptolemaic counterrevolution—Attempt to place mind at the center of reality, analogous to attempting to go back to Ptolemy's view that the sun and planets revolve around the earth.

Reductionism—View that explanations of phenomena should always be stated in terms of component entities and processes.

Reflective equilibrium—Philosophical method that reaches normative conclusions by mutual adjustment of principles and intuitions.

Relatedness—Psychological need for social attachments and feelings of security, belongingness, and intimacy with others.

Representation—Structure intended to stand for something.

Responsibility—Being held morally accountable for one's actions.

Science—The experimental and theoretical investigation of the world.

Skepticism—Philosophical view that knowledge is unattainable.

Slacker serenity—A state of happiness that comes from having only minimal goals. (A slacker is a person who shirks work and other duties.)

Synapse—Space in which a signal passes from one neuron to another.

Telic rationality—Consideration of how goals ought to be acquired, abandoned, and revalued.

Theory—A collection of hypotheses that together explain a range of evidence.

Thought experiment—Mental construction of an imaginary situation in the absence of attempts to make observations of the world.

Transcranial magnetic stimulation—Use of magnetic pulses to affect neural activation in the cortex.

Vital need—Something without which a person cannot function as a human being.

Wisdom—Knowledge about what matters, why it matters, and how to achieve it.

Zombie argument—Claim that minds cannot be brains, because we can imagine beings (zombies) who are physically identical to us but lack consciousness.

References

Akerlof, G. A., & Shiller, R. J. (2009). *Animal spirits: How human psychology drives the economy, and why it matters for global capitalism.* Princeton: Princeton University Press.

Anderson, J. R. (2007). *How can the mind occur in the physical universe?* Oxford: Oxford University Press.

Angell, M. (2004). *The truth about the drug companies: How they deceive us and what to do about it.* New York: Random House.

Appiah, A. (2008). *Experiments in ethics.* Cambridge, MA: Harvard University Press.

Ariely, D. (2008). *Predictably irrational.* New York: HarperCollins.

Aron, A., Fisher, H., Mashek, D. J., Strong, G., Li, H., & Brown, L. L. (2005). Reward, motivation, and emotion systems associated with early-stage intense romantic love. *Journal of Neurophysiology, 94,* 327–337.

Baillargeon, R., Kotovsky, L., & Needham, A. (1995). The acquisition of physical knowledge in infancy. In D. Sperber, D. Premack & A. J. Premack (Eds.), *Causal cognition: A multidisciplinary debate* (pp. 79–116). Oxford: Clarendon Press.

Balcetis, E., & Dunning, D. (2006). See what you want to see: Motivational influences on visual perception. *Journal of Personality and Social Psychology, 91,* 612–625.

Banich, M. T. (2004). *Cognitive neuroscience and neuropsychology.* Boston: Houghton Mifflin.

Barnes, A., & Thagard, P. (1997). Empathy and analogy. *Dialogue: Canadian Philosophical Review, 36,* 705–720.

Barnes, J. (2008). *Nothing to be frightened of.* London: Jonathan Cape.

Barnes, T. D., Kubota, Y., Hu, D., Jin, D. Z., & Graybiel, A. M. (2005). Activity of striatal neurons reflects dynamic encoding and recoding of procedural memories. *Nature, 437*(7062), 1158–1161.

Barrett, L. F. (2006). Are emotions natural kinds? *Perspectives on psychological science, 1,* 28–58.

Barsalou, L. W., Simmons, W. K., Barbey, A. K., & Wilson, C. D. (2003). Grounding conceptual knowledge in modality-specific systems. *Trends in Cognitive Sciences, 7,* 84–91.

Bartels, A., & Zeki, S. (2000). The neural basis of romantic love. *NeuroReport, 11,* 3829–3834.

Batson, C. D. (1991). *The altruism question.* Hillsdale, NJ: Lawrence Erlbaum Associates.

Baumeister, R. F. (1991). *Meanings of life.* New York: Guilford Press.

Baumeister, R. F., & Leary, M. R. (1995). The need to belong: Desire for interpersonal attachments as a fundamental human motivation. *Psychological Bulletin, 117,* 497–529.

Bazerman, M. H. (1994). *Judgment in managerial decision making.* New York: John Wiley.

Bechtel, W. (2008). *Mental mechanisms: Philosophical perspectives on cognitive neuroscience*. New York: Routledge.

Bechtel, W., & Abrahamsen, A. A. (2005). Explanation: A mechanistic alternative. *Studies in History and Philosophy of Biology and Biomedical Sciences, 36*, 421–441.

Bechtel, W., & Richardson, R. C. (1993). *Discovering complexity*. Princeton: Princeton University Press.

Behrendt, R., & Young, C. (2005). Hallucinations in schizophrenia, sensory impairment, and brain disease: A unifying model. *Behavioral and Brain Sciences, 27*, 771–830.

Benatar, D. (2006). *Better never to have been born*. Oxford: Clarendon Press.

Bennett, M., Dennett, D., Hacker, P., & Searle, J. (2007). *Neuroscience and philosophy*. New York: Columbia University Press.

Benson, H., Dusek, J. A., Sherwood, J. B., Lam, P., Bethea, C. F., Carpenter, W., et al. (2006). Study of the Therapeutic Effects of Intercessory Prayer (STEP) in cardiac bypass patients: A multicenter randomized trial of uncertainty and certainty of receiving intercessory prayer. *American Heart Journal, 151*(4), 934–942.

Bentham, J., & Mill, J. S. (1973). *The utilitarians*. New York: Anchor Books.

Biswas-Diener, R., Vittersø, J., & Diener, E. (2005). Most people are pretty happy, but there is cultural variation: The Inughuit, the Amish, and the Masai. *Journal of happiness studies, 6*, 205–226.

Blair, J., Mitchell, D. R., & Blair, K. (2005). *The psychopath: Emotion and the brain*. Malden, MA: Blackwell.

Blanke, O., et al. (2005). Linking out-of-body experience and self processing to mental own-body imagery at the temporoparietal junction. *Journal of Neuroscience, 25*, 550–557.

Bloom, P. (2004). *Descartes's baby*. New York: Basic Books.

Boden, M. (2006). *Mind as machine: A history of cognitive science*. Oxford: Oxford University Press.

Braybrooke, D. (1987). *Meeting needs*. Princeton, NJ: Princeton University Press.

Bugliosi, V. (1997). *Outrage: The five reasons why O. J. Simpson got away with murder*. New York: Island Books.

Bunge, M. (2003). *Emergence and convergence: Qualitative novelty and the unity of knowledge*. Toronto: University of Toronto Press.

Bunge, M. (2006). *Chasing reality: Strife over realism*. Toronto: University of Toronto Press.

Byrne, R. (2006). *The secret*. New York: Simon and Schuster.

Camerer, C., Loewenstein, G. F., & Prelec, D. (2005). Neuroeconomics: How neuroscience can inform economics. *Journal of Economic Literature, 34*, 9–64.

Camus, A. (2000a). *The myth of Sysyphus* (J. O'Brien, Trans.). London: Penguin.

Camus, A. (2000b). *The outsider*. London: Penguin.

Capaldi, N. (2004). *John Stuart Mill: A biography*. Cambridge: Cambridge University Press.

Casebeer, W. D., & Churchland, P. S. (2003). The neural mechanisms of moral cognition: A multiple-aspect approach. *Biology and philosophy, 18*, 169–194.

Chalmers, D. J. (1996). *The conscious mind*. Oxford: Oxford University Press.

Changeux, J.-P. (2004). *The physiology of truth: Neuroscience and human knowledge.* Cambridge, MA: Harvard University Press.

Chi, M.T.H. (2005). Commonsense conceptions of emergent processes: Why some misconceptions are robust. *Journal of the Learning Sciences, 14*, 161–199.

Churchland, P. M. (1995). *The engine of reason: The seat of the soul.* Cambridge, MA: MIT Press.

Churchland, P. M. (2007). *Neurophilosophy at work.* Cambridge: Cambridge University Press.

Churchland, P. S. (1986). *Neurophilosophy.* Cambridge, MA: MIT Press.

Churchland, P. S. (2002). *Brain-wise: Studies in neurophilosophy.* Cambridge, MA: MIT Press.

Churchland, P. S. (2009). Inference to the best decision. In J. Bickle (Ed.), *Oxford handbook of philosophy and neuroscience* (pp. 419–430). Oxford: Oxford University Press.

Churchland, P. S., & Sejnowski, T. (1992). *The computational brain.* Cambridge, MA: MIT Press.

Clark, A. (2008). *Supersizing the mind: Embodiment, action, and cognitive extension.* Oxford: Oxford University Press.

Craver, C. F. (2007). *Explaining the brain.* Oxford: Oxford University Press.

Csikszentmihalyi, M. (1997). *Finding flow: The psychology of engagement with everyday life.* New York: Basic Books.

Damasio, A. R. (1994). *Descartes' error.* New York: G. P. Putnam's Sons.

Damasio, A. R. (1999). *The feeling of what happens: Body and emotion in the making of consciousness.* New York: Harcourt Brace.

Davidson, R. J., Scherer, K. R., & Goldsmith, H. H. (Eds.). (2003). *Handbook of affective sciences.* New York: Oxford University Press.

Dawis, R. V. (2004). Job satisfaction. In J. C. Thomas (Ed.), *Comprehensive handbook of psychological assessment. Vol. 4, Industrial and organizational assessment* (pp. 470–481). Hoboken, NJ: John Wiley and Sons.

Dawkins, R. (2006). *The God delusion.* New York: Houghton Mifflin.

de Sousa, R. (1988). *The rationality of emotion.* Cambridge, MA: MIT Press.

Deaton, A. (2008). Income, health, and well-being around the world: Evidence from the Gallup World Poll. *Journal of Economic Perspectives, 22*, 53–72.

Decety, J., & Jackson, P. L. (2004). The functional architecture of human empathy. *Behavioral and Cognitive Neuroscience Reviews, 3*(2), 71–100.

Deci, E. L., & Ryan, R. M. (2000). The "what" and "why" of goal pursuits: Human needs and the self-determination of behavior. *Psychological Inquiry, 11*, 227–268.

Deci, E. L., & Ryan, R. M. (Eds.). (2002). *Handbook of self-determination research.* Rochester: University of Rochester Press.

Dennett, D. (2003). *Freedom evolves.* New York: Penguin.

Dennett, D. (2005). *Sweet dreams: Philosophical obstacles to a science of consciousness.* Cambridge, MA: MIT Press.

Dennett, D. (2006). *Breaking the spell: Religion as a natural phenomenon.* New York: Penguin.

Depue, R. A., & Morrone-Strupinsky, J. V. (2005). A neurobehavioral model of affiliative bonding: Implications for conceptualizing a human trait of affiliation. *Behavioral and Brain Sciences, 28*, 313–350.

Diaconis, P. (1978). Statistical problems in ESP research. *Science, 201*, 131–136.

Diener, E., & Seligman, M. E. (2004). Beyond money: Toward an economy of well-being. *Psychological Science in the Public Interest, 5*(1–31).

Dijksterhuis, A. (2004). Think different: The merits of unconscious thought in preference development and decision making. *Journal of Personality and Social Psychology, 87*, 586–598.

Doidge, N. (2007). *The brain that changes itself*. New York: Penguin.

Drake, S. (1978). *Galileo at work: His scientific biography*. Chicago: University of Chicago Press.

Dreyfus, H. L. (2007). Why Heideggerian AI failed and how fixing it would require making it more Heideggerian. *Philosophical Psychology, 20*, 247–268.

Eagleton, T. (2007). *The meaning of life*. Oxford: Oxford University Press.

Easterlin, R. A. (2006). Life cycle happiness and its sources: Intersections of psychology, economics, and demography. *Journal of Economic Psychology, 27*, 463–482.

Ehrsson, H. H. (2007). The experimental induction of out-of-body experiences. *Science, 317*(5841), 1048.

Eisenberger, N. I., & Lieberman, M. D. (2004). Why rejection hurts: A common neural alarm system for physical and social pain. *Trends in Cognitive Sciences, 8*, 294–300.

Eisenberger, N. I., Lieberman, M. D., & Williams, K. D. (2003). Does rejection hurt? An fMRI study of social exclusion. *Science, 302*(5643), 290–292.

Eliasmith, C. (2005a). Cognition with neurons: A large-scale, biologically realistic model of the Wason task. In B. Bara, L. Barasalou & M. Bucciarelli (Eds.), *Proceedings of the XXVII Annual Conference of the Cognitive Science Society* (pp. 624–629). Mahwah, NJ: Lawrence Erlbaum Associates.

Eliasmith, C. (2005b). Neurosemantics and categories. In H. Cohen & C. Lefebvre (Eds.), *Handbook of categorization in cognitive science* (pp. 1035–1054). Amsterdam: Elsevier.

Eliasmith, C., & Anderson, C. H. (2003). *Neural engineering: Computation, representation and dynamics in neurobiological systems*. Cambridge, MA: MIT Press.

Eliasmith, C., Stewart, T. C., & Conklin, J. (forthcoming). A new biologically implemented cognitive architecture.

Eliasmith, C., & Thagard, P. (1997). Waves, particles, and explanatory coherence. *British Journal for the Philosophy of Science, 48*, 1–19.

Eliasmith, C., & Thagard, P. (2001). Integrating structure and meaning: A distributed model of analogical mapping. *Cognitive Science, 25*, 245–286.

Engels, F. (1947). *Anti-Dühring*. Moscow: Progress Publishers.

Fazio, R. H. (2001). On the automatic activation of associated evaluations: An overview. *Cognition and Emotion, 15*, 115–141.

Feigl, H. (1958). The "mental" and the "physical." In H. Feigl, M. Scriven & G. Maxwell (Eds.), *Concepts, theories and the mind-body problem. Minnesota Studies in the Philosophy of Science, vol. 2* (pp. 370–497). Minneapolis: University of Minnesota Press.

Feldman, J. A. (2006). *From molecule to metaphor: A neural theory of language*. Cambridge, MA: MIT Press.

Finger, S. (1994). *Origins of neuroscience: A history of explorations into brain function.* New York: Oxford University Press.

Fisher, H. (2004). *Why we love: The nature and chemistry of romantic love.* New York: Henry Holt.

Fisher, H., Aron, A., & Brown, L. L. (2005). Romantic love: An fMRI study of a neural mechanism for mate choice. *Journal of Comparative Neurology, 493,* 58–62.

Flanagan, O. (2002). *The problem of the soul.* New York: Basic Books.

Flanagan, O. (2007). *The really hard problem: Meaning in a material world.* Cambridge, MA: MIT Press.

Fodor, J. (1975). *The language of thought.* New York: Crowell.

Fodor, J. A. (1998). *Concepts: Where cognitive science went wrong.* Oxford: Oxford University Press.

Frank, R. H. (1988). *Passions within reason.* New York: Norton.

Frankfurt, H. G. (2004). *The reasons of love.* Princeton: Princeton University Press.

Freud, S. (1962). *Civilization and its discontents.* New York: W. W. Norton.

Frey, B. S., & Stutzer, A. (2002). *Happiness and economics.* Princeton, NJ: Princeton University Press.

Gazzaniga, M. S. (2005). *The ethical brain.* New York: Dana Press.

Gibbs, R. W. (2006). *Embodiment and cognitive science.* Cambridge: Cambridge University Press.

Giere, R. N. (1999). *Science without laws.* Chicago: University of Chicago Press.

Gigerenzer, G. (2000). *Adaptive thinking: Rationality in the real world.* New York: Oxford University Press.

Gilbert, D. (2006). *Stumbling on happiness.* New York: Alfred A. Knopf.

Gilovich, T. (1991). *How we know what isn't so.* New York: Free Press.

Gladwell, M. (2005). *Blink.* New York: Little Brown.

Goel, V. (2005). Cognitive neuroscience of deductive reasoning. In K. J. Holyoak & R. G. Morrison (Eds.), *The Cambridge handbook of thinking and reasoning* (pp. 475–492). Cambridge: Cambridge University Press.

Goldman, A. I. (2006). *Simulating minds.* New York: Oxford University Press.

Goodwin, F. K., & Jamison, K. R. (2007). *Manic-depressive illness: Bipolar disorders and recurrent depression* (2nd ed.). Oxford: Oxford University Press.

Gordon, D. (Ed.). (2008). *Your brain on Cubs: Inside the heads of players and fans.* New York: Dana Press.

Gould, S. J. (1999). *Rock of ages: Science and religion in the fullness of life.* New York: Ballantine.

Grandjean, D., Sander, D., & Scherer, K. R. (2008). Conscious emotional experience emerges as a function of multilevel, appraisal-driven response synchronization. *Consciousness and Cognition, 17,* 484–495.

Greene, J. D., & Cohen, J. (2006). For the law, neuroscience changes nothing and everything. In S. Zeki & O. Goodenough (Eds.), *Law and the brain* (pp. 207–226). Oxford: Oxford University Press.

Greene, J. D., Sommerville, R. B., Nystrom, L. E., Darley, J. M., & Cohen, J. D. (2001). An fMRI investigation of emotional engagement in moral judgment. *Science, 293,* 2105–2108.

Groopman, J. (2007). *How doctors think*. Boston: Houghton Mifflin.

Guyatt, G. et al. (1992). Evidence-based medicine: A new approach to teaching the practice of medicine. *Journal of the American Medical Association, 268*, 2420–2425.

Hacking, I. (1999). *The social construction of what?* Cambridge, MA: Harvard University Press.

Haidt, J. (2006). *The happiness hypothesis*. New York: Basic Books.

Hall, A. R. (1962). *The scientific revolution 1500–1800*. London: Longmans.

Hardy-Vallée, B., & Thagard, P. (2008). How to play the ultimatum game: An engineering approach to metanormativity. *Philosophical Psychology, 21*, 173–192.

Hare, R. D. (1993). *Without conscience: The disturbing world of the psychopaths among us*. New York: Pocket Books.

Harman, G. (1973). *Thought*. Princeton: Princeton University Press.

Harman, G. (1986). *Change in view: Principles of reasoning*. Cambridge, MA: MIT Press/Bradford Books.

Harman, G., & Kulkarni, S. (2007). *Reliable reasoning: Induction and statistical learning theory*. Cambridge, MA: MIT Press.

Harrington, A. (1997). *The placebo effect: An interdisciplinary exploration*. Cambridge, MA: Harvard University Press.

Harris, S., Sheth, S. A., & Cohen, M. S. (2008). Functional neuroimaging of belief, disbelief, and uncertainty. *Annals of Neurology, 63*, 141–147.

Hatfield, E., Cacioppo, J. T., & Rapson, R. L. (1994). *Emotional contagion*. Cambridge: Cambridge University Press.

Hauser, M. D. (2006). *Moral minds: How nature designed our universal sense of right and wrong*. New York: Ecco.

Hebb, D. O. (1949). *The organization of behavior: A neuropsychological theory*. New York: Wiley.

Hebb, D. O. (1980). *Essay on mind*. Hillsdale, NJ: Lawrence Erlbaum.

Hegel, G.W.F. (1969). *Science of logic* (A. V. Miller, Trans.). London: George, Allen and Unwin.

Held, V. (2006). *The ethics of care: Personal, political, global*. Oxford: Oxford University Press.

Hoffman, M. L. (2000). *Empathy and moral development: Implications for caring and justice*. Cambridge: Cambridge University Press.

Hofstadter, D. (2007). *I am a strange loop*. New York: Basic Books.

Hofstadter, D. R. (1979). *Gödel, Escher, Bach: An eternal golden braid*. New York: Basic Books.

Holyoak, K. J., & Thagard, P. (1995). *Mental leaps: Analogy in creative thought*. Cambridge, MA: MIT Press/Bradford Books.

Homer-Dixon, T. (2007). *The upside of down: Catastrophe, creativity, and the renewal of civilization*. Toronto: Vintage Canada.

Hume, D. (1888). *A treatise of human nature*. Oxford: Clarendon Press.

Iacoboni, M. (2008). *Mirroring people: The new science of how we connect with others*. New York: Farrar, Straus and Giroux.

Ignatieff, M. (1985). *The needs of strangers*. New York: Viking.

Inglehart, R., Foa, R., Peterson, C., & Welzel, C. (2008). Development, freedom, and rising happiness: A global perspective. *Perspectives on psychological science, 3*, 264–285.

Insel, T. R., & Young, L. J. (2001). The neurobiology of attachment. *Nature Reviews Neuroscience, 2*, 129–136.

Jackson, P. L., Brunet, E., Meltzoff, A. N., & Decety, J. (2006). Empathy examined through the neural mechanisms involved in imagining how I feel versus how you feel pain. *Neuropsychologia, 44*(5), 752–761.

James, W. (1884). What is an emotion? *Mind, 9*, 188–205.

James, W. (1961). *Psychology: The briefer course.* New York: Harper.

Jamison, K. R. (2000). *Night falls fast: Understanding suicide.* New York: Vintage Books.

Josephs, R. A., Larrick, R. P., Steele, C. M., & Nisbett, R. E. (1992). Protecting the self from the negative consequences of risky decisions. *Journal of Personality and Social Psychology, 62*, 26–37.

Judge, T. A., Thoreson, C. J., Bono, J. E., & Patton, G. K. (2001). The job satisfaction job performance relationship: A qualitative and quantitative review. *Psychological Bulletin, 127*, 376–407.

Juslin, P. N., & Västfjäll, D. (2008). Emotional responses to music: The need to consider underlying mechanisms. *Behavioral and Brain Sciences, 31*, 559–575.

Kadosh, R. C., & Walsh, V. (2009). Numerical representation in the parietal lobes: Abstract or not abstract? *Behavioral and Brain Sciences, in press.*

Kahneman, D., & Tversky, A. (Eds.). (2000). *Choices, values, and frames.* Cambridge: Cambridge University Press.

Kandel, E. R. (2006). *In search of memory: The emergence of a new science of mind.* New York: W. W. Norton.

Kant, I. (1959). *Foundations of the metaphysics of morals* (L. W. Beck, Trans.). Indianapolis: Bobbs-Merrill.

Kant, I. (1965). *Critique of pure reason* (N. K. Smith, Trans. 2nd ed.). London: Macmillan.

Kaufman, S. (2008). *Reinventing the sacred: A new view of science, reason, and religion.* New York: Basic Books.

Klemke, E. D., & Cahn, S. M. (Eds.). (2007). *The meaning of life: A reader.* Oxford: Oxford University Press.

Knobe, J., & Nichols, S. (2008). *Experimental philosophy.* Oxford: Oxford University Press.

Knutson, B., Adams, C. M., Fong, G. W., & Hommer, D. (2001). Anticipation of increasing monetary reward selectively recruits nucleus accumbens. *Journal of Neuroscience, 21*, RC159: 151–155.

Knutson, B., & Greer, S. M. (2008). Anticipatory affect: neural correlates and consequences for choice. *Philosophical Transactions of the Royal Society of London B, 363*, 3771–3786.

Knutson, B., Rick, S., Wimmer, G. E., Prelec, D., & Loewenstein, G. (2007). Neural predictors of purchases. *Neuron, 53*, 147–156.

Koch, C. (2004). *The quest for consciousness: A neurobiological approach*. Englewood, CO: Roberts and Company.

Koelsch, S., & Siebel, W. A. (2005). Towards a neural basis of music perception. *Trends in Cognitive Sciences, 9*, 578–584.

Koenigs, M., Young, L., Adolphs, R., Tranel, D., Cushman, F., Hauser, M., et al. (2007). Damage to the prefrontal cortex increases utilitarian moral judgements. *Nature, 446*, 908–911.

Koggel, C. M. (1998). *Perspectives on equality: Constructing a relational theory*. Lanham, MD: Rowman and Littlefield.

Kolnai, A. (1978). Deliberation is of ends. In *Ethics, value, and reality* (pp. 44–62). Indianapolis: Hackett.

Kosfeld, M., Heinrichs, M., Zak, P. J., Fischbacher, U., & Fehr, E. (2005). Oxytocin increases trust in humans. *Nature, 435*, 673–676.

Kramer, P. D. (2005). *Against depression*. New York: Penguin.

Kringelbach, M. L., Lehtonen, A., Squire, S., Harvey, A. G., Craske, M. G., Holliday, I. E., et al. (2008). A specific and rapid neural signature for parental instinct. *PLoS ONE, 3*(2), e1664.

Kronman, A. T. (2007). *Education's end: Why our colleges and universities have given up on the meaning of life*. New Haven: Yale University Press.

Krueger, F., McCabe, K., Moll, J., Kriegeskorte, N., Zahn, R., Strenziok, M., et al. (2007). Neural correlates of trust. *Proceedings of the National Academy of Sciences USA, 104*(50), 20084–20089.

Kruschke, J. K. (1992). ALCOVE: An exemplar-based connectionist model of category learning. *Psychological Review, 99*, 22–44.

Kunda, Z. (1990). The case for motivated inference. *Psychological Bulletin, 108*, 480–498.

Kunda, Z. (1999). *Social cognition: Making sense of people*. Cambridge, MA: MIT Press.

Kurtz, P. (Ed.). (1985). *A skeptic's handbook of parapsychology*. Amherst, NY: Prometheus Books.

Lakatos, I. (1970). Falsification and the methodology of scientific research programs. In I. Lakatos & A. Musgrave (Eds.), *Criticism and the growth of knowledge* (pp. 91–195). Cambridge: Cambridge University Press.

Lambert, K. G. (2006). Rising rates of depression in today's society: Considerations of effort-based rewards and enhanced resilience in day-to-day functioning. *Neuroscience and Biobehavioral Reviews, 30*, 497–510.

Larson, E. J., & Witham, L. (1998). Leading scientists still reject God. *Nature, 394*, 313.

Latour, B. (1987). *Science in action: How to follow scientists and engineers through society*. Cambridge, MA: Harvard University Press.

Latour, B., & Woolgar, S. (1986). *Laboratory life: The construction of scientific facts*. Princeton, N.J.: Princeton University Press.

Lazarus, R. S. (1999). Hope: An emotion and a vital coping resource against despair. *Social Research, 66*, 653–678.

Lazarus, R. S. (2003). Does the positive psychology movement have legs? *Psychological inquiry, 14*, 93–109.

LeDoux, J. (1996). *The emotional brain*. New York: Simon and Schuster.

LeDoux, J. (2002). *The synaptic self*. New York: Viking.

Levinson, D. (1978). *The seasons of a man's life*. New York: Alfred A. Knopf.

Levinson, D. (1996). *The seasons of a woman's life*. New York: Alfred A. Knopf.

Levitin, D. (2006). *This is your brain on music*. New York: Dutton.

Levitin, D. (2008). *The world in six songs: How the musical brain created human nature*. New York: Penguin.

Lipton, P. (2004). *Inference to the best explanation* (2nd ed.). London: Routledge.

Litt, A., Eliasmith, C., & Thagard, P. (2008). Neural affective decision theory: Choices, brains, and emotions. *Cognitive Systems Research, 9*, 252–273.

Locke, E. A., & Latham, G. P. (1990). *A theory of goal setting and task performance*. Englewood Cliffs, NJ: Prentice Hall.

Locke, E. A., Shaw, K. N., Saari, L. M., & Latham, G. P. (1981). Goal setting and task performance: 1969–1980. *Psychological Bulletin, 90*, 125–152.

Lodish, H., Berk, A., Zipursky, S. L., Matsudaira, P., Baltimore, D., & Darnell, J. (2000). *Molecular cell biology* (4th ed.). New York: W. H. Freeman.

Loewenstein, G. F., Weber, E. U., Hsee, C. K., & Welch, N. (2001). Risk as feelings. *Psychological Bulletin, 127*, 267–286.

Lucas, R. E., Clark, A. E., Georgellis, Y., & Diener, E. (2003). Reexamining adaptation and the set point model of happiness: Reactions to changes in marital status. *Journal of Personality and Social Psychology, 2003*(527–539).

Luce, R. D., & Raiffa, H. (1957). *Games and decisions*. New York: Wiley.

Lutz, A., Greischar, L. L., Rawlings, N. B., Ricard, M., & Davidson, R. J. (2004). Long-term meditators self-induce high-amplitude gamma synchrony during mental practice. *Proceedings of the National Academy of Sciences, 101*, 16369–16373.

Lyubomirsky, S. (2008). *The how of happiness: A scientific approach to getting the life you want*. New York: Penguin.

MacDonald, G., & Leary, M. R. (2005). Why does social exclusion hurt? The relationship between social and physical pain. *Psychological Bulletin, 131*, 202–223.

Macdonald, P. S. (2003). *History of the concept of mind*. Aldershot: Ashgate.

Machamer, P., Darden, L., & Craver, C. F. (2000). Thinking about mechanisms. *Philosophy of Science, 67*, 1–25.

Maddy, P. (2007). *Second philosophy: A naturalistic method*. Oxford: Oxford University Press.

Mansfield, S. (2003). *The faith of George W. Bush*. New York: Penguin.

Mar, R. A., & Oatley, K. (2008). The function of fiction is the abstraction and simulation of social experience. *Perspectives on Psychological Science, 3*, 173–192.

Martin, R. A. (2007). *The psychology of humor: An integrative approach*. Amsterdam: Elsevier.

McCauley, R. N. (2007). Reduction: Models of cross-scientific relations and their implications for the psychology-neuroscience interface. In P. Thagard (Ed.), *Philosophy of psychology and cognitive science* (pp. 105–158). Amsterdam: Elsevier.

McCauley, R. N., & Lawson, E. T. (2002). *Bringing ritual to mind: Psychological foundations of cultural forms*. Cambridge: Cambridge University Press.

McClure, S. M., Laibson, D. I., Loewenstein, G., & Cohen, J. D. (2004). Separate neural systems value immediate and delayed monetary rewards. *Science, 306*(5695), 503–507.

McClure, S. M., Li, J., Tomlin, D., Cypert, K. S., Montague, L. M., & Montague, P. R. (2004). Neural correlates of behavioral preference for culturally familiar drinks. *Neuron, 44*, 379–387.

Medin, D. L. (1989). Concepts and conceptual structure. *American Psychologist, 44*, 1469–1481.

Meyer, J. S., & Quenzer, L. F. (2005). *Psychopharmacology: Drugs, the brain, and behavior.* Sunderland, MA: Sinauer Associates.

Mikhail, J. (2007). Universal moral grammar: Theory, evidence and the future. *Trends in Cognitive Sciences, 11*(4), 143–152.

Millgram, E., & Thagard, P. (1996). Deliberative coherence. *Synthese, 108*, 63–88.

Minsky, M. (1975). A framework for representing knowledge. In P. H. Winston (Ed.), *The psychology of computer vision* (pp. 211–277). New York: McGraw-Hill.

Minsky, M. (2006). *The emotion machine: Commonsense thinking, artificial intelligence, and the future of the human mind.* New York: Simon & Schuster.

Moll, J., Zahn, R., de Oliveira-Souza, R., Krueger, F., & Grafman, J. (2005). The neural basis of human moral cognition. *Nature Reviews Neuroscience, 6*(10), 799–809.

Montague, R. (2006). *Why choose this book? How we make decisions.* New York: Penguin.

Murphy, G. L. (2002). *The big book of concepts.* Cambridge, MA: MIT Press.

Nagel, T. (1979). *Mortal questions.* Cambridge: Cambridge University Press.

Nersessian, N. (2008). *Creating scientific concepts.* Cambridge, MA: MIT Press.

Nichols, S. (2004). *Sentimental rules: On the natural foundations of moral judgment.* Oxford: Oxford University Press.

Nowak, G., & Thagard, P. (1992a). Copernicus, Ptolemy, and explanatory coherence. In R. Giere (Ed.), *Cognitive models of science,* (Vol. 15, pp. 274–309). Minneapolis: University of Minnesota Press.

Nowak, G., & Thagard, P. (1992b). Newton, Descartes, and explanatory coherence. In R. Duschl & R. Hamilton (Eds.), *Philosophy of Science, Cognitive Psychology and Educational Theory and Practice.* (pp. 69–115). Albany: SUNY Press.

Nussbaum, M. (2001). *Upheavals of thought.* Cambridge: Cambridge University Press.

Nussbaum, M. C. (2000). *Women and human development: The capabilities approach.* Cambridge: Cambridge University Press.

O'Connor, M. F., Wellisch, D. K., Stanton, A. L., Eisenberger, N. I., Irwin, M. R., & Lieberman, M. D. (2008). Craving love? Enduring grief activates brain's reward center. *NeuroImage, 42*(2), 969–972.

Oatley, K. (1992). *Best laid schemes: The psychology of emotions.* Cambridge: Cambridge University Press.

Orend, B. (2002). *Human rights: Concept and context.* Peterborough: Broadview.

Panksepp, J. (1998). *Affective neuroscience: The foundations of human and animal emotions.* Oxford: Oxford University Press.

Parisien, C., & Thagard, P. (2008). Robosemantics: How Stanley the Volkswagen represents the world. *Minds and Machines, 18*, 169–178.

Pearl, J. (2000). *Causality: Models, reasoning, and inference*. Cambridge: Cambridge University Press.

Penn, D. C., Holyoak, K. J., & Povinelli, D. J. (2008). Darwin's mistake: Explaining the discontinuity between human and nonhuman minds. *Behavioral and Brain Sciences, 31*, 109–178.

Phan, K. L., Taylor, S. F., Welsh, R. C., Ho, S. H., Britton, J. C., & Liberzon, I. (2004). Neural correlates of individual ratings of emotional salience: A trial-related fMRI study. *Neuroimage, 21*(2), 768–780.

Phelps, A. C., et al. (2009). Religious coping and use of intensive life-prolonging care near death in patients with advanced cancer. *Journal of the American Medical Association, 301*, 1140–1147.

Phelps, E. A. (2006). Emotion and cognition: Insights from studies of the human amygdala. *Annual Review of Psychology, 24*, 27–53.

Place, U. T. (1956). Is consciousness a brain process? *British Journal of Psychology, 47*, 44–50.

Plate, T. (2003). *Holographic reduced representations*. Stanford: CSLI.

Plato (1961). *The collected dialogues*. Princeton: Princeton University Press.

Popper, K. (1959). *The logic of scientific discovery*. London: Hutchinson.

Posner, M. I., & Rothbart, M. K. (2007). *Educating the human brain*. Washington: American Psychological Association.

Preston, S. D., & de Waal, F. B. (2002). Empathy: Its ultimate and proximate bases. *Behavioral and Brain Sciences, 25*, 1–20.

Priest, G. (2006). *In contradiction: A study of the transconsistent* (2nd ed.). Oxford: Oxford University Press.

Prinz, J. (2004). *Gut reactions: A perceptual theory of emotion*. Oxford: Oxford University Press.

Prinz, J. J. (2007). *The emotional construction of morals*. Oxford: Oxford University Press.

Putnam, H. (1975). *Mind, language, and reality*. Cambridge: Cambridge University Press.

Putnam, H. (1983). There is at least one *a priori* truth. In H. Putnam (Ed.), *Realism and reason: Philosophical papers, vol. 3* (pp. 98–114). Cambridge: Cambridge University Press.

Quartz, S. R., & Sejnowski, T. J. (2002). *Liars, lovers, and heroes: What the new brain science reveals about how we become who we are*. New York: Morrow, William.

Quine, W.V.O. (1968). Epistemology naturalized. In W.V.O. Quine (Ed.), *Ontological relativity and other essays* (pp. 69–90). New York: Columbia University Press.

Railton, P. (2003). *Facts, values, and norms: Essays toward a morality of consequence*. Cambridge: Cambridge University Press.

Randal, J. C. (2004). *Osama: The making of a terrorist*. New York: Alfred A. Knopf.

Raney, A. A. (2006). Why we watch and enjoy mediated sports. In A. A. Raney (Ed.), *Handbook of sports and media* (pp. 313–331). Mahwah, NJ: Lawrence Erlbaum Associates.

Rawls, J. (1971). *A theory of justice*. Cambridge, MA: Harvard University Press.

Richard, M. (1990). *Propositional attitudes: An essay on thoughts and how we ascribe them*. Cambridge: Cambridge University Press.

Richardson, R. C. (2007). *Evolutionary psychology as maladapted psychology*. Cambridge, MA: MIT Press.

Rizzolatti, G., & Craighero, L. (2004). The mirror-neuron system. *Annual Review of Neuroscience, 27*, 169–192.

Rolls, E. R. (2005). *Emotion explained*. Oxford: Oxford University Press.

Rosch, E. B., & Mervis, C. B. (1975). Family resemblances: Studies in the internal structure of categories. *Cognitive Psychology, 7*, 573–605.

Rosenblatt, R. (2000). *Rules for aging*. San Diego: Harcourt.

Roskies, A. (2006). Neuroscientific challenges to free will and responsibility. *Trends in Cognitive Sciences, 10*, 419–423.

Rumelhart, D. E., & McClelland, J. L. (Eds.). (1986). *Parallel distributed processing: Explorations in the microstructure of cognition*. Cambridge MA: MIT Press/Bradford Books.

Russell, B. (1948). *Human knowledge: Its scope and limits*. London: Allen and Unwin.

Russell, S., & Norvig, P. (2003). *Artificial intelligence: A modern approach* (2nd ed.). Upper Saddle River, NJ: Prentice Hall.

Russo, J. E., & Schoemaker, P. J. H. (1989). *Decision traps*. New York: Simon & Schuster.

Ryan, R. M., & Deci, E. L. (2000). Self-determination theory and the facilitation of intrinsic motivation, social development, and well-being. *American Psychologist, 55*, 68–78.

Ryan, R. M., Deci, E. L., Grolnick, W. S., & La Guardia, J. G. (2006). The significance of autonomy and autonomy support in psychological development and psychopathology. In D. Cicchetti & D. Cohen (Eds.), *Developmental psychopathology: Vol. 1, Theory and methods* (pp. 795–849). New York: John Wiley.

Salmon, W. (1984). *Scientific explanation and the causal structure of the world*. Princeton: Princeton University Press.

Salmon, W. C. (1989). Four decades of scientific explanation. In P. Kitcher & W. C. Salmon (Eds.), *Scientific explanation. Minnesota Studies in the Philosophy of Science, vol. 13* (pp. 3–219). Minneapolis: University of Minnesota Press.

Scherer, K. R., Schorr, A., & Johnstone, T. (2001). *Appraisal processes in emotion*. New York: Oxford University Press.

Schwartz, N., & Clore, G. L. (2003). Mood as information: 20 years later. *Psychological Inquiry, 14*, 296–303.

Seligman, M. (2003). *Authentic happiness*. New York: Free Press.

Sen, A. (1999). *Development as freedom*. New York: Random House.

Sheldon, K. M. (2002). The self-concordance model of healthy goal striving: When personal goals correctly represent the person. In E. L. Deci & R. M. Ryan (Eds.), *Handbook of self-determination research*. Rochester: University of Rochester Press.

Sheldon, K. M., Elliot, A. J., Kim, Y., & Kasser, T. (2001). What is satisfying about satisfying events? Testing 10 candidate psychological needs. *Journal of Personality and Social Psychology, 80*, 325–339.

Shepard, R. N. (2008). The step to rationality: The efficacy of thought experiments in science, ethics, and free will. *Cognitive Science, 32*, 3–35.

Simon, D., Krawczyk, D. C., & Holyoak, K., J. (2004). Construction of preferences by constraint satisfaction. *Psychological Science, 15*, 331–336.

Singer, T., Seymour, B., O'Doherty, J., Kaube, H., Dolan, R. J., & Frith, C. D. (2004). Empathy for pain involves the affective but not sensory components of pain. *Science, 303*(5661), 1157–1162.

Singer, T., Seymour, B., O'Doherty, J. P., Stephan, K. E., Dolan, R. J., & Frith, C. D. (2006). Empathic neural responses are modulated by the perceived fairness of others. *Nature, 439*(7075), 466–469.

Skinner, B. F. (1972). *Beyond freedom and dignity*. New York: Bantam.

Sloan, R. P., & Bagiella, E. (2002). Claims about religious involvement and health outcomes. *Annals of Behavioral Medicine, 24*(1), 14–21.

Slote, M. (2007). *The ethics of care and empathy*. London: Routledge.

Smart, J. J. C. (1959). Sensations and brain processes. *Philosophical Review, 68*, 141–156.

Smith, E. E., & Kosslyn, S. M. (2007). *Cognitive psychology: Mind and brain*. Upper Saddle River, NJ: Pearson Prentice Hall.

Sober, E., & Wilson, D. S. (1998). *Unto others: The evolution and psychology of unselfish behavior*. Cambridge, MA: Harvard University Press.

Soon, C. S., Brass, M., Heinze, H. J., & Haynes, J. D. (2008). Unconscious determinants of free decisions in the human brain. *Nature Neuroscience, 11*(5), 543–545.

Spector, P. E. (1997). *Job satisfaction: Application, assessment, causes, and consequences*. Thousand Oaks, CA: Sage.

Spreitzer, G., Sutcliffe, K., Duttion, J., Sonenshein, J., & Grant, A. M. (2005). A socially embedded model of thriving at work. *Organization science, 16*, 537–549.

Steinhardt, P. J., & Turok, N. (2007). *Endless universe: Beyond the big bang*. New York: Doubleday.

Sternberg, R. J. (2003). *Wisdom, intelligence, and creativity synthesized*. Cambridge: Cambridge University Press.

Stich, S., & Nisbett, R. E. (1980). Justification and the psychology of human reasoning. *Philosophy of Science, 47*, 188–202.

Stiles, J. (2008). *The fundamentals of brain development*. Cambridge, MA: Harvard University Press.

Stroud, S., & Tappolet, C. (Eds.). (2003). *Weakness of will and practical irrationality*. Oxford: Clarendon Press.

Swinburne, R. (1990). *The existence of God* (2nd ed.). Oxford: Oxford University Press.

Sylwester, P. (2007). *The adolescent brain: Reaching for autonomy*. Thousand Oaks, CA: Corwin Press.

Taylor, C. (2007). *A secular age*. Cambridge, MA: Harvard University Press.

Taylor, C., Funk, C., & Craighill, P. (2006). Are we happy yet? Retrieved May 22, 2008, from http://pewresearch.org/assets/social/pdf/AreWeHappyYet.pdf.

Thagard, P. (1986). Parallel computation and the mind-body problem. *Cognitive Science, 10*, 301–318.

Thagard, P. (1988). *Computational philosophy of science*. Cambridge, MA: MIT Press/Bradford Books.

Thagard, P. (1989). Explanatory coherence. *Behavioral and Brain Sciences, 12,* 435–467.

Thagard, P. (1991). The dinosaur debate: Explanatory coherence and the problem of competing hypotheses. In J. Pollock & R. Cummins (Eds.), *Philosophy and AI: Essays at the Interface* (pp. 279–300). Cambridge, MA: MIT Press/Bradford Books.

Thagard, P. (1992). *Conceptual revolutions.* Princeton: Princeton University Press.

Thagard, P. (1999). *How scientists explain disease.* Princeton: Princeton University Press.

Thagard, P. (2000). *Coherence in thought and action.* Cambridge, MA: MIT Press.

Thagard, P. (2003). Why wasn't O. J. convicted? Emotional coherence in legal inference. *Cognition and Emotion, 17,* 361–383.

Thagard, P. (2004). Causal inference in legal decision making: Explanatory coherence vs. Bayesian networks. *Applied Artificial Intelligence, 18,* 231–249.

Thagard, P. (2005a). *Mind: Introduction to cognitive science* (2nd ed.). Cambridge, MA: MIT Press.

Thagard, P. (2005b). Testimony, credibility, and explanatory coherence. *Erkenntnis, 63,* 295–316.

Thagard, P. (2006). *Hot thought: Mechanisms and applications of emotional cognition.* Cambridge, MA: MIT Press.

Thagard, P. (2007a). Coherence, truth, and the development of scientific knowledge. *Philosophy of Science, 74,* 28–47.

Thagard, P. (2007b). I feel your pain: Mirror neurons, empathy, and moral motivation. *Journal of Cognitive Science, 8,* 109–136.

Thagard, P. (2007c). The moral psychology of conflicts of interest: Insights from affective neuroscience. *Journal of Applied Philosophy, 24,* 367–380.

Thagard, P. (2008). How cognition meets emotion: Beliefs, desires, and feelings as neural activity. In G. Brun, U. Doguoglu & D. Kuenzle (Eds.), *Epistemology and emotions* (pp. 167–184). Aldershot: Ashgate.

Thagard, P. (2009). Why cognitive science needs philosophy and vice versa. *Topics in Cognitive Science, 1,* 237–254.

Thagard, P. (forthcoming). The brain is wider than the sky: Analogy, emotion, and allegory.

Thagard, P., & Aubie, B. (2008). Emotional consciousness: A neural model of how cognitive appraisal and somatic perception interact to produce qualitative experience. *Consciousness and Cognition, 17,* 811–834.

Thagard, P., & Beam, C. (2004). Epistemological metaphors and the nature of philosophy. *Metaphilosophy, 35,* 504–516.

Thagard, P., & Findlay, S. (forthcoming-a). Changing minds about climate change: Belief revision, coherence, and emotion. In E. Olsson (Ed.), *Scientific belief revision.*

Thagard, P., & Findlay, S. (forthcoming-b). Getting to Darwin: Obstacles to accepting evolution by natural selection. *Science & Education.*

Thagard, P., & Finn, T. (forthcoming). Conscience: What is moral intuition?

Thagard, P., & Litt, A. (2008). Models of scientific explanation. In R. Sun (Ed.), *The Cambridge handbook of computational psychology* (pp. 549–564). Cambridge: Cambridge University Press.

Thagard, P., & Millgram, E. (1995). Inference to the best plan: A coherence theory of decision. In A. Ram & D. B. Leake (Eds.), *Goal-driven learninge* (pp. 439–454). Cambridge, MA: MIT Press.

Thagard, P., & Stewart, T. C. (forthcoming). The Aha! experience: Creativity and consciousness by emergent binding in neural networks. *in preparation*.

Thompson, E. (2007). *Mind in life: Biology, phenomenology, and the science of mind*. Cambridge, MA: Harvard University Press.

Thoren, P., Floras, J. S., Hoffmann, P., & Seals, D. R. (1990). Endorphins and exercise: Physiological mechanisms and clinical implications. *Medicine & science in sports & exercise, 22*, 417–428.

Todd, O. (1997). *Albert Camus: A life*. New York: Knopf.

Tononi, G., & Koch, C. (2008). The neural correlates of consciousness: An update. *Annals of the New York Academy of Sciences, 1124*, 239–261.

Trigger, B. G. (2003). *Understanding early civilizations*. Cambridge: Cambridge University Press.

Vohs, K. D., Baumeister, R. F., & Loewenstein, G. (Eds.). (2007). *Do emotions help or hurt decision making? A hedgefoxian perspective*. New York: Russell Sage Foundation.

Wagar, B. M., & Thagard, P. (2004). Spiking Phineas Gage: A neurocomputational theory of cognitive-affective integration in decision making. *Psychological Review, 111*, 67–79.

Walton, M. E., Devlin, J. T., & Rushworth, M. F. (2004). Interactions between decision making and performance monitoring within prefrontal cortex. *Nature Neuroscience, 7*(11), 1259–1265.

Ward, J. (2006). *Student's guide to cognitive neuroscience*. Hove, East Sussex: Psychology Press.

Wegner, D. M. (2003). *The illusion of conscious will*. Cambridge, MA: MIT Press.

Westen, D. (2007). *The political brain: The role of emotion in deciding the fate of the nation*. New York: Public Affairs.

Wiese, B. S. (2007). Successful pursuit of goals and subjective well-being. In B. R. Little, I. Salmelo-Aro & S. D. Phillips (Eds.), *Personal project pursuit* (pp. 301–328). Mahwah, NJ: Lawrence Erlbaum Associates.

Wiggins, D. (1987). *Needs, values, truth*. Oxford: Basil Blackwell.

Wild, T. C., & Enzle, M. E. (2002). Social contagion of motivational orientations. In E. L. Deci & R. M. Ryan (Eds.), *Handbook of self-determination research* (pp. 140–157). Rochester: University of Rochester Press.

Williamson, T. (2007). *The philosophy of philosophy*. Malden, MA: Blackwell.

Wittgenstein, L. (1968). *Philosophical investigations* (G.E.M. Anscombe, Trans. 2nd ed.). Oxford: Blackwell.

Wittgenstein, L. (1971). *Tractatus logico-philosophicus* (D. F. Pears & B. F. McGuinness, Trans. 2nd ed.). London: Routledge & Kegan Paul.

Wolf, M. (2007). *Proust and the squid: The story and science of the reading brain*. New York: HarperCollins.

Woodward, J. (2004). *Making things happen: A theory of causal explanation*. Oxford: Oxford University Press.

Worrall, J. (2007). Evidence in medicine and evidence-based medicine. *Philosophy Compass, 2*, 981–1022.

Wrosch, C., Miller, G. E., Scheier, M. F., & Brun de Pontet, S. (2007). Giving up on unattainable goals: benefits for health? *Personality and Social Psychology Bulletin, 33*, 251–265.

Xiaohe, X., & White, M. K. (1990). Love matches and arranged marriages: A Chinese replication. *Journal of marriage and the family, 52*, 709–722.

Zajonc, R. (1980). Feeling and thinking: Preferences need no inferences. *American Psychologist, 35*, 151–175.

Zeki, S., & Romaya, J. P. (2008). Neural correlates of hate. *PLoS ONE, 3*(10), e3556.

Zunshine, L. (2006). *Why we read fiction: Theory of mind and the novel*. Columbus: Ohio State University Press

Index

a priori, 5, 35–39, 196, 221, 251
Aaron, A., 152
Aesop, 131
affective afflictions, 112
Allen, W., 56, 166
amygdala, 96–99, 125, 163, 185–186, 251
analogy, 127–128, 134, 190
Anderson, J., 50
Anselm, 35
anthropic principle, 226, 251
anxiety, 12
Aquinas, T., 7, 13
Aristotle, 7, 13, 14, 39, 44, 58, 131
autonomy, 170–174, 251
Averroes, 13
Ayer, A., 55

balance, 176–177
Barnes, A., 190, 191, 192
Barnes, J., 224, 229
Barsalou, L., 78
Bartles, A., 153
Baumeister, R., 170
Bechtel, W., 233, 236, 248
Bentham, J., 126, 196
bin Laden, O., 16, 40
Blair, 194
bodily perception, 98–100, 102, 106, 251
Boyle, R., 14
brain revolution, 42–43, 60–61, 64–65, 80,
    138, 205, 213, 230, 251
brains, 44–54, 95–98, 123–125
Brown, L., 152
Browne, S., 55
Bush, G., 16, 40, 134

Cacioppo, J., 192
Camus, A., 1, 2, 3, 12, 142, 143, 144, 145,
    146
Cantor, G., 222
Carnap, R., 68
causality, 78, 86–87, 219
Chopra, D., 19
Churchland, P. M., 75, 231, 235, 248

Churchland, P. S., 231, 235, 248
Cochrane, A., 28
cognitive appraisal, 98–100, 103, 107, 186,
    190, 251
cognitive science, 7, 251
Cohen, J., 205
coherence, 22, 74, 85, 87, 90–92, 104, 140,
    176–177, 209
coherentism, 90, 228, 251
Colbert, S., 44
color, 75
competence, 170–174, 251
concepts, 76–81, 110, 222
confirmation bias, 16–17, 28, 251
conscience, 184–188
consciousness, 57–59, 105–108, 251
consequentialism, 196–201, 206, 208, 251
constructive realism, 67, 75–76, 84, 228, 251
Copernicus, N., xii, 7, 42, 89
creativity, 51, 217–218
Crow, S., 132
Csikszentmihalyi, M., 160

Dahmer, J., 187
Darwin, C., xii, 23, 42, 218
death, 55–56, 181
Deci, E., 169–172, 174, 177, 199
decisions, 119–141, 183
Dennett, D., 138
depression, 113, 219
Descartes, R., 35, 38, 42
descriptive, 142, 174, 251
despair, 178, 181
Dewey, J., 39
Doidge, N., 50
dopamine, 52–53, 101–102, 109, 131,
    153–154, 156, 159, 162, 164, 173, 186,
    197, 219
Dowd, M., 134
drugs, 52–53, 72, 116, 135
dualism, 54–59, 251

Easterlin, R., 147
Einstein, A., 23, 36, 38, 39, 58, 89

Eliasmith, C., 79, 86

embodiment, 63, 104, 236, 252

EMOCON, 100–108, 153, 155, 185–186, 191, 252

emotion, 94–118, 120, 123, 159, 190, 252

emotional consciousness, 34, 105–108, 166, 185–186

empathy, 190–192, 198, 252

empiricism, 67–69, 75–76, 81, 84, 91, 252

Epicurus, 4, 56

epistemology, 9, 252

ethics, 183–208

evidence, 13–14, 19–32, 210, 252

evil, 17

evolution, 33, 42, 212–213, 245

experiments, 25–26, 28, 175, 234

explanation, 87, 219, 252

faith, 13–19, 31–35, 56, 107, 210, 252

falsifiability, 40–41

Feldman, J., 51

Feynman, R., 229

Fields, W., 129

Fisher, H., 152, 153, 157

Flanagan, O., 138

Fodor, J., 5, 69, 80

Frankfurt, H., 156, 157

Franklin, B., 43, 44

free will, 137–140, 172–174, 252

Freud, S., 161

functionalism, 62, 252

Galileo, 6, 7, 16, 25, 26, 38

Gandhi, M., 127

Gazzaniga, M., 204, 205

Gilbert, D., 148

goal, 98, 121–132, 135, 144, 149–151, 156, 159, 174, 186, 205, 211, 252

God, 1, 32–35

Goel, V., 51

Gould, S., 14

Greene, J., 205

Guyatt, G., 28

happiness, 146–149, 180–181, 197–198, 252

Hatfield, E., 192

Hawthorne, N., 146

Hebb, D., 50

Hebbian learning, 50, 131, 252

Herodotus, 135

Hofstadter, D., 38, 157

Hooke, R., 14

hope, 11, 177–179, 214, 252

Hume, D., 14, 39, 63, 68, 183

Husserl, E., 226

hypothesis, 20, 85, 252

idealism, 67–69, 75–76, 84, 91, 252

identity theory, 42, 235, 252

immortality, 55, 139

inference to the best explanation, 21, 24, 26, 28–29, 31–32, 41, 74, 83–85, 88, 91, 103, 121, 134, 175, 222, 252

inference to the best plan, 120–123, 252

instruments, 25, 74–75

insula, 99–100, 189, 193

intuition, 107–108, 137, 184–188, 200, 202, 210, 242, 253

James, W., 99, 129

Jamison, K., 145

Kandel, E., 49, 50

Kant, I., 38, 63, 68, 72, 196, 198, 226

Kepler, J., 7

Keynes, J., 229

Kronman, A., 228

Kunda, Z., 232

Lambert, K., 172

Lavoisier, A., 82, 83

Lazaridis, M., 217

learning, 49–50

Leary, M., 154, 170

LeDoux, J., 64

legal reasoning, 20–21

Leibniz, G., 35

Levinson, D., 177

Levitin, D., 163, 164

Locke, J., 39, 68

love, 152–158, 171–172

Lyubomirsky, S., 180–182

MacDonald, G., 154

Maimonides, 13

materialism, 37, 253

mathematics, 24, 221–223

meaning of concepts, 80, 82, 150

meaning of life, 1–2, 80, 139, 142–168, 228

mechanism, 23, 253
medicine, 13, 21–22, 27–32
memory, 48–49
mental illness, 53
metaphysics, 9, 253
Mill, J., xi, 39, 126, 149, 182, 196
Minsky, M., 127
mirror neurons, 127, 155–156, 188–193, 198, 253
Montague, R., 131
motivated inference, 17, 28, 56, 114, 116, 134, 229, 232, 253
Muhammad, 15
multilevel explanations, 108–110, 218–219
multimodal representation, 9, 77–78, 90, 116–117, 253
Murphy, G., 76
music, 163–164

Nagel, E., 119
naturalism, xii, 8, 11, 39, 253
necessary truth, 38
need, 168–177, 200, 203, 207, 216, 253
neural naturalism, xii, 11–12, 253
neuron, 44–46, 71, 95–96, 109
neuropsychology, 9, 253
New Age, 17, 226
Newton, I., 7, 14, 23–24, 65
Nichols, S., 193
Nietzsche, F., 183
nihilism, 143–146, 253
normative, 142, 168, 174–175, 182, 210–211, 253
nucleus accumbens, 96–98, 125, 156, 163–164, 172–173, 191, 253
Nussbaum, M., 175

Obama, B., 141, 177
objectivity, 68, 183, 185, 201–203, 207, 210
Orend, B., 198–199, 203

Panksepp, J., 161–162
parallel constraint satisfaction, 88–89, 104, 108, 125, 130–131, 135, 140–141, 253
parapsychology, 56–57
Paul, 15
Peirce, C., 39
perception, 46, 48, 69–72, 91–92
philosophy, 1–6, 8, 10, 12, 35–40, 168, 228–230, 253

Pinker, S., 44
Plato, 5–6, 12–13, 35–36, 42, 76, 95, 112, 221
play, 161–165, 171–172
politics, 141, 215–217
Pollan, M., 115
Popper, K., 40, 41
positivism, 27
postmodernism, 59, 68, 226, 250
Prinz, J., 201, 203
Ptolemaic counterrevolution, 68, 91, 226, 253
Ptolemy, 42

Quine, W., 39

Raiffa, H., 119, 120, 137
Railton, P., 175
Ramón y Cajal, S., 7
Rapson, R., 192
rationality, 111–116, 131–132, 193
Rawls, J., 185, 198, 202
reading, 51, 164
realism, 67, 69, 75–76
reality, 67, 72–76
reductionism, 111, 213, 219–220, 253
reflective equilibrium, 185, 202, 253
relatedness, 170–174, 253
religion, 1, 13–19, 32–34, 179–180, 195, 234
responsibility, 204–206, 253
rights, 196, 198–199
Rizzolatti, G., 188
Rosenblatt, R., 144–145
Rowling, J., 223
Russell, B., xi
Ryan, R., 169–172, 174, 177, 199

Sackett, D., 28
Santayana, G., 229
Sartre, J., xi
Schiavo, T., 144, 150
science, 23–27, 253
self, 63–64, 206
self-deception, 112–113
Seligman, M., 2
Sen, A., 175
Shakespeare, W., 223
Shields, C., 223
Simpson, N., 21, 85–86, 88, 89
Simpson, O., 20, 21, 85–86, 88–90
Singer, T., 190–191

skepticism, 68, 184–185, 254
Skinner, B., 204
slacker serenity, 132, 149, 161, 173, 254
social explanations, 110
Socrates, 149, 196
Spears, B., 128
spirituality, 180–181
Steinhardt, P., 224–226

Taylor, C., 17
telic rationality, 131–133, 254
Tennyson, A., 139
testimony, 74
Thales, 58
thought experiment, 35–39, 209, 254
Tolstoy, L., 223
Tomlin, L., 67
truth, 90–92
Turok, N., 224–226

universe, 224

values, 95
van Fraassen, B., 68
van Musschenbroek, P., 43
vital need, 169, 203, 254
Voltaire, F., 14

weakness of will, 113
Wegner, D., 137
Weil, A., 19
Westen, D., 141
Wiggins, D., 169, 198
wisdom, 3–5, 93–94, 115, 118, 141,
    213–214, 226–228, 254
Wittgenstein, L., 5
Wolf, M., 51, 164
work, 158–161, 170–172
Wundt, W., 7

Zeki, S., 153
Zeno, 37
zombie argument, 60–61, 254